The Watcher Angel Tarot Guidebook

myth, meaning, and creation

written by Michelle Belanger

illustrated by Jackie Williams

The Watcher Angel Tarot Guidebook
© 2011 Michelle Belanger

Images of the cards are © 2011 Jackie Williams
and Michelle Belanger

Additional images in Creation part II: Jackie's Story
are © 2006-2011 Jackie Williams

ISBN: 978-0-9838169-1-1

Published by Emerald Tablet Press
PO Box 1120, Brunswick, OH 44212

Copies of the Watcher Angel Tarot can be obtained at:

www.spiralfirestudio.com
www.michellebelanger.com

This book is lovingly dedicated to our founders.
We couldn't have done it without you!

Theresa Vaughn; Robert Crook; Boris Jocoy; Anne Wallace; Morgan Felidae; S. Rune Emerson; Rosalie J. Williams; Jennifer Sporer; Patricia A. Davenport; Patricia Boswith; Ties that Bynde Designs, Inc., Jeff Varble; Greg Radabaugh; Bradley Winn; Shannon Sais; Diane Seager; Valerie Bell; Kayla Bell; Morgana Bondig; K. Kiera Fischer; Kellie Wiley; Jinx.

Thanks also to all the members of House Kheperu and its associates who have helped along the way, and especially to those who modeled for cards in the deck, providing both image and energy to bring them into being.

Table of Contents

0. Introduction

The Watcher Angel Tarot is an ambitious project ten years in the making. Combining concepts and material from the mythos of the Watchers, the works of Joseph Campbell and Carl Jung, and the Western magickal tradition with the Tarot, this project is a synthesis of several different streams of thought which all converge at the juncture of myth itself. Many of the concepts presented in the deck are based upon in-depth research into early Christian and Jewish angelology as well as the roots of these beliefs in Biblical and extra-Biblical texts. There is a lot of material to cover, and a lot of concepts to explain that go above and beyond the complexities of the Tarot (which is an extensive topic of study all by itself!).

Because of the sheer amount of information at hand, this book has been difficult to organize. Narrowing the scope while at the same time providing enough well-substantiated research to help readers understand not only the concepts behind the Watcher Angel Tarot but also the decisions behind these concepts' integration with the deck has been a challenge. I've gone back and forth with several sections in this book – particularly those sections that address the *Book of Enoch,* its history and origins – expanding them at times and, at other times, cutting entire chapters. I want to be certain that this book provides all the information essential to understanding the Watcher Angel Tarot without overwhelming readers – especially those readers who are new to both the Tarot and the myth of the Watcher Angels.

Because of the issues raised by the scope of this book (and, by extension, the deck itself), I have divided this book into three major sections. These sections each address a different aspect of the Watcher Angel Tarot and/or its development. They are I. *Creation,* II. *Mythos*, and III. *Tarot.*

The first section of this book, Creation, tells the story of the deck itself: its development, initial concepts, artistic influences, and a little about its creators, Jackie Williams and myself. While this story is not essential to understanding the deck itself, a great many of you have likely followed the development of the deck as updates were posted online between 2006 and 2011 via a variety of social networking sites. Several fans have asked to hear a little more of that story, but please realize that you can gloss over this section and still

7

understand the deck itself by reading the other portions of this book. We enjoy sharing our stories, however, and some of our personal experiences with the deck's creation offer insight into choices about meaning and iconography.

The next section is Mythos. This section covers the myth of the Watcher Angels, delving into the complexities of Biblical and extra-Biblical texts such as the *Book of Enoch, Chronicles of Jerahmeel,* and the *Dead Sea Scrolls* (better known to scholars as the Qumran manuscripts). I have danced back and forth with this section more than any other because the topic of the Watchers is a complicated one, and their mythic tradition is spread throughout a variety of Christian and Jewish (and possibly Muslim) texts – many of which are fragmentary or questionably transmitted. The very existence of the Watcher Angel myth has significant ramifications upon modern beliefs about angels, demons, and heavenly retribution. I think the full scope of the Watcher myth, its history, and its relation to Enochic literature is too big for this book. So, in the interest of maintaining focus, I have kept this section as concise as possible, providing what I feel is information essential to understanding to the Watcher Angels in context with this Tarot.

The final section of this book covers the Tarot itself – our deck as well as basic concepts about the Tarot as a whole. If your interest in this book lies solely with its usefulness as a guide to the Watcher Angel Tarot, you will probably want to skip straight to this section. If you skip ahead like this, you may miss some details about the story that unfolds throughout the deck, but you will nevertheless be able to start reading with our Tarot. All of the extended meanings of the cards are presented in this third section, along with interpretations, insights into Tarot basics, and some of the history of the Tarot. As far as the Tarot itself is concerned, this section is the real meat of this book.

Finally, because I can never resist sharing details from my research, you will also find two appendices at the end of this book. One addresses the names used in the Tarot, the other presents findings on traditional astrological and Kabalistic associations with the Trumps of the Major Arcana. I have included them because they elaborate on ideas, information, and/or research addressed within the greater work.

I. Creation

Creation Part I: Michelle's Story
Discovering the Tarot

The Tarot has been a spiritual and creative influence in my life since my early teens. My very first introduction to the Tarot was through the medium of fiction. I was thirteen or fourteen when I read the young adult novel *Eyes of the Tarot* by Bruce Coville. It was a spooky little tale about a haunted pack of cards, and the gimmick was that the eyes of the figures in this particular deck seemed to track whoever was looking at them. It was tween fiction, and most of the details about the cards being haunted and causing frightening events were clearly just a plot device. But the book also had enough details about the Tarot, describing iconic cards like the Hanged Man and the Tower, that it made me curious about Tarot in general. And anyone who knows me knows that when I'm curious about something, I erupt into a research frenzy that usually involves digging through countless books. So I started searching for information about these fascinating cards, albeit in my small Ohio town with limited access to anything that might even be associated with the Tarot, years before the establishment of the Internet,.

My local library had a few scattered references in encyclopedias and a series or two of Time/Life books, but it was a trip to the mall with friends that netted me my very own deck. It was a Rider-Waite-Smith deck (practically everyone's starter deck, at least in the English-speaking world), and while I did not understand the history of that particular deck at the time, I felt immediately drawn to the colorful images. I found myself especially fascinated by the repeated motif of lilies and roses observable throughout the deck, which I later learned were intended as symbols of spirit and flesh. At that point, I could only afford the deck itself, not any of the books that explained it, but I comforted myself with the knowledge that at least the deck came with a little guide inside the box – albeit a teeny, tiny guide that didn't define any of the cards so much as it teased with abbreviated snippets of information.

Thereafter, I became the *de facto* Tarot reader among my little circle of friends. It didn't matter that I barely had any of the meanings memorized. It didn't matter that I was still trying to hunt down a book that would expand upon those meanings beyond the tantalizing summaries in the abbreviated guidebook. My friends and I were instantly captivated by the Tarot, in part because of its novelty, and in part because of the implied magick of working with something that might be able to foretell the future. Eventually, I tracked down a book or two on the Tarot. The one I found most useful at the time was Eden Gray's *Mastering the Tarot*. It featured the same deck that I happened to own and by reading it, I started to understand more of the history of the Tarot as well as more of the concepts behind its use. It's a resource I consult still, alongside several others noted at the back of this book.

At fourteen, I struggled with concepts like reversed cards, where the meaning of a card is essentially turned on its head if it comes into a spread upside-down (a concept pioneered by Etteilla). And I made the mistake of a lot of Tarot newbies in thinking that learning the Tarot meant memorizing the expanded definitions of the cards word for word. To facilitate this, I added notes to my deck, writing in the tiniest lettering possible (and using a mechanical pencil so I could erase it all later!) in the little white borders of the cards. I picked key words and phrases from Eden Gray's book, listing these at the top and bottom of the card so I had prompts for when the card was read right-side up and when it showed up reversed.

I won't lie – this early trick for learning the Tarot, which essentially turned my starter deck into Tarot flashcards, was a primary inspiration for the use of key words in the Watcher Angel Tarot (of course, it's a time-honored tradition: the Golden Dawn system featured key words for each card, though these do not appear on the Rider-Waite-Smith deck, and Crowley also included verbal keys to expand upon the meaning of the cards). Those prompts – especially once I realized that they were suggestions only and meant to be flexible in readings – really helped me to get a handle on the Tarot. In less than a year, I was reading without the prompts, although I kept the summaries lettered in the margins so my friends could check the meanings of the cards whenever they wanted to learn more about a particular card when it came up in a reading.

I think it's important for me to acknowledge that my initial interest in the Tarot arose from my exposure to the concept through fiction. As you will see as we progress through this section of the book (as well as through this book as a whole), I place a good deal of value upon the art of storytelling. I see storytelling as a form of magick in its own right: the stories we imagine in creative and even fantastic works of fiction can nevertheless convey universal truths. Storytelling is really just modern myth-making and it arises from and simultaneously speaks to that deep, fertile, and primal portion of our minds known as the unconscious.

The Tarot and Fortune-Telling
The Tarot is most widely known to people as a method of fortune-telling. However, from the start, I did not like reading the Tarot to foretell the future. Or rather, I should say, I did not gravitate naturally toward this application of the Tarot. Rather, whenever I did readings, the information that came up was always introspective. It tended to have more to do with revealing the querent's past, or bringing to light current issues that were weighing on their minds and needed further cogitation. The conclusions of my readings were never "such and such is *definitely* going to happen to you three days from now" but rather foretold of overarching influences moving into a person's path and possible outcomes of that person's decisions. Whenever a friend approached me thinking that the Tarot could explicitly tell their future, I remained skeptical. As a matter of fact, I remain skeptical on that topic to this day, and this is another portion of my early work with Tarot that has most definitely found its way into the Watcher Angel Tarot.

Regardless of anyone else's opinion on the matter, I cannot bring myself to perceive the future as fixed. That there are guideposts, pathways, and sometimes clear boundaries between which one's future may unfold – these concepts I understand and can accept. But as for a single, linear thread of future unfolding, irrevocable, inarguable, and unavoidable – I don't buy it. There is an overall pattern, but we play a role in how that pattern unfolds. Our future is created collectively with each choice, each action, and each inaction. It – like we ourselves – is constantly changing.

The Language of the Tarot
While still a teen, as I grew more comfortable with the Tarot, I began to think about designing my own deck. I think everyone who is into the Tarot considers this at some point in their relationship with the system. Tarot symbolism is a deeply held tradition, but as one reads

and grows familiar with the cards, it becomes clear that the real power of the Tarot's imagery resides not in tradition but in how it speaks to the reader him or herself. This is a large reason for the many different packs of cards out there: dragon Tarots, elven Tarots, Shakespeare-themed and Art Nouveau – to mention only a few. The art and symbolism of the Tarot serve as psychological touchstones that help the reader tune in to his or her intuitive reading of the cards. This unlocks the deep reservoirs of myth and symbols we each carry in our own minds.

What we have in the Tarot is language beyond language, deeper than words. It is a remnant of that atavistic impulse to draw on the cave walls – only now, the arched interior surfaces of that dark and womb-like space have become nothing less than the insides of our own skulls. This is the grotto of the mind and from its deepest levels springs the well of ancient memory. Consider that the earliest language started not as letters to form words but as pictograms – hieroglyphs, abstract and nuanced. The Tarot retains this pathway into communication, encapsulating complex ideas within richly textured images, thus speaking to us from the unconscious mind outward.

Another detail that is important to note is that my understanding of the Tarot, once it progressed beyond the mere curiosity inspired by fiction, was steeped in concepts of Jungian archetypes and universal myth. Most Tarot traditionalists tie the cards to astrological or kabalistic symbolism, but deeper than this, there is a profound connection between Tarot imagery and analytical psychology as defined by Carl Jung. The Tarot – especially the Major Arcana – eloquently expresses in images fundamental archetypes that reside in the collective unconscious. This Jungian character of the Tarot is really how I came to understand and bond with this system. I see the Tarot of a potent method for expressing personal myth and the truths which are carried at the heart of such myth like the sleeping embers of a flame – ready to spring to life when catalyzed by recognition.

Because there is a very personal aspect to symbols, even when we're talking about the archetypal and colossal forms that slumber in our collective unconscious, I didn't want simply to design another Tarot built upon the bones of the Rider-Waite-Smith. I wanted to *revision* the Tarot entirely, allowing the symbols to speak through me and to find expression in some vital and personal myth. This was a powerful and early impulse. My senior year of high school saw my first attempt in the *Tarot of the Birds* – which was entered (and stolen from) a local art show. I only produced the Major Arcana, and although they earned me a ribbon in the show, it's probably for the best that this early deck has not survived through the years. Even at the time, I was unhappy with its execution, mainly because my own artistic skills were not up to the scope of expression I felt the deck – *any* deck – deserved.

I went to college and continued in my studies (notably not in art), further exploring the power of myth and the language of symbols both in and out of the classroom. My inquiries into the meaning and power of our mythic imagination led me to study a variety of world religious traditions, as well as the practices of mysticism and magick. My own spiritual journey was in full swing at this time, and my relation with the Tarot was a part of this. The *leit-motif* resounding through everything harkened back to the teachings of Joseph Campbell and Carl Jung. Various myths stood out to me, speaking to both my personal vision and my experience of the world: tales of the Hindu god Shiva, in his aspect of *Nataraja* whose dance simultaneously creates and unmakes the world, the echoes of ancient systems – Babylon and Egypt, Etruria and Greece … But the story I came back to again and again was that of the Watcher Angels.

Watching the Watchers

The theme of the Watchers appears in a number of my creative works and has been a source of both fascination and inspiration for many years. It serves as the underlying narrative connecting the various songs in my CD *Blood of Angels* (with *Nox Arcana*). It has emerged in fiction, in poetry, and it sees its most complete expression in the Watcher Angel Tarot. My interest in the Watcher Angel myth is many-layered, much like the myth itself, and I think in order to best understand why I've felt so compelled to tell the story of the Watchers, it is first necessary to explain how I learned about the Watcher Angels in the first place.

The seed of my long-standing fascination with the Watcher Angels was planted my freshman year of college when Dr. Joseph Kelley took our Religion 101 class on a wild and ambitious romp through the field of angelology. I had never heard of the Watcher Angels until that time, but what I learned in that class electrified me, and I needed to learn more. At the time, I would not have been able to fully explain *why* the Watchers grabbed me so. However, a few years later, I learned that my fascination was something of a family affair. I met my maternal grandfather for the first time when I was in my twenties – he was estranged from the rest of the family, with the exception of my mother, due to a very bitter divorce between himself and my maternal grandmother. Grandfather and I did not sit down immediately and have a discussion on angelology (although we did end up talking about magick and past lives relatively quickly). Rather, I learned of his own interest in the Watcher Angel mythos rather discursively. My mother battled breast cancer on and off for nearly thirteen years and my grandfather moved near her in order to help care for her through this experience. During one the many hospital stays during which her life hung in the balance, my grandfather sought to comfort Mom by telling her something that puzzled her at the time. It was strange enough that she didn't ask him to explain but instead called me up once she was out of the hospital to run it past me. Imagine my surprise when she asked in all my studies whether I'd ever heard stories of angels coming down to marry and have children among mortals.

I was in the middle of one of my Enochic kicks at the time, digging through references in the *Testament of the Twelve Patriarchs* and the *Book of Jubilees.* The question totally threw me for a loop – especially when I found out why my mother was asking. This is one of those things that is really too weird and if it hadn't happened directly to me, I would never give it credit. Apparently my grandfather had been brought up to believe that our family line had some connection with the Watchers' story. The French name *Belanger* is generally a derivative of *boulangier,* meaning "baker." It's a tradeskill name. But grandfather had been taught that our version of the name derived not from *boulangier* but from a contraction of two other French words: *bel* and *ange,* "beautiful angel." Given that the other branch of his family were Luciers, one can readily see where he might develop some curious notions about angelic heritage.

This was actually not the strangest conversation my mother and I ever had (childhood ghosts and past life memories randomly spouted at the age of two rank up there), but it certainly went beyond the pale. By her own admission, Mom had been half out of it when grandfather talked to her, so she only imperfectly remembered the details of their discussion concerning tall, charismatic, and musically-gifted angel-people (notably, my grandfather was a veritable giant of a man standing 6'8" with a lean and ropey build packed with muscle even in his 80s). I, of course, was compelled to address him directly on the issue. I mean – come on, *seriously?!?*

But my grandfather talked about the topic as if it were the most normal thing in the world to claim direct lineage back to rebel angels who chose to leave heaven for earth. According to him, his grandfather was the one who taught him about it, and it was a point of family pride. I felt like I'd suddenly fallen into a Dan Brown novel where the bloodline of the Holy Grail had been replaced with the bloodline of the Watcher Angels. I have no idea how far this tradition actually goes back on the French side of my family – or whether to credit it at all. Honestly, if the whole concept of the Watchers wasn't such uncommon knowledge for most people, I'd say my grandfather was pulling my leg. But he was deadly serious and – bless his blue-collar heart – he had never even heard of the *Book of Enoch* when I asked him about it. Even so, he rattled off various details about giants and their hybrid angelic qualities as powerful warriors, charismatic leaders, psychics, and gifted artists. One thing I can say for certain: Grandfather believed it. It was not only normal in his mind, it was a point of pride.

That my grandfather was a powerful psychic, a will-working magickian, and a psychic vampire like myself I have no doubt (and gods, I know the skeptics are rolling their eyes as they read this passage!). Grandfather and I traded experiences and techniques and even some past life memories we had in common over the small span of years we were allowed to share in our lives. Do I believe his family history about the Watchers? The best I can say is this: it's a story, and stories don't need to be true in order to have meaning – even if it's only the meaning which we project upon them. The story certainly had meaning for my grandfather: it gave him a reason for why he was so tall, why he could pick up and beautifully play any musical instrument he laid hands on, and why he possessed an easy, scintillating charisma that inspired people to take interest in him wherever he went. This is the whole purpose of myth-making. Myths allow us to contextualize qualities, forces, and events in our lives that otherwise would seem frustratingly inexplicable.

For me, grandfather's stories served as an inspiration to dig even deeper into the Watcher myth, seeking any related textual material that seemed to shed light on where and how the belief in these earthly angels originated. I am not likely to ever get hard answers for any of it, but I have certainly discovered a lot of great stories along the way. Marrying the Watchers to the Tarot allows me to tell these stories in a rich and vital way, sharing the meaning I have found within the mythos of both. (One thing I will say in my grandfather's defense is that there was a fad at one time, particularly among French royal families, to validate their nobility by fabricating a family history that tied them originally to some supernatural creature: angels, faeries, and in the case of the Merovingians, a peculiar sea-creature known as a *quinotaur*. Whether or not my grandfather's story was merely a remnant of such a tradition, I'll never know. He died a few months before my mother in 2004, and everyone else from his generation or before has also passed on). But that's enough of my weird family stories. Let's get back to the Tarot.

Finding the Artist
Electrified with the desire to create my own deck, I filled journals with notes and rough sketches, but every time I tried to map out the images of a card, I was reminded of my own inadequacies for bringing such a work into being. My mother was a skilled sculptor and painter, and while I had certainly inherited her artistic temperament (which she, in turn, had clearly gotten from Grandfather), I knew, when it came to the visual arts, I was at best mediocre. If I ever really wanted to design my own Tarot, I would eventually have to find a gifted artist who shared my passion and my vision – not to mention a dogged desire to see the project through to completion. Creating seventy-eight individual and unique works of art is no small task!

You know that person as Jackie Williams. I met Jackie in 2005 at the Kheprian Gathering that year (the Gathering is a yearly event hosted by my magickal group, House Kheperu). Her boyfriend had brought her to meet me and the rest of House Kheperu. He was an old friend and an early member of HK, but he and I had fallen out of touch for a while as life took him in a different direction. I can't imagine what it was like for Jackie that first time she was introduced to all of us. The members of House Kheperu are a colorful lot, and the Gathering itself attracts a very diverse group of Pagans, energy workers, and magickal practitioners. Jackie was down in the consuite looking a little overwhelmed – not by the subject matter of the Gathering so much as the sheer number of unfamiliar people. That first meeting was admittedly awkward, largely because neither Jackie nor myself are particularly adept at making small talk with strangers.

Over time I learned that Jackie had a degree in Classics and that she was an artist. She was also involved in the Society for Creative Anachronism, known widely as the SCA. The SCA is a group devoted to historical re-enactment, with a focus on Medieval and early Renaissance time periods. Costuming, research, and a love of history come together in the SCA, and each member has his or her own persona – a fictional identity tied to a specific time in history and exhaustively researched for authenticity. Like many individuals involved in the SCA, Jackie poured a lot of her creativity into sewing costumes, creating cotehardies and chemises and even full Elizabethan dresses based upon patterns drawn from historical research. But, in addition to her skill as a seamstress, I learned also that Jackie was a scribe. In fact, she was one of the official scribes for her region, crafting manuscript illuminations, certificates, and awards for other members of the SCA. Painstakingly done in colors and styles according to each region and time period, only a well-trained eye can distinguish her work from the real deal.

The Right Person, the Right Time
One of the first pieces of art Jackie did for me was a gift to me & House Kheperu: a Celtic knotwork design in lush greens and blues integrating the two initials of the group, H and K. It's still hanging on a wall in my living room. The other piece of early art Jackie did for me is perhaps more telling with regard to our later work together. You see, in addition to being educated and artistic, Jackie is also a spirit medium. She has a pretty clear perception of spirits – a very visual perception. And, as an artist, she has the skill not only to perceive spirits but she can also sketch what she is seeing. At the time, I had a particular spirit show up in my room again and again. I had a solid image of him in my head, and in an attempt to compare my perception with that of another medium, I asked him to drop in on Jackie. She drew what she "saw" with her inner vision. The resulting sketch captured what I myself had been seeing, right down

to what he habitually wore. I still have the sketch in my room. The spirit himself – something of a personal guardian – has also continued to stick around. You don't need to see the sketch to know what he looks like: he shows up as a recurring character in the suit of Swords. He's the Celtic warrior we follow through the story woven throughout that suit.

After this experience, it was really only a matter of time before I approached Jackie with my proposal for the Tarot. I didn't have any expectation that she would commit to the project: as observed before, a Tarot deck is no small undertaking, especially for the artist. Seventy-eight individual cards means seventy-eight individual paintings. Even if the artist is working full-time at break-neck speed, that is still many months of work – and, feasibly, years. At the time, I didn't have a lot to offer in terms of compensation, beyond the opportunity to produce something fresh and unique. I knew asking anyone to participate in the project was asking for a leap of faith. But it turns out Jackie is as crazy as me – at least when it comes to working on creative projects.

Jackie was not the first person I had approached to work with me on the deck. I had been carting around my notes on the Watcher Angel Tarot (called variously the Fallen Angel Tarot, the Dark Angel Tarot, and the Tarot of the Nephilim) since 2000 or so. Around that time, my friends at Monolith Graphics, Joseph Vargo and Christine Filipak, started laying the groundwork for their own Tarot. As both a friend and a fan of their art, I offered some input on their project. The resulting work – the Gothic Tarot – is gorgeous. The deck showcases both Vargo's dark, atmospheric fantasy art and Christine's enviable skills at graphic design. It remains one of my favorite decks to work with. But offering a suggestion here and there just wasn't the same as creating my own deck from start to finish (I do owe Joseph and Christine a great deal for all of their helpful input as they have essentially mentored me and Jackie through the process of getting our deck printed and out to the world).

The first potential artist for the Watcher Angel Tarot was Jenn Bechtel. I met Jenn at KinVention North, a convention we both attended in the early 2000s. We had converging interests in magick and angelology, and I liked her use of color and form (the fact that she tends to draw angels also worked in her favor for this particular project). Life, however, had other plans for what Jenn was to be doing with her time. After an initial work-up of the Fool, she found she couldn't devote herself to another seventy-seven cards. Life comes first, so I tabled the project until I could find another promising candidate. (If you're curious about Jenn's art and the Tarot that never was, I highly recommend that you look her up on DeviantArt.com under her ID, GoldRonin.). I had plenty of other projects to keep me busy (it was during this time that I was putting the finishing touches on *The Psychic Vampire Codex* and writing *The Vampire Ritual Book* for the Sanguinarium), so I set the notes aside, adding to them only when some flash of inspiration grabbed me from out of the blue.

And along came Jackie. Like Jenn, Jackie started with the Fool. I had notes on all of the Major Arcana at that point, and rough sketches for a number of the cards. Some of my suggestions were more specific than others. For the Fool, I mostly had blocking recorded, plus details involving severed wings and a lone feather drifting to the ground. But from this, Jackie serendipitously came up with an image of the Fool that echoed the work Jenn had done – right down to the background colors of greens and blues (colors that weren't specified in the notes, but nevertheless fit). It wasn't as if Jackie had copied Jenn's work – in truth, she had never seen the first version of the card. This was purposeful on my part: I didn't want to taint her vision or lead her into recreating someone else's art. Instead, it was like she tuned into the same creative flow where the ideal image of the Fool of the Watcher Angel Tarot resided, somewhere in the realm of visions and dreams. That made me confident that I had found the right person to bring the rest of the deck out of that realm and into reality.

Tarot and Magick

I won't lie and say that this deck was merely the product of detached academic research. There is a great deal of vision and inspiration, myth, dream, and magick woven into this work. But that should become apparent the further along you read in this book and the further along you get in your relationship with the deck. My story really is the deck itself. It is a synthesis of my personal philosophies and beliefs. Notions of history, identity, and incarnation pertinent to my worldview (and by extension, that of my group House Kheperu) are all embodied in the cards. You just need to know how to look.

The process of bringing these cards into being was profoundly magickal. In the weeks that I worked on the extended definitions of the Major Arcana, I dreamed them each night, each Trump unfolding – sometimes in unexpected ways – within my unconscious mind. Pathworking the Tarot like this helped bring out further layers and nuances of meaning to the cards that even I hadn't intended to put there. But such is the nature of dream, and the Tarot truly does speak the language of our dreams.

But I think that's enough about me. I'll let the deck itself tell the rest of the story. One thing that's always bugged me about the Rider-Waite-Smith and the Crowley-Harris decks is that most people don't even know the names of the artists who painted those decks. In the vast majority of references, the artists are left out entirely: it's usually the Crowley Thoth deck, and I grew up knowing my deck only as the Rider-Waite deck. The artist of the RWS, Pamela Colman Smith – Pixie to her friends – had been so eclipsed that I spent some time trying to puzzle out this really strange and serpentine glyph that appeared again and again on the cards. I couldn't find reference to it in any of the books. None of the other Tarot readers I asked about it (several of them professionals), had any insight into the matter. And it turned out to be the *artist's signature!*

I don't want that happening with my deck. Jackie Williams brought a great deal to this work, and without her talent and dedication, my vision would not have come to life. So I think it's time to let her recount some of her own process of creating the Watcher Angel Tarot. Her story has much to add to this unfolding tale.

Creation Part II: Jackie's Story
The Making of the Watcher Angel Tarot

When it comes to a tarot deck, it's important to choose one that is right for you - a deck where the images capture your imagination and intuition. Most people never think about the art though. They like the pictures but don't have any sense of how the image was created. To most people, the art process isn't all that important, it's the final outcome that matters most. But to those very connected to the tarot and divination, getting to know a deck through a personal understanding of the art process is an integral part of choosing their deck. To some, especially fellow artists or those aspiring to make their own deck, learning about the art process itself is a part of art appreciation. As an artist, I am always fascinated by the art process. I want to know the size of the original piece, the medium used, the references explored. To me, learning how someone else created a piece educates and inspires me. I have a deeper appreciation of the art, I can marvel at the complexity of the technique and wonder at the difficulty of the medium. Learning about another's technique helps me to consider my own art and how I could incorporate similar techniques or ideas into my own process. I grow in understanding, I develop new artistic skills, and I feel that my art is better for it.

About the Artist

I have been drawing since two years of age, a talent that my mother Rosalie – also an artist – strongly encouraged. I loved art and frequently won art competitions exploring a variety of mediums beyond pencil and paint including ceramics, enameling, weaving and textile arts, though it was in drawing and painting that my talent really shined. I loved school too and recognized that there was only a slim chance I would ever be a professional artist, so I decided to pursue an academic interest and always keep my art as a beloved hobby. I chose to major in Classical Studies in college, studying the history of ancient Greece and Rome, Latin, and ancient culture. I knew it was a field that would lead to many different career paths, but more than that, I truly loved the subject.

After college I got into the field of academia, always keeping my art as a hobby and using my artistic talents for marketing my department. I became very involved with the Society for Creative

Anachronism and my artistic talent and degree in Classics came in very handy when I began to explore medieval manuscript illumination as the newest area of interest in art. But it wasn't until I met Michelle Belanger in 2005 that I began to pursue art as more than a hobby. At the same time, I also began to pursue my psychic ability as a medium and energy worker – skills which I had all my life but remained very reserved about it. With Michelle's help, I became more confident and open about it and worked to develop those talents.

Michelle is of course a very talented writer and we paired up to make the Watcher Angel Tarot deck. I also worked with her on her book, *The Dictionary of Demons,* and its fun compendium, *D is for Demon.* In doing so, I was introduced to study of ancient and medieval textual amulets and sigils, and brought both my Classics background and artistic talents together to recreate amuletic talismans for publication. My art has been published in several books including: Brad Steiger's *Real Zombies,* 2010; Lon Milo DuQuette's *Low Magic,* 2010; Michelle Belanger's *Dictionary of Demons,* 2010 and *D is for Demon,* 2010; Ellen Dugan's *Practical Protection Magic,* 2011; and Christopher Penczak's *The Witches Heart,* 2011.

Artist to Artist
If there was something I could say to aspiring artists it would be this – when considering the work of others, never compare yourself to anyone but you. It's a simple concept but a difficult one to learn to accept. It is probably the thing that took me the longest to learn and seriously hampered me when I was in college. Everyone has their own skill level, everyone has a different experience. You cannot compare yourself and your style to someone who has been working all their lives in the professional art world. Doing so only sets you up for failure and despair. Instead of comparing yourself to others, keep a portfolio of your work. Date each piece in your portfolio and refer back to older pieces from time to time. You will see improvement in yourself as you continue to work and practice, and it will amaze you how far you have come in only a few months or years. A portfolio is like a roadmap to your artistic life, a journal of your development and style.

I learn a great deal from the artists I admire. Studying the art of others is very useful in the development of your own style and technique because in studying art, you are encouraged and inspired to try new things. Your own personal style grows as you incorporate ideas into your art. You are not copying or duplicating the work of another, you are learning and utilizing an art technique and marrying it to your existing style. Don't try to be someone else, for we all have artists we aspire to be like, but instead appreciate their talent and try and learn from them. Your style is personal to you, why would you want your art to look exactly like someone else? Bottom line – it's okay to be unique. Give yourself permission to be different. While I no longer wish that my art looks identical to those I respect, I do wish to be as respected in the art community as they are, and to be a mentor to others as they are to me. I think that is the most any artist can hope for.

How the Tarot Deck Came to Me
I first met Michelle around 2005, but it wasn't until late 2006 that we first began talking about the deck. Sitting in her living room one night, she began telling me about this tarot deck that she wanted to make. Her other artist had fallen through and the deck was once again at a standstill. So I asked her for the notes and after flipping through them, I asked if I could take a crack at it. Michelle knew I had some artistic skill – she had seen a few things I had done, some portraiture, some illumination work, and other things. So she let me to give it a try, probably figuring that she didn't have anything to lose. After all, what is one more disappointment after you have had so many artists attempt and fail? I had some experience with the tarot. As a psychic and energy worker, I had myself used the Rider & Waite deck for years as a divination tool. I did not feel particularly connected to the images of the tarot deck; I did not understand the symbols and subtle meanings of the cards. The deck was a tool. It worked well enough and my readings were good, but I never really cared to investigate the meanings of the cards any further than the basic meaning I got in my *How to Read the Tarot* book.

I started playing around with images for the deck in late 2006, though the first surviving card wasn't completed until March 2007. I laugh at myself every time I look back at those early attempts, I was such an amateur! No, really, I was completely amateurish in my style and technique. Part of the problem was though I had skills in portraiture and fantasy art, I had only marginal experience with painting (mostly acrylics). Most of my art, with the obvious exception of the medieval illumination, was in black and white, pencil or pen & ink. I had no idea what I was in for on so many levels. I had read that illustrators preferred to use watercolors, and so I dove into that medium – head first and without any life preserver! I had not used watercolor as a serious medium. I had screwed around with it a couple of times in college and of course there was the old school watercolors in elementary school. But I hadn't really *used* watercolors. Acrylics sure, and charcoals, pencils, and gouache paint – but watercolor... not so much.

Now, you artists out there who know what gouache is, are probably sitting there saying, "But gouache is just opaque watercolor!" Well, yes that's true. But I use gouache in place of period pigments in my medieval illumination art, and the medieval artists applied their pigment straight out of the shell (or out of the tube in this case). In medieval art, paint is thinned out only enough to be spreadable (like melted ice cream) and is treated very like acrylics. There isn't really color blending, though there is some shading occasionally. So yes, there I was with a brand new medium and a whole tarot deck to do. I was in WAY over my head but too excited at the prospect of being a published artist to really understand what I had gotten in to. It is fitting, in retrospect, that the first card I chose to do in the deck was The Fool.

Gathering Reference Materials
One of the first things Michelle and I discussed was the overall style for the art. Michelle had a particular liking for the artists Alphonse Mucha and Arthur Rackham. Both men were illustrators of the late nineteenth and early twentieth century, and Michelle had a fondness for the color usage and stylistic design of their art. Mucha was a Slavic artist whose illustrative art in advertisements and magazines in Paris lead the way in the Art Nouveau movement. And Rackham was an illustrator whose unique style utilized pen and ink, coupling it with light color washes to illustrate fairy tales as well as works of Shakespeare.

I began as a good artist should: I assembled reference materials and began examining the style of those two artists. And as this was an Angel tarot, I also looked at the representation of angels in art, looking at everything from the winged *daemones* of the ancient world, to Fra Angelico and Jean Pucelle, to Gustav Doré, to the Pre-Raphaelites, and even to angelic depictions on Christmas cards. I also purchased a bird book to exam wing structure in a variety of positions. I also began looking outside this sphere of the classics to the modern fantasy artists, such as Brian Froud and John Howe, for watercolor technique. Each artist inspired me, and I drew upon all of their art for ideas on color application, drapery, style and technique. As you look at the images in the tarot, you will note some direct nods to these artists and art styles as I learned and incorporated aspects of these various art forms into my own style.

The Original Notes

As I began designing the card images, I tried to keep in mind the overall concept for the tarot that Michelle had begun work on in 2002. Even though she had lent me her notebook with her original ideas, it wasn't much to go on, making my job even more difficult. The original notes only sketched out basic ideas for some of the Major Arcana with only rough concepts for the minors and the court cards. As I worked, I was able to incorporate some aspects of her original concepts into the design, but it was easy to see that this deck was going to diverge significantly from the original concept. Each conversation we had brought new ideas for the cards, fleshing out the deck into a fully designed concept. We discussed colors for each suit, costumes, hair, even eye color and skin tone, making notations of each decision to aid us as we tried to establish a unified style for each suit. We quickly realized that one of the best ways for the art to happen was for Michelle to explain to me the core idea of each card and let me create an image within the overall style of the deck based on my interpretation of that idea. So she wrote up a document of key words associated with each card. Sometimes she added a few of her own notes, suggestions for card designs, but generally there were just one or two key words in which

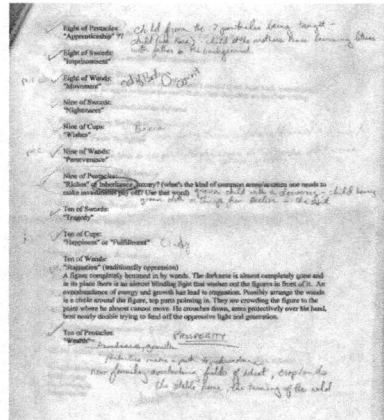

to proceed. I used the key word associated with each card to provide me a guideline for the overall emotion and design of the card. I would frequently add my notes to this outline sheet, identifying a person to model the card, design ideas, colors to use, and scenes to depict. These notes were the first things I would review before beginning any card and were important in helping to maintain a cohesive style to the deck.

A page from Michelle's main notebook on the Tarot

Inspiration and Models

I gathered collections of reference photos for assistance with figure drawing. It's important to have references to work from, whether you're drawing a potted plant or a seated figure – all good artists have references and study object form. Using a reference, especially for figure drawing, ensures that your proportions, positioning, and shading are correct. Even the masters used models and references for their paintings. It is necessary to be cautious of where your images come from due to copyright and usage issues. When possible, have your friends model for you and take your own photographs. Even if you are not planning on publishing or selling

your art, make sure you have a standard model contract or release form to ensure their permission of image usage and that you are free of future compensation. Standard art model release forms are readily available on the internet. If you don't have people willing to model, there are a variety of artist modeling books available for purchase, but mind the usage rules of the book! I highly recommend the *Virtual Pose* book series by Mario Henri Chakkour.

Each card began with a meditation on the concept behind the card. With each card, a key word or idea is associated, and it was my task as the artist to find the best way to represent that idea. Not an easy task when you consider the esoteric nature of some of the card meanings. I would boil down the idea into a single concept using the image key-word, and then translate that meaning into a single still life image. I would come up with a rough idea of what I wanted for the image, and then begin pawing through my reference photos looking for an image to fit the concept. I would frequently select friends to model for me, telling them the meaning of the card, my basic idea for an image, and then ask them to pose in a way that they felt embodied the emotion and concept of the card. Some cards images were quick to reveal themselves and only a few photos were needed. Some images though, like the Nine of Cups, required a photo session where over 60 pictures were taken as I tried to find the right image for the card.

The Psychic Factor

One thing that most people do not know is that apart from being an artist, I am also a medium and energy worker. I think this rather made me an ideal choice for making a tarot deck because it allowed me a more intimate connection to the essences behind the cards like the Major Arcana. This was a good and bad thing. So, let this serve as a warning to all of you who deign to take on such a task unawares – be prepared for the consequences *before* you say, "Wow, I think it would be NEAT to make a tarot deck!"

I went into the project thinking of this only as an art project and dreaming of the day when I might finally be published. I did not realize that I began the *journey* of the tarot when I took on this project, and I what I got was well more than I bargained for. What I found was that true creation of a tarot deck is a magical act, one which I was unprepared for. The meditation on the meaning of each card was like an invocation, and with some of the Major Arcana, more like a summoning. The cards were reflecting themselves in my life and sometimes the lives of some of my friends, and in turn my life affected the development of the deck. It really is difficult to know which came first. I lived each and every card in this way, each card a personal journey and experience. I painted my life and emotions into these cards.

Some cards were easy to deal with, some were very painful. The creation of some cards went very quickly, like The Chariot, which seemed to almost draw itself, like a whisper in my head speaking to me demanding to be drawn in a particular way. It was like having a demanding client stand behind you as you draw saying, "Okay yeah, now, put a line there and make the hand like that... No! Not that way!" And then a 'thwap' on the head. Cards like that were so demanding that twelve to fifteen hours behind my art desk were not unheard of. Images were frequently completed in my head even before I laid pencil to paper and I often felt like I was just coloring in a sheet of paper – as though I had seen the future of card and I was but the hand to lay the paint. Some cards were arduously slow, like The Hanged Man. The creation of that card dragged on and on until I finally realized the truth in my life and not in the card – that I had to surrender to my situation and the bonds that held me would loosen. I did, and suddenly the card just "popped" and it was finished in no time. It was frequently exhausting and I went through a lot of energy in making each card and it seemed often as though I were taking pieces of my soul and embedding them in the cards.

Being psychic was incredibly useful though, as Michelle and I conspired on a number of cards. More than occasionally, Michelle would have an idea for a card and I would see the image in my head, or vice versa. That was the case for Justice. We were struggling to find an idea for the card, and suddenly Michelle had the image in her head. She stood there trying to describe it as I sat trying to draw it, but I didn't quite understand where she was going. In her description of the card, she quoted, "The veil that conceals the face of mercy." And just like that, I had the image that she was picturing. As the deck progressed, the mental collaboration became so instantaneous that it was nearly impossible to know who had an idea first. Michelle would come running into the art room with a great idea only to find me already sketching what she was thinking of. Or she would have an idea and only need to say a few words and I would be able to describe the image in detail that she was thinking of. It was a unique experience and one which I find makes the deck that much better – a deck designed by two psychics with input from the universe.

Materials

I chose watercolor as my medium for the deck primarily because I knew it to be the preferred paint of many illustrators. But it has been pointed out to me by my friend Trystia – a gifted artist, sassy lady and a leader in the pagan community – that watercolors happen to be the perfect medium for a tarot deck. Watercolors are of earth and water, and when you create a tarot card you add in your spirit (air) and power (fire). The sheer perfection of this combination for the creation of a divinational tool is startling to comprehend. As Trystia has told me, "I know the heart and soul that goes into these pieces, and the process weaves into every aspect of your life. It weaves in traits of those you love, moments in time that you recall every time you see one, and people whose faith in you, whose love for you is deeply interwoven in time with those pieces. It's not surprising really, when you consider the heart of the medium. Water and earthly elements. It is scrying, conjuring, invoking and weaving in every primal way ever done in history. It *is* the perfect medium for Tarot, and for the creation of the images... as well as the intent of the cards."

Paints: I use Winsor & Newton Artists Water Colour as much as possible due to the purity of color and longevity of the paint, but will also use the student grade Cotman Water Colour for a number of hues. To those starting out with water color, don't spend your money on the expensive paints until you know for sure that water color is for you. Student grade paints are perfectly acceptable and yield a beautiful result. The difference between the professional grade and student grade paint is the quantity of pigment (ground stone or chemical) in the paint. Because there is more pigment in the professional grade paint, the paint will be more brilliant and last much longer than the student grade. The elevated quantity of pigment also raises the price of the paint because processing some of these chemicals is very expensive for the small amount of pigment actually produced. One tiny tube of professional grade water color can cost as much as five or six times the price of a student grade tube. As a professional artist, I feel that the end result was well worth the price. If you want to branch into the more expensive pigments, I would suggest buying one basic color in each hue that can be modified up or down on the color wheel. You can fill in your color wheel gaps with the student grade pigment or try to mix up your own with existing professional paints.

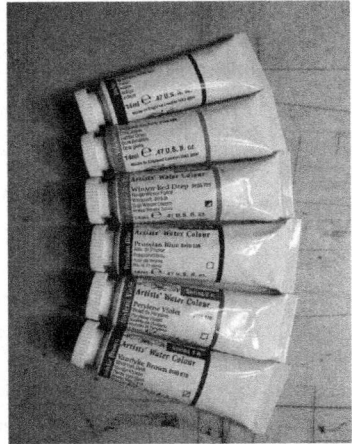

Paper: I use Winsor & Newton or Arches 140 pound hot press paper, 30x22 inch sheets. This gives me a very smooth surface with very little tooth. I do not recommend the common cold press water color paper with the irregular surface for any kind of detail work. What is the difference between "hot press" vs. "cold press"? Hot press is paper pressed between two hot rollers, essentially ironed flat, creating a very smooth surface. A smooth surface allows for more detail and prevents the paint from absorbing as fast into the fibers which means you can work blending the paint much longer. Cold press paper is paper rolled between cold rollers which leaves a very rough irregular surface. A rough surface allows you to have more texture in your image, but it also means that the paper will absorb the paint like a sponge. You don't have as much time to work with it, and a high amount of detail work is very difficult to accomplish. There are surface textures in between, and if you are looking for something with a slight amount of texture but still allowing for a good amount of detail, choose a vellum surface. A vellum surface has the texture of an egg shell – almost smooth but with just a little bit of surface tooth.

Brushes: Paint brushes vary in size and shape. I do prefer buying a better quality brush because the brush lasts longer and doesn't shed bristles on your canvas while you're working. That does not mean you need to run out and buy the pricey Winsor & Newton Series 7 brushes, but choosing a better brush can make the difference in your satisfaction while painting - to not be fighting your brush to keep its shape or picking bristles off of wet paint. As with pigments, so too with brushes – you get what you pay for. Brush shape is entirely at your discretion; use what gets you the desired result. My favorite brushes are those with an angular or wedge shape, and round brushes with a thick well at the base narrowing to a point. I also used a variety of flat, filbert and liner brushes, as well as the fan brush though infrequently. Brush choice really depends on where you want to go with your painting.

Other Materials: Other materials include Sanford Drawing pencils, primarily HB, 3B and 4B for drawing, gridded ruler, and a standard Canson 65 pound sketch book. I will also use 6B to transfer an image to the canvas, using the softer graphite to shade the back of the transfer paper. Kneaded rubber erasers are the eraser of choice for me. They lift the graphite without damaging the pager, and can be easily molded to remove very small areas of detail. I use a pipette (a laboratory style eye dropper) to wet the page or splatter paint in the background. I found the pipette to be the best tool for moving paint around too because it didn't drip. I use regular masking tape to tape the paper to the backing board (artists tape doesn't stick well), and I also use a variety of salts (iodized, sea salt, and kosher salt) to accomplish the strange mottled background on many of the images.

So if you have ever wondered why an original painting costs so much, there's your answer – material prices are phenomenally expensive. Most artists barely recoup the cost of their materials, to say nothing of payment for the time involved. Next time you're at an art fair, don't gripe about the price, think about what went into making that painting.

The Painting Process

Once reference materials are selected, the sketching process begins. In my sketch book, I begin by blocking out the image on the page, creating a basic skeleton of the image. I then add in as many details of the images as I feel are needed to complete the concept. Sometimes I draw out the entire card image, but more often than not I draw out only the main figure of the page. Because so much of the detail is done with paints, I will generally only worry most about the details of the face and hands and leave all the other details for the canvas. Once the sketch is done, I may choose to resize it on the scanner, adjusting up or down depending on what I want to see in the finished image. I print out the resized black and white sketch and shade the back of the print with a 6B pencil, which will transfer easily to the canvas.

Canvas Preparation: Prepping the canvas is a step usually done during the sketching phase. I don't like to prepare large numbers of the watercolor sheets ahead of time, I prefer to leave my paper protected in its wrapping or in a drawer to keep in clean. I cut down the large water color sheets (30x22 inches) into 5 smaller canvases measuring a little better than 8.5x12 inches (extra .125 to .25 to allow for shrinkage). When scaled down in the computer and added to the card border, the image is the perfect tarot card size for a standard deck. I then take two of the cut sheets and soak them in a large clean basin full of warm water for 10-15 minutes. A presoak is necessary to remove the sizing in the paper. The sizing is a chemical that keeps the paper nice and crisp, but it prevents even paint absorption if not removed. This will affect your color washes, leaving a strange splotchiness as you paint (some areas of the page will absorb paint more than others). Presoaking is also good for slightly shrinking your paper before you work with it. This is especially important in watercolor work, as the last thing you want to happen is to have your paper shrinking on the backing board *while* you're working on it.

The ten minutes in the bath are up – now to test the paper. Put your finger tip under a corner and bend it back slightly. If the paper springs back to place right away, the paper hasn't soaked long enough. If the paper returns to place slowly, your paper is just right. Remove it from the tub and lay it on your backing board. A backing board is just a piece of treated plywood, something that won't warp as easily. My backing boards were a standard wood cutting board, and a chunk from the back of a church door. Yes, the tarot deck was painted (especially the Major Arcana) on a piece of wood cut from an old church door being upcycled. Gives the deck a little something extra, don't you think? I place my cut sheets on the backing board and blot them dry just a little with a paper towel. Next I tape the paper edges down with long strips of masking tape to stretch it. The paper stays taped to the board throughout the entire painting process to prevent further shrinkage or warping.

Once the newly stretched paper is thoroughly dry on the board, I can proceed to transfer the image onto it. I position my image where I want it on the canvas and being to trace on top of the image. The graphite on the back transfers easily and can be removed easily from the canvas if needed. I fill in any other details to the sketch on the canvas, and clean up any dirty areas to ensure the paints adhere to a clean white surface. If I am working with light colors like yellows, I do not want my pigments muddied by loose graphite on the page.

Water Colors Technique
The painting process is frequently the longest step in the process, second only to finding the appropriate reference images. Unlike

acrylics, water colors are a completely unforgiving medium but with uncompromising beauty. With acrylics, if you make a mistake, you just paint over it. If you hate a huge section of the image, your gesso is only an arm's reach away and you can white out the entire section. But with water color, if you make a mistake, you must either make it work, try to touch it up with white gouache, lift the color, or with a large mistake you must scrap the entire piece and start over. I cannot tell you how many pieces I had to scrap and start over on during the first two years of the deck when I was still learning. With water colors, you must plan out each painting in your head ahead of time, knowing precisely where all the light and dark areas on a page will be. Water colors are transparent, which means you can see the white of the page or pencil lines under a wash. But because water colors are transparent, you can also do remarkable things with color layering and gradient washes. You can use the white of the page for your highlights, and continue to blend color into color or smooth out edges even after the paint has dried. That is a flexibility that acrylics do not have - once dried, it's dried forever. Water color only needs to be rewet to make it workable.

With water colors, you must proceed from lightest to darkest, building up your layers of color for rich full colors. I always start with the background, building up the layers of color, sometimes letting my page dry before the next blending, sometimes working wet to wet as when I applied the salt technique to give a "starry" look to the background. If I needed to work on something and didn't have time for a natural drying, I pulled out my hair dryer and set to rapidly drying the page being careful not to apply to much heat. I always planned in my head where I wanted

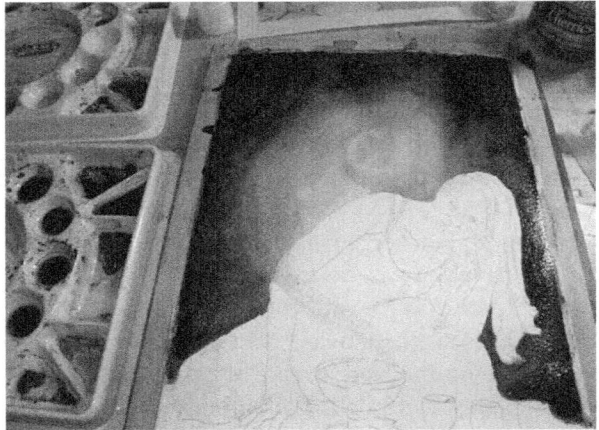

white space on the page and did not use a masking fluid to reserve spaces after several very poor results with the masking fluid.

I always enjoyed painting the backgrounds of the cards, especially the Major Arcana. I would use the pipette to drop paints onto the wet surface, letting them mingle as they would. The background was free-flowing, colors upon colors, seemingly creating the shapes and swirls itself but with subtle structure built in. The background is where I imbedded a lot of the power of the card by using layers of colors to represent the emotional context of the card meaning. The backgrounds feel alive in some respect, and have as much weight and meaning in the card as the main figure. I feel that color representative to the meaning will make the cards easier to read for people who are more meditative or instinctual in their reads. Instead of focusing on the figure, they can instead choose to reflect on the colors of the card and read from that. Color meaning is present throughout the deck and not limited to the Major Arcana. If doing a reading with these cards, try it out – do your standard card spread and then instead of reading each card, unfocus your eyes and rise above the image. Just try to see the shades and hues, the lights and darks, and disregard the figures seeing them only as another color. Feel the overall emotion of the spread using only the color and read intuitively from that information.

After layering up and completing the background, I would begin to work the foreground and the main figures. As with the background, layer after layer was placed, building up the shading and delicately gradating washes between the shadows and highlights. Skin tone was the easiest once I got the hang of the watercolors. Skin tone in watercolors is a matter of adding in your mid-tones and blending in the shadows. The highlights are all the white of the page. Pale skin is easily done with a light brown to let the white of the page shine through, and darker skin utilizes a darker brown tone. Details were carefully added, the most delicate of which like the eyes, costume details or jewelry I always saved for the last.

Development of Style
As you will note, there is a distinct difference in some of the card art. The earliest cards are easy to identify as they are obviously different in technique from the later cards. This was an unavoidable issue as an artist, for you cannot help but grow and improve your technique

the more you practice. Even if I had gone back to re-do cards that bug me, it would be a perpetual cycle because where could I really stop? Old cards redone become better than the new cards and so I have to remake even more? No, I decided that I should accept my art as being depictive of my tarot journey. When I thought about it, even the images I was not particularly proud of as an artist when compared to the latest and greatest were still integral to the deck as a whole. The images had interwoven themselves into a unified whole! Remake cards and you poke holes in your tapestry. There were two cards that I did choose to remake – the High Priestess and the Five of Cups. When looking at the deck as a whole interwoven tapestry, those two previous cards did not fit the deck any longer. They were image aberrations, they did not weave themselves into the cohesive whole. And so losing them was not a difficulty. The cards that replaced them were perfect additions to the deck, and the image tapestry which had previously rejected those two cards suddenly became whole. I do not regret the choice.

Card Completion
Now the card is finished with the painting stage. The last thing I do to a card before calling it done is to sign my name at the bottom. Unbelievably, the question of, "How do I want to sign my name?" was something I struggled with for the first several of months painting. Ridiculous, isn't it? I wonder if every artist has this problem. For the record, I decided to go with a simple "J. Williams" printed neatly at the bottom (usually right) of the piece, feeling that my shortened name would interrupt the piece less. I had also been researching Arthur Rackham's art, and I noticed his signature at the bottom of his paintings was encased in a little scroll like box. I thought such a flourish was both charming and distinctive, so for some of my paintings I signed my name "J. Williams" with the date and encased it in a scroll box. I gave up on that after a while not wishing to interrupt details in the image, and would occasionally add a little flourish line under my signature, or none at all depending on space. Consistently though, I signed my name, "J. Williams" with the year next to my signature.

Once complete, the card is then scanned at a high resolution to preserve the color integrity in digital form. The card image is then merged with the card border in Photoshop, and the card name and meaning added.

Behind the Cards: Friends as Models
Perhaps you recognize some of the people in the deck? That may be true - models for a number of the cards are personal friends and acquaintances, chosen for the card based on the individual's personality, past life, or generally embodying the nature of the card. I used a number of stock images for some of the body models, and features of most of them are altered to give the card the necessary look and feel. Likenesses other than what are listed here are purely coincidental. For the Major Arcanca (in order): I posed for the High Priestess, Jane and her daughter Katie posed for the Empress, Jay posed for the Emperor, Michelle posed for the Devil, Andrea posed for the Star (a very distinct tribute to Mucha), and Jason posed for Judgment. For the Pentacles Suit: Jessica and Aaron posed for the Two of Pentacles, Jason for the Three, Kate for the Six, Aaron and Kira for the Eight, me for the Nine, Rhiannon for the Page and the Knight, and Matthew for the King. For the Wands Suit: Michelle posed as the body model for the Two, Four, and Five, though her likeness only truly appears once in the deck as the Devil. Shawn posed for the Eight and Nine, and Sarah was a body model for the pose of the Page. For the Cups Suit: Sarah posed for the Five of Cups, Michaela posed for the Six, Becca posed for the Nine of Cups, and Cindy, Shawn, Adrienne, Jessica, and Andrea, as well as my dog Penny posed for the Ten. Stephanie posed for the second incarnation of the Page, Rhiannon again posed for the Knight, and Kate posed for the Queen.

For the Sword Suit: A dead guy posed for the Three (yes, that's right, a ghost), Andrea posed for the Four, Polina posed for the Page, Chuck (Midair) posed for the Knight, Jason again posed for the King, and Eilfie Music (whom you might recognize from *Paranormal State*) posed for the Seeker card.

Music and Movie Influences

During the five year painting process, I watched (or more appropriately *listened to*) a ton of movies and TV shows to get me through the endless hours at the art table. *The West Wing* series carried me through the entire deck, and I bless the people who decided to put the series onto DVD. I watched the series at least eight full times, re-watching a couple of the seasons independently. Why did I obsess over *The West Wing*? Apart from the spectacular writing, acting, and political satire, the story was fantastic and I didn't have to watch the show to enjoy it. It's not always convenient when painting to continually look up from the canvas to stare at whatever is going on, and with shows and movies that were not so dependent on action, I was able to listen to the story while working. I would also occasionally listen to songs while working.

Many people want to know if I was influenced by music while painting the deck or in general. Music does inspire me and I frequently see colors when I hear music. This is especially true when I hear classical music and I tend to see swirls of colors much like the backgrounds of the Major Arcana. There are even some classical composers where I think I can actually hear math equations. But my favorite songs to be inspired by are the ballads such as those found among the artists in the Filk genre. Having spent so many years in the SCA (Society for Creative Anachronism), this is hardly surprising. There is one such artist whose music single-handedly influenced and inspired the entire feel of the Sword Suit, and that is Heather Dale. Songs from her album *The Trial of Lancelet*, as well as songs from several other of her albums were particularly inspirational in setting the mood for the swords. Of note, there is a song called *Measure of a Man* which specifically inspired the Ten of Swords. I painted her music in that card and hear that song in my head every time I see that image. The song *Exile* from her album *May Queen* was also particularly inspirational to the suit and reminds me of the Six of Swords. If you want to experience the Swords from a musical perspective, immerse yourself in that album and you will understand (www.heatherdale.com). To Heather – thank you for your wonderful music, you will never know how much it inspires me.

What Took So Long?
Most people cannot imagine spending five years on a single project. Some may be thinking, "Five years? I could get it done in half that time!" If anyone had told me that I would be at this so long when I first agreed to the project, I would have laughed and said, "no way will it take that long." In fact, I was re-reading my blog back to when I had first started the deck. At that time I was making such swift progress on the first few cards that I mused that at the present rate, I would be done in a year! Yeah… that was 2008.

So what took me so long? Well, first off, art is not my professional career (at this time of writing this). I worked a full time job during the time I was working on the deck, which meant that I could not dedicate all day every day to painting. I gave up my hobbies to focus on painting, but that still only meant nights and weekends. Additionally, decks… well… they seem to have a life of their own. There were periods of time when no image would work for a particular card, periods of time when I was uninspired to paint no matter how much I wanted to. I fought and struggled with the deck, refusing to let it just go about its own merry pace, but still, it didn't matter. The cards came to me as they would, in their own due course at the right time – sometimes quickly with periods of intense creativity, and sometimes weeks would go by with barely anything to show. I worked on a few small projects while doing the deck, something to break up the monotony and give me something to do when the cards wouldn't come. But all in all, the last five years, most specifically the last three has seen me at the art desk nights and weekends. The last year was the hardest as I pushed to complete the deck. But it is done and as Michelle says with projects like these, "They take as long as they are going to take." In the end though, I am almost glad it took five years. My artistic style improved so much, I think the deck would have been an inferior product if I hadn't allowed my art to mature.

The SCA Influence

For those who do not know what the SCA is, it is the Society for Creative Anachronism, a worldwide organization whose members seek to recreate aspects of the Middle Ages and Renaissance. We enjoy all varieties of the arts like scribal work, dancing, wood working, cooking (medieval style of course), sewing, fencing and sword play, and various other things. I was involved with the SCA for about seven years before beginning the deck and enjoyed the dancing, fencing, sewing and the scribal arts. I was a scribe for the Middle Kingdom (different regions of the world are organized into kingdoms and baronies, echoing the old European feudal system) for several years, earning my Order of the Evergreen for my illumination art and teaching. The SCA was and continues to be a huge part of my life, which is why you will notice the strong medieval influences in some of the costumes and props. I even included a few SCA friends into the deck – Kate as the Queen of Cups, Chuck as the Knight of Swords, Jason as Judgment and the King of Swords, Matthew as the King of Pentacles, and Michaela as the Six of Cups. The sword used in the Sword suit is actually Jason's officer's sword, and the cup used in the Cups suit is my personal wooden goblet that I use at events. There are even scenes from events – if you've ever been to Pennsic War in Pennsylvania, you may be reminded of the Coopers Lake Campground lake in the Two of Cups, and the Seven of Swords will bring fond memories to anyone who has seen the tents of Pennsic illuminated on a warm summer's night.

Fur Child

The Ten of Cups has the only animal within the deck – my dog Penny. Penny, a rat terrier, is my loving fur child. As the deck began to consume my free time, I had less time to play with her. Though we did play often and go for walks, the times when I had long painting spells were difficult on my small one, for she was lonely and bored and no amount of toys could replace my attention. Her love and companionship was desperately needed by me as I wound my way through the painting process, and I cherish every moment spent with her. I felt she was owed a place in history and so put her into the tarot.

Running the Tarot Marathon

I'd like to say that painting the tarot was an easy thing to do. I would like to say that I never struggled with the painting process, was never frustrated, never had internal battles, never wanted to quit. I cannot say those things though, because I experienced all of it in great amounts. Finding the deck style was very frustrating, and accepting my personal style even worse. I *hated* my art in that first year. For an artist, I think there is nothing more depressing than despising your own style.

What made things extremely difficult was that Michelle had particular ideas of what she wanted for the style, but couldn't adequately describe it to me. She continued to point to the examples of Mucha and Rackham as what she liked. But she didn't actually want the stylized Mucha and didn't want the ink art of Rackham but somehow more of an internal *feel* which those artists inspired. I was in a conundrum, and I tried and failed time and time again to achieve her wholly subjective idea of the style. I went through a lot of failed cards during this period and one card in particular was The Sun card. I had already had a number of failed cards previous to this card, and even for the Sun I had painted three designs – all of which garnered a, "No, doesn't really work" from Michelle. Finally, I painted the image that is the present Sun card – painted it and emailed her the file thinking to myself, "If she says she doesn't like this one too, I

41

am done. I quit." This was the make-it or break-it card and I was serious about quitting if this one failed to fly. Michelle opened the file... and loved it. Loved it and I don't know why. It didn't follow either Mucha or Rackham in design. But she gave a thumbs up, and I had found tone of the deck. The rest is history.

But despite finding the right tone of the deck, I cannot tell you how many times I beat my head against my art desk. There were times when I was very frustrated with a card or my developing style that I just wanted to tear it to shreds. And there were times when I was so overwhelmed with the enormity of the deck, or unhappy with a card, that I gave serious thought to burning the deck. I honestly considered saying to Michelle, "Please, take the portfolio and hide it from me, I'm going to destroy it." But of course, I did not destroy the deck, and once I got to the halfway point, my style had vastly improved and the deck was no longer giving me as many problems. That's not to say that I didn't want to tear my hair out over certain cards thereafter, but things were infinitely better.

As I neared the final twenty cards, I started to set goals for myself – milestones that I could look forward to as I counted down to zero, like my "Sweet Sixteen" party when I reached sixteen cards to go. The last three cards were the hardest and I felt like a marathon runner in that last mile. Once I finished that last card, I was relieved... for about five seconds. I took a month off but I realized that although I had crossed the finish line, there was still so much to do to prepare the deck for printing. The thought of finishing the marathon only to have to run another race was exhausting and I think the time following card zero was the most difficult part of the entire deck creation process. I had difficulty finding the strength to finish what ultimately became the last mile. Not only did I have to worry about formatting the deck, I had to re-create two cards. Emotionally I was just spent, but I knew I just had a little more to go. I pushed myself through and with the help of Christine Filipak and Joseph Vargo of Monolith Graphics, I was able to finish the tarot and get it to the printer. I can honestly say that creating a Tarot deck of seventy eight hand-painted cards was a daunting task that tested me as an artist and a person. It was an exercise in perseverance and internal fortitude that few can achieve and I am honored to stand in the ranks of Tarot artists.

Favorite Cards

I am frequently asked if I have a favorite card. It is difficult to choose one favorite card and as I progressed along in the deck, my "favorite card" would change as my technique improved. My favorite cards had nothing to do with the subject matter of each card. As an artist my favorite card became the card in which the art I was most proud at the time – an evaluation of color, design, and technique. Early on, my favorite cards had been the Three of Swords, Death, and the Ace of Cups. As my technique improved and more cards were made, I then also prized the Knight of Swords and the Seven of Cups. Then came the Wheel and The Hanged Man to add to my list of favorites. Now, here at the end of the deck, I can appreciate each and every card, each in its own right. It is as hard to select a single favorite card, but the cards that I am most artistically proud of (at the moment) are the following:

The High Priestess: I appreciate this card for the use of light and dark, and my ability to paint a sheer curtain as well as believable smoke from the incense.

The Chariot: This card is loved for the glowing sky behind the clouds, the look upon the faces, and its true Pre-Raphaelite style.

The Wheel: This is probably the most unique card of the deck. I really stepped outside myself to paint this. I appreciate this card for the design as well as the background blending and overall concept.

Justice: This card was an exercise in using the white of the canvas and only painting shadows.

Death: This card was an exercise in gray-scale and I loved the statuesque design.

Three of Swords: I like this card for the use of gray and white in contrast to the red.

Nine of Cups: I loved the background of this card with the smoke and the ghostly cups.

Knight of Pentacles: In this card I am most probably the most proud. The skin tones and shading are perfect, the hands of the figure are perfect, and the background colors are rich and vibrant.

Appearance of Ancient Locales

I studied the ancient world for my undergraduate degree and a few years after my graduation, I was at last able to travel to Greece where

I spent ten days running around Athens, Delphi, Mycenae, and Thebes. This was at a point in my life where my medium skills still controlled me, and before I had even begun to explore the possibility of past lives. Travelling in Greece, there wasn't a place in that country that didn't touch me deeply and profoundly. My experience in the country moved me literally to tears, and I wouldn't be joking to say that in many places, I walked around with a camera in one hand and tissue in the other. There was something very familiar about the land and the cityscape, and I walked around Athens with a strange innate sense of direction. I knew approximately where everything was – without a map. It was the strangest feeling to walk the streets, never getting lost and always feeling as though I belonged there. I had never had that before, not in all the places I had visited. But there in Athens I felt that at last I had come home.

Two of the places I visited while in Greece make their appearance here in the tarot. One is in the Three of Cups. The grotto where the girls are washing was inspired by my visit to Delphi and the Castalian Spring. The spring was the place where the Pythia and the priests of the temple of Apollo washed, as well as where the patrons to the temple purified themselves before seeking consultation of the gods. According to the archaeologists, the Castalian Spring is located at the foot of a rocky crag and the stream from it runs into the valley. The much pictured "Lower Castalian" was built well below the source of the spring itself. The structure has been built and refurbished several times over the last 2,500 years or so, and is in its present state a large rectangular basin. Though I did not get to venture to the actual spring's source, for the card I pictured water issuing from rocks into a rough built basin surrounded by the deep green trees of the mountainside. Perhaps this is what it might have looked like long ago when the first oracles of Delphi prepared themselves for the ritual of divine communication.

The second ancient place appearing in the deck is in the Four of Pentacles. Depicted here is a tribute to the Lion's Gate at Mycenae. Mycenae is perhaps the most profound place I had ever or will ever visit. I made a pilgrimage to the archaeological site for Mycenae, walking the long dirt road from the bus stop at the small town of Φιχτι some four miles to the ruins. I reached the site, and as I walked up the dirt path, there it was, the site from my history books, the Lion's Gate. The site itself is thousands of years old, with Mycenae itself inhabited since the Neolithic period and first walls of the ancient palace itself and other construction dating to the middle of the second millennium B.C.E. It was truly magnificent to behold, and walking under the massive lintel, I stretched out my arms on the wall of the city entrance and sobbed. Mycenae is unimaginably special to me, and I felt it appropriate that I use it in the Four of Pentacles.

Past Life Memories
One of my talents as a medium and an artist is to be able to draw and paint the images that I am seeing – from spirit portraits to memory scenes from past lives. I put this skill to use in the tarot, incorporating spirit portraits and past life images and ideas into the cards. Images inspired by spirit and memory are scattered throughout the deck. One such example is in the Three of Swords where the man in the painting is actually a dead Celtic warrior who hangs about. The Six of Swords is an example of a past life memory – it was a vision I received doing some energy work with a friend. A particularly personal example though is the image of the Queen of Wands, which is a self-portrait of me from a long time ago. I have a memory of looking like that – the way my face looked, the gold combs in my hair, the way my hair and earrings brushed on my neck, and the sheer silk drapery. For those seeking their own past life memories and connections, I have no wish to divulge too much. Rather, I would say to reflect on the images in the deck and meditate on what touches you.

The Alpha and Omega
The first card completed in the deck was The Fool. Appropriate in retrospect that I – the fool – should jump into a tarot deck so blithely unaware. But actually the Fool was chosen because when I first began the deck, I thought I should go in order of the cards and so the Fool came first. But the deck soon took on a life of its own and I jumped around from card to card in a seemingly random fashion at first. It was later I realized that I was in fact giving myself a tarot reading by painting the cards in the order I in which I was inspired to. Again, the deck influenced my life as much as my life influenced the deck. Sometimes it's hard to know which came first. The last

card to be painted was The World. That was planned for. I needed a capstone, and the World would serve to sum up the deck for me.

The Wheel

The Wheel card has a very interpretive quality to it. The Wheels on the outside of the great wheel between the two angels represent the realms and influences outside our own plane of existence. The angels themselves are forces of the universe acting upon the influences. Those wheels move, which in turn moves the big wheel – our universe, that which contains our plane of existence – and as those forces move the big wheel, the smaller wheels inside our realm also begin to move, indirectly acted upon by the universal force. The globe at the top right of the image in the center of the big wheel represents our world, and so represents us. There was a painful realization that I made as I meditated on the image. It made me want to throw my sketch book across the room and beat my hands onto the ground and scream and cry like a child. The realization was – sometimes you're the cog, and sometimes you're the hand that moves the cog. Complicated? No. But a painfully hard realization when you actually sit down and think about it. And the moral of the story is? Be the hand.

Bookends

Death and Justice were not planned as an image set. They were actually drawn one year apart and it is a coincidence that they reflect one another. That is to say, it was not consciously planned out by me. I drew the Death card after a vision that I had before a massive natural disaster occurred. The image itself of the Death figure is not what I saw in the vision; what I saw were the colors of the

background towards the bottom of the figure – colors of teal blue, black and grays mottled together like a storm cloud. I saw it so closely, it was as though I were looking at something so big, that all I could see was a tiny part. Like holding your arm up in front of your eyes and all you see is your sleeve. You know there's more, but all you are seeing is a close-up of the sleeve. I had to find a way to create an image that would flow with the style of the deck yet incorporate my vision. So

I sketched out the figure you see, inspired by the idea of funerary statues. I used the colors of my vision for the colors of the card, building it into the background, making it part of the figure itself. The Justice card followed a full year later, drawn from a vision Michelle had and showed to me. The figures oddly complement each other, light versus dark, both figures tall and cold almost like statues themselves but somehow alive; aspects of measurement and balance, each in their own right.

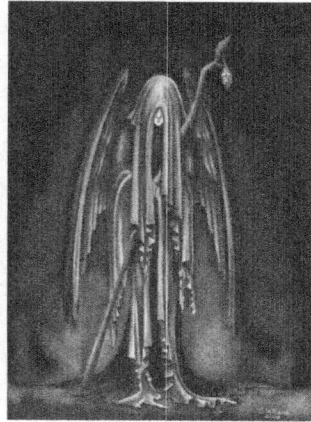

The World

The World card was the last card in the tarot to be painted. It was a capstone and a summation of all I had been through over the five year journey. I struggled, literally for months, to find the right image idea for this card, but the card just wasn't ready to reveal itself. In the struggle to find the right idea, The World began to represent the culmination of my very personal journey. I had to spend time to consider what the meaning of the card meant to me. To me, the World is what happens *after* Judgment, so I then had to go back and decide what Judgment meant. I decided that Judgment is the old world thrown down – the world you knew or thought you knew brought into the stark harsh light of reality, and truth and lie revealed. What you once trusted, relied on, believed in, held dear or true now crumbles as you are forced to see things as they are. It is the ultimate "big decision world upheaval" kind of change card for me. And so the World card had to serve as what comes *after* the storm, a culmination of the journey. But how do you conclude the entire deck in a single card?

After much consideration, I depicted a figure walking out of the ruin and rubble of a destroyed city, the crumbled statues of dead gods and temples littering the road. He has made the long journey and survived Judgment, but as he reaches the end of the path you can see that he is not unscathed from his journey. Blood drips from his wings and legs, some of it his and some not, for no one can walk a path of change and remain untouched by the experience. Wounds will heal over time but the scars will remain to serve as a reminder lest he forget and the lessons become lost. He is not the same as when he began, he walked through fire, suffered, triumphed, won and lost. The journey has changed him, the journey made him wise.

The angel's hair is cut short, representative of a release – a re-initiation. He walks from the old path, its colors already fading into the past and we see a new path before him. His face angles down reflecting on his old path. He does not know where this new path will take him, but walks acceptingly and resolutely forward, changed but stronger and wiser for his journey. There was some discussion as to whether the angel should be depicted as returning to heaven, as Enoch was supposed to do in the story. That would certainly have held true to the story of the Watcher Angels but not, in my opinion, true to the card. The World is both an ending and a beginning, and for the angel who was Enoch to return to heaven implies an ending and completion of the journey in total. So I tried for a compromise. I drew a new city before him in the distance, a city awash in warm golden tones reminiscent of Elysium, and the light of God shining down upon the angel and the city. For some people, this may represent Elysium or the City of Heaven – that Enoch/Metatron is walking into the Light and returning home. And for others, the image may represent God illuminating the new path and the city only an arbitrary representation of a new destination. Some may interpret the image as the path leading to another incarnation of the body, the life after this life. Howsoever one chooses to interpret my painting, one thing is true: One path is completed and a new one lies ahead, be it in this life or in lifetimes to come – always a new path.

Conclusion

My journey with the creation of the Tarot has come to a conclusion, and the deck at long last has come to fruition. I am greatly changed from my experience with this project. I have made the journey, won, lost, and grew in knowledge and experience. I am older and wiser than when I began, and my artistic style will forever be changed, made better by all the many hours of work on the tarot. I am grateful to all of my wonderful friends and family for supporting me on this journey. Your love and support has been and will always be tremendously important to me. I could not have walked this path without you. With all my heart, I thank you.

-- Jackie Williams

II. Mythos

Mythos Part I: The Tarot as Monomyth

I wasn't sure what to think about Tarot cards when I bought my first deck. My introduction to the very concept of the Tarot had come through young adult fiction, so my initial relationship with my deck was light-hearted: I wanted to play around with the cards, learn how to do readings for friends, and see what all the fuss was about. I was one of those kids (who turned into one of those adults) who asks questions about everything – especially when it comes to beliefs. People believed that the Tarot could foretell the future, and as I learned to work with the cards, I had to admit that there was something going on. My cards never foretold specific world events or anything as exciting as that. But they did frequently provide insight into details about people that I did not previously know.

Some of my readers will immediately think, "Well, you're psychic, so it wasn't the cards. It was you." But that's the thing: sure, I'm sensitive and I have an intuitive grasp of emotions. I can pick a lot of things out of peoples' heads if I'm trying. But I was working with a set of cards, randomly shuffled and randomly placed. While there is some wiggle room in the nuances of the cards, and proper interpretation of these nuances relies on the intuitive capabilities of the reader, the cards are still set quantities. The Three of Swords is an unhappy card, and no amount of interpretive wiggle room is going to turn it suddenly cheery. Yet, with all the random probability involved in laying cards out for a reading, those readings nevertheless had useful information time and again.

Some people would be content with the idea that it's magick. Among the anecdotal reports about Tarot cards that I've heard over the years is the idea that there is a spirit or spirits within the deck. Supposedly, these spirits are what power the deck, influencing the fall of the cards to predict the future. This notion of spirits that literally inhabit the cards is one of the primary reasons that individuals of conservative faiths fear the Tarot. The reasoning goes something like this: all spirits that aren't working for God are working for the Devil; the Tarot is not a part of the teachings of God; any spirits inhabiting a Tarot deck must then be working for the Devil. And following exactly that logic, a great many people still look upon the Tarot as an instrument of evil. Further, they see individuals who work with the cards as unwitting pawns of that evil, to the point where they may go so far as to store decks of Tarot cards among haunted items as if the deck itself could have a malignant influence over onlookers simply by existing.

I could regale you with a long-winded explanation of how this belief ties back to notions that were prevalent in the Middle Ages with regards to books of magick and grimoires. I could cite instances where superstitious clergy operating during the reactionary period of the witchcraft hysteria went so far as to put actual books on trial on the basis that these magickal texts were powered by and inhabited by evil spirits. But professor Richard Kieckheffer does a bang-up job of this himself in his book, *Forbidden Rites,* saving me the ink and you the tangent. Suffice to say that the notion that evil spirits inhabit the tools of magick and ritual is generally a belief held only by those individuals who do not practice such, and are on the outside of the tradition, looking in with confusion. While I won't argue that certain decks seem to possess a kind of personality, especially the more a reader works with that particular deck, it's not quite the same thing as having each individual card imbued with some otherworldly intelligence. That's literally the stuff of fiction: it was the very premise of the young adult novel that brought me to the Tarot.

If the Tarot is not inhabited by an intelligent spirit or spirits with the miraculous power of controlling the otherwise random action of the cards in order to foretell the future, then why does the Tarot seem to work? Moreover, why do we tend to personalize it when we're reading it? If you're not sure what I mean by that, take a few moments to get a seasoned Tarot reader gushing about their deck. It won't take long for them to start talking about their deck as if it were intelligent, like a person. I do it myself, even though I don't believe that there's a spirit inhabiting my (or any other) deck. I describe the ways in which certain decks "talk" to me, and I approach my readings rather like a conversation – with the deck, not with the querent.

These were questions I asked myself as I was learning the Tarot. And then an intrepid high school English teacher had my class read Joseph Campbell's *The Hero With a Thousand Faces.* That made everything about the Tarot fall into place, at least for me. The insights I gained from Campbell's work form the very foundation of the Watcher Angel Tarot. To understand the core concept behind this deck, it's necessary first to learn a little about Joseph Campbell and his notion of the Monomyth.

The Master of Stories

Joseph Campbell was the master mythologist of the 20th century – at least for the English-speaking world (I have no idea if he had a counterpart elsewhere). His playful yet intense personality, together with his encyclopedic knowledge of world mythology, come through vibrantly in a series of televised interviews with journalist Bill Moyer. The series is called *The Power of Myth*. There are book versions of this series, but I highly recommend looking up the televised series itself. A book simply cannot adequately capture the seamless way in which Campbell's scintillating intellect will leap from the *Bhagavad-Gita* to the Eleusinian mysteries to the Jedis of *Star Wars* without skipping a beat, tying it all together conceptually along the way. You will get to experience the interconnectedness of world mythologies directly if you choose to watch the series, because Campbell carries all of it in his head, effortlessly relating stories and legends of heroes from every corner of the globe and often finding meaning in unexpected places, such as *Star Wars.*

Campbell approached all beliefs and religious systems in terms of myth, but that's not to say that he viewed these myths as mere fantasy. Rather, he felt that myth – as well as fairy tales and all the stories that we tell ourselves (including, in the modern day, novels and movies) – is a fundamental expression of human truths. In his view, myth is an ageless method for encoding our collective experiences with the world. Myths make use of symbols and metaphors to present universal truths about human experience, in much the same way that dreams use images and symbols to present to each individual half-forgotten emotions, insights, and memories stored in the unconscious mind. Notably, Campbell says, "Dream is the personalized myth. Myth is the depersonalized dream." Taking a page or two from Carl Jung with regards to dreams and the unconscious mind – specifically the collective unconscious – Campbell then points out the underlying themes and archetypal figures that emerge in myth time and again.

Of course, you're probably wondering what all of this has to do with the Tarot. For those of you who are not new to the Tarot, you are likely aware that there are two "types" of cards in a Tarot deck: the numbered suits, which include the Court Cards, and a series of twenty-two Tarot Trumps. The suits are called the Minor Arcana (meaning lesser mystery) and the Trumps are called the Major Arcana (greater mystery). When using the Tarot for divination, the Major Arcana are generally approached as a kind of cycle of human experience, with certain key figures and encounters represented within the cards. The trumps start with The Fool, numbered zero, and end with The World, numbered twenty-one (often using Roman numerals, to distinguish them from the suits of the Minor Arcana). When approached as a cycle of experience, The Fool marks the beginning of the journey and The World marks its completion.

The journey thus represented is nothing less than the story of innocence and experience. The Fool marks, after a fashion, childhood's end. Here, an individual leaps off into the unknown in pursuit of a life-altering experience. It is the pursuit of knowledge, the pursuit of growth, and the pursuit of personal transformation. It is of course not limited to the end of childhood but can be symbolically applied to each and every new endeavor, because we are children again with each new thing we seek to learn, starting from the ground up. And, if you happen to have read Campbell's *The Hero with a Thousand Faces* in college or in high school, you will also see that this cycle of experience holds echoes of the archetypal hero's journey recounted in innumerable world myths.

Campbell, working in the tradition of scholars like Sir James Frazer, author of *The Golden Bough,* compared story after story and myth after myth from every world culture, seeking the details these had in common. And ultimately, Campbell developed a theory of what he calls the Monomyth*: the one underlying story that repeats in fairy tales, legends, and myths the world over. And Campbell's Monomyth applies neatly to the Major Arcana of the Tarot. It was with this in mind that I designed that aspect of my deck, choosing to highlight the process by marrying the already pregnant Tarot imagery with the legend of the Watcher Angels.

---

*The term *Monomyth* itself was borrowed by Campbell from James Joyce's oft-inscrutable work, *Finnegan's Wake*

Fundamentals of the Monomyth

Campbell wrote an entire book on the Monomyth, which I heartily suggest that you consider reading. There is a lot of ground to cover when considering the fundamental story behind all the stories that we tell. In the interest of brevity, I am going to reduce this down as far as I can to a format that is easily understood and relevant to our current topic, the Tarot. Fortunately, Campbell provides key points within the story as chapters in his book, outlining the stages of the hero's journey as he sees them. The over-arching process can be boiled down to three basic steps: *Departure; Initiation;* and *Return.* Every journey begins with a first step, and every hero's tale begins with that hero leaving a familiar and controlled environment to answer the call to adventure. It doesn't matter if that adventure involves the slaying of dragons or taking a new job with a different company or going off to college and living on one's own for the first time: all of these are adventures. They carry risks, they take us out of our comfort zones, and they demand that, if we desire to succeed, we must learn, adapt, and grow. This is the fundamental process of the hero's tale, what Campbell labeled the Monomyth. Notably, in the tales that fit the Monomyth structure, there are key experiences and encounters that typically occur along each of these three stages. Those encounters, as presented in Campbell's *The Hero with a Thousand Faces,* are outlined below:

Departure
- The Call to Adventure
- Supernatural Aid
- Crossing the Threshold
- The Belly of the Whale

Initiation
- The Road of Trials
- Meeting the Powers*
- Atonement and Apotheosis

Return
- Refusal to Return
- Crossing the Return Threshold
- Master of the Two Worlds
- The Freedom to Live

The stage called "Meeting the Powers" is, in Campbell's original schema, called "Meeting the Goddess." At times, he approaches the Universal powers in a regrettably binary fashion, including stages such as "Woman as Temptress." Because Campbell himself is working from a Judeo-Christian background, he envisions the highest power in terms of the Father, with the Goddess as a suppressed power discovered along the way. Campbell is far from a sexist; he is merely a product of his time and culture, as are we all. Just as there is an obvious Jungian influence on his ideologies, his parsing of myth also reveals certain Freudian aspects as well. This is evidenced particularly in the tensions Campbell sees between the hero and God-as-Father and the attraction/repulsion with Goddess-as-Mother. Like Freud, Campbell specifically describes this in terms of Oedipus. For a variety of reasons (not the least of which is the fact that my own worldview *doesn't* involve a binary reduction of God to male or female) I've chosen to leave out these specifics. Broadly speaking, the gender of the powers encountered by the hero in the initiatory phase of the journey is not relevant unless the journey is specifically about gender, or it involves a resolution with traditional parental figures.

Departure: The Call to Adventure
In the Departure portion of Campbell's Monomyth, the first step, or the "Call to Adventure," is pretty straight-forward. Think of every fairy tale you've ever heard. Consider that point when the hero (or heroine) of the tale is sitting at home or working on the family farm then encounters something wondrous. There is that breathless moment where the hero then has to decide whether or not to leave behind everything familiar in order to pursue the remarkable and the unknown. Sometimes the main character becomes a hero by necessity: the home, or the family, or something he or she loves is in peril, and the only salvation involves plunging into the abyss to challenge the monsters lurking there. Sometimes, the protagonist is an accidental hero, stumbling unwittingly through a door to fairy-land or some other otherworldly place, and there is no going back until the journey forward (and all its accompanying trials) is complete. Although there are many variations to the specifics of the departure, the fact that the hero must depart what he or she knows is

the key here. And this process is eloquently captured in the Tarot through card zero, The Fool.

In most traditional Tarot decks, following the example of the Rider-Waite-Smith, The Fool is depicted as a wanderer blithely walking toward the edge of a cliff. A small dog chases after the Fool, offering a warning, which presumably the wanderer does not heed. The cliff is not always obvious. In the Marseille deck (published circa 1650), the Fool is simply a transient with a walking stick and a sack of belongings slung over his back. There may be a cliff somewhere beyond the boundaries of the card, but we don't get to see it. And maybe the Fool doesn't either – notably, the name of The Fool card in the Marseille deck is *Le Mat,* which means "the beggar" but also "the madman." He is a person in transit (internally as well as externally). He may have no set destination in mind, but he is certainly engaged in the journey. The little dog appears in the Marseille deck also, nipping at the Fool's heels, possibly in warning or chasing him off, but it is equally possible that the dog seeks to call him back home. With this, The Fool captures the very moment of Departure – right before the hero takes the leap, plunges into the abyss, or walks through the otherworldly door and crosses the threshold of adventure.

The next step outlined by Campbell in the process of the hero's journey is Supernatural Aid. In myths and fairytales, the hero is often approached by people and powers that offer guidance of one form or another. They teach things or give tokens that will help along the way: magickal talismans, enchanted swords, or, in the case of Ariadne with the hero Theseus, something as simple as a skein of thread to help him escape the labyrinth after slaying the Minotaur. These figures are archetypal (and have ties to similar figures in dreams as well as shamanic visions): the Old Wise Woman; the Hermit in the Wilderness; sometimes also the Trickster, who challenges the hero to separate good advice from bad, thus offering a deeper lesson in the long run. The Tarot depicts each of these as individual cards: The Magician; The Priestess; The High Priest; The Emperor; The Empress. Each represent powers and people encountered along the way, and each has a lesson to teach to anyone willing to learn. They are, in many ways, glorified (or magnified) versions of figures the hero undoubtedly has interacted with back in the ordinary world.

Like Dorothy over the rainbow, these otherworldly beings are familiar faces clothed in the raiment of myth: The Emperor is really the father; The Empress is the mother, perceived in a different yet not altogether inaccurate light. The High Priest and the Priestess represent different approaches to religious experience, and thus represent the individuals who serve to initiate or to dictate the terms of that experience. The Magician is the Trickster – every man Jack who appears over and over again in fairy tales, an ambiguous figure who is often simultaneously a simpleton and a master manipulator. He operates by the seat of his pants and can be seen as a reflection of The Fool immediately after the beginning of the journey. Except that The Magician is The Fool arrested: having gotten a mere taste of the Otherworld and its potential, he mistakenly believes he is its master already, and he plays with his sword and his wand, weaving magick because he's still too ignorant to believe that he *can't*. Mythically speaking, The Magician echoes those moments where the hero gets to view himself, either in the past or in an alternate timeline, and both his strengths and his flaws become painfully obvious – hopefully inspiring choices to grow beyond that point of sophomoric bliss.

Among these familiar faces reframed as otherworldly powers there is often an unfamiliar face as well: the love interest. Most fairy tales* (and Campbell's Monomyth is eloquently realized in his readings of the various fairy tales recorded by the brothers Grimm) have a fair maiden who becomes tied to the hero in the course of his quest. We see this in the heroic cycles of Greek myth as well: Theseus has his Ariadne; Perseus has his Andromeda; Jason has his Medea. In Campbell's analysis, this fair maiden is really another aspect of the hero, projected outside of himself: in Jungian terms, she is his *anima,* or soul. In the mythology of dreams, Jung tells us that we each project our equal and opposite as a partner and a guide.

*Fairy tales are far more ancient than previously assumed. Adopting a technique used by biologists to create a taxonomic tree of life, cultural anthropologist Dr. Jamie Tehrani, at Durham University, compared thirty-five different versions of the classic "Little Red Riding Hood" from around the world. Tehrani discovered that all versions of the tale share a common ancestor dating back to the sixth century BCE -- that's more than 2600 of vibrant, evolving oral tradition. Tehrani's fascinating work was reported in the UK *Telegraph,* September 5, 2009.

For the masculine mind, this takes the form of the *anima,* a female. For the feminine mind, the figure is the *animus,* a male. However, the identity of this other half is less about gender and more about completion: it represents all those qualities that we think we do not possess when, in fact, we do. They are merely forgotten, suppressed, or hidden. Part of the journey to completion, then, relies upon bringing these qualities into the conscious self, which often requires externalization.

This concept that one's subconscious or inner will may be projected outward as a male or female figure which then serves as the other half to complete a whole has ancient roots and powerful implications. Our modern concept of soul mates is derived from Platonic teachings that humans were originally created as a conjoined male and female: one body, two faces. But, as Aristophanes recounts in *The Symposium,* the Greek all-father Zeus feared the power of these beings so much that he eventually split them in half. Thus scattered, the halves become twin flames, each seeking the other and always feeling incomplete until reunited.

The notion of original, perfected hermaphroditism is not exclusive to Greek myth and can be found echoed in creation myths the world over. In Tantric teachings, sexual union is the natural physical expression of this spiritual reunion of the two halves that complete a mystic whole. Notably, we also see this expressed within the Tarot. The Lovers card is not really about romance, although sometimes it can be interpreted as such depending on how it comes up in a reading. But the real message of The Lovers is concerned with opposites and union – or re-union, if we're taking the Platonic approach. Viewed in terms of the Monomyth, The Lovers are the hero and the fair maiden that he rescues from the dragon – only to realize that the fair maiden is really another half of himself, lost until the very moment when he risked his life to save hers.

Crossing the Threshold
Once the hero has heard the call to adventure and started the process of departing from his or her familiar world to the otherworldly realm of initiatory experience, there is a necessary moment of transition. Here, the traveler crosses the threshold from one world to the next. Sometimes the crossing is made with his or her own power, but more often, the transition requires some level of help. A guiding spirit

appears to point the way to the door under the hill, the messenger of the gods must lead the hero to the cave that leads to the Underworld, or, in the case of the Patriarch Enoch, an angel appears and carries him up to the Seven Heavens and, ultimately, to the very Throne of God. In the Tarot, the card that marks this this archetypal crossing of the threshold is The Chariot. Traditionally depicted as a literal charioteer, this card represents not simply the journey but also the delicate balance of powers or states of being required to manage that journey successfully. In traditional representations of this card, the chariot is drawn by two creatures: horses or, in the case of the Rider-Waite-Smith and several other decks, sphinxes. One animal is black, the other white, and they represent oppositional forces: darkness and light; spirit and flesh; death and life. The key to the meaning of this card is that these animals are yoked together and it is only through their combined power that the chariot is drawn forward. This means that the charioteer, in order to safely complete his journey, must find a way to ameliorate these oppositional forces, to balance their power, and to make them work in unison for him. Our deck has a very different take on the visual representation of The Chariot, yet the key meanings remain the same and hold special significance within the context of the Watcher Angel myth. But I'll talk more about that when we get to the section outlining the meanings and interpretations of our particular cards. When the forces are properly harnessed, they propel the hero into his journey.

In Campbell's method of parsing world myth, the act of crossing the threshold brings the hero directly into the "belly of the whale." This is a visceral representation of the Otherworld itself, into which the hero often *descends*. The Otherworld – be it Hades or Fairyland or even the high Heavens themselves – is, within the context of the hero's journey, a location that exists as much *within* as it does without, for all of this journey is a process meant ultimately to change the hero from the Fool to the World. Campbell distinguishes the moment of submersion in life-altering experience from the process: the Belly of the Whale is the end of his Departure phase, and The Road of Trials marks the beginning of Initiation. However, within the Tarot, a great deal more of the process is revealed. There are further stages and lessons and experiences within each of these steps along the way. So, by my reading of things, the true "Belly of the Whale" experience – that moment wherein the hero has been suspended in his or her own interior world, simultaneously struggling with and integrating the new experiences and lessons – comes a little later, and serves as the key point of the Initiation phase.

Once the threshold has been crossed, the hero then encounters "the road of trials." This represents the challenges, tests, and obstacles the hero must overcome in order to proceed on the journey through the Otherworld in pursuit of the final goal. Often, if the hero attempts to overcome many of these challenges by main force alone, he or she will quickly be laid low: more than strength of arms is required to survive and to thrive along this journey. The process of journeying along the Road of Trials is alchemical in nature: the hero or heroine is being tempered like a fine blade, tossed into the fire and exposed to greater and greater intensities of heat until all that is unworthy (alchemically speaking, all of the dross) is burned away. Card eight in the progression of the Tarot reflects the first lesson learned along the Road of Trials: true strength comes from within. The Strength card traditionally depicts a woman holding shut the jaws of a lion. She clearly does not manage this through brute strength, but rather through a subtle application of power. The catch-phrase for this card can be seen to be "Beauty conquers the beast," and it represents a discovery of inner strength that empowers the hero far more than mere physical strength alone.

As the hero walks the Road of Trials, he or she often meets along the way a supernatural guide – someone who holds up a light in the darkness at the moment in which the hero feels most desperately lost. This is The Hermit, often shown as a robed and bearded man standing alone in some desolate place and, Diogenes-like, holding a lantern aloft. The Hermit represents a guide or a teacher who does not walk the path for the hero but rather helps to light the way. In truth, the Road of Trials is a solitary path and no one but the hero can walk it to its end.

After The Hermit helps to light the way, the hero has the first of several life-altering encounters with the Otherworldly Powers. These reveal truths about the Universe, but also interior truths relevant to the hero's understanding of his or her own circumstance. First is The Wheel. This is nothing less than the macrocosmic force of the Universe itself, the very gears of reality upon which the hero is ground. Traditionally, this card represents Fortune, though it is more clearly stated as Fate. The phrase one can associate with this card is "God *is* the machine." It is no coincidence that this card is the tenth in the Tarot sequence. It marks the mid-point between the start of the journey, with The Fool, and its conclusion, with The World. It serves as the fulcrum of the entire experience. Traditional representations call this card The Wheel of Fortune and show figures (sometimes only partially human) being spun around or caught within the spokes of the wheel. They are powerless to resist the turns of fate. This is the card where the hero realizes that he or she is part of something far bigger than the self. Although a choice was made to leap into this experience, the experience itself is a part of destiny or fate.

With Justice, the hero finds himself weighed in the balance by powers in a position to judge. And, no matter how good or pure of heart the hero believes himself to be, he knows he will be found wanting, for he fears that he is inadequate to the task at hand. It is this very fear that leads inevitably to the next stage of the journey: Initiation, the true "belly of the whale." This is The Hanged Man, the hero suspended within him or herself, fighting an inner battle to overcome the fears and the doubts and the imperfections. The key to surviving the rigors of the initiatory experience is simply to give in to them: to surrender doubt and fear and even hope and accept the free-fall into the abyss. What waits after this stage of the Hanged Man is nothing less than Death, which itself is not an end but a change. Having surrendered to the experience of the Hanged Man, the hero emerges irrevocably changed: reborn in a purer state. This is represented by the card Temperance, which traditionally depicts an angel mixing water or wine between two goblets. The meaning of the card is in the mixing itself: it is water tempered with wine, the two parts joining to create something new. On a cosmic scale, it is not water and wine but spirit and flesh achieving balance and union, and this admixture of Heaven and Earth is the very core of the initiatory process. The hero undertakes the journey a mortal, untempered, naïve, and flawed. Through the various encounters along the Road of Trials, he or she is broken down and prepared for the ultimate journey: the journey within. Dragged into his or her own inner abyss, the hero dies to his or her existence as a purely physical being, touches the powers that lie beyond and returns as being with a foot in both worlds: spirit and flesh.

Even after Temperance, there is still the temptation posed by The Devil: the call to fall back into one's base nature, allowing the purity of spirit to be lost, ignored, or obscured. The key to escaping The Devil is volition. As seemingly inescapable temptation looms, the hero must realize that he or she holds the power of choice, to fall or to fly. Even after all of these lessons and transformational experiences, most who follow the hero's journey must learn the lesson of The Devil the hard way: before they learn to make a choice, they find themselves pulled back into the trap of ignorance and fear. This brings us to The Tower, which in many ways is the darkest card of the entire Tarot cycle, for The Tower represents the ruin that we bring upon ourselves. If the Devil is the instigator, the Tower is the consequence. After all he or she has been through up to this point, the hero should truly know better, and now, as a being initiated into the mysteries, mistakes are not made lightly. Any backsliding has dire consequences, as demonstrated by the card whose best catch phrase is "Pride cometh before a fall."

Following Campbell's Monomyth, this takes us to the steps along the initiatory process known as Atonement and Apotheosis. Campbell parses "atonement," which is a reconciliation and forgiveness of sin, as simultaneously meaning *"at-one-ment."* This is to say, as one reconciles with the essence of the Universe, one also achieves union with that essence. In keeping with his Judeo-Christian framework, Campbell presents this as a reconciliation with the Father, symbolized as reconciliation with the God. Apotheosis, then, is the union itself. The word means "to become god-like" or sometimes literally, "to become a god."

Apotheosis is the fundamental goal of mystical experience – the experience unwittingly pursued by our Fool as he tumbles blithely into the unknown. At the heart of mystical experience is a pursuit of union with the infinite. We can call this the Universe or God or Goddess – the exact name is immaterial to the experience itself. There are, in the various mystical traditions the world over, two general schools of thought when it comes to this pursuit of union. On one hand, as mortals are finite, some students of mysticism insist that perfect union can never be achieved. At best, one can manage a vision or a taste of this union. We see this in the Merkaba* tradition

*Merkaba means "chariot" and is a reference to the throne-chariot of God, supported and carried by the four *chayot,* or "living creatures."

of Jewish mysticism, where the culmination of the experience is a *vision* of the throne of God. This is as close as a mere mortal can get to union. The other school of thought is best expressed in the teachings of the Gnostics, where the pursuit of mystical experience is the pursuit of gnosis itself: knowledge or, more appropriately, *knowing* of God. In the Gnostic tradition, the true achievement of gnosis occurs when the knower becomes the known: that sense of awareness of a concept or thing that is so complete, it manifests as an internal knowledge or feeling that is too profound for any expression in words. This is more of a pure union. In this system, the mind is seen as pure enough to not merely contain a vision of God but to merge with the very essence of infinity itself in its pursuit to reconnect with the source from which it came. A side effect of the Gnostic approach to mysticism is the realization that ultimately we are all God, because we all came from and have the potential to return to that quintessential source.

Campbell, and the Tarot itself, really, belong to the second school of mystical thought. The finite can become refined enough to not only perceive but also encompass the infinite. Spiritually speaking, you can go home again. And this process of apotheosis following the tragedy of the Tower is expressed in stages through the three celestial cards of the Tarot: The Star, The Moon, and The Sun. It is no mistake that these are three manifestations of celestial light, and that they progress in order from the weakest to the brightest. If the Tower is the dark night of the soul, the Star is that little glimmer of hope shining in the darkness. And if our hero can seize upon that star as a guide to navigate his way through the darkness, he will ultimately find his way back from darkness to the light.

Where the Star represents the promise of hope and renewal in the wake of the Tower, the Moon is an ambivalent card that contains as much warning as it does potential hope. Astronomically speaking, the Moon's light is not its own: the light of the Moon is merely a reflection of the light of the Sun, and while it allows some of the Sun's light to shine in the darkness, that light is nevertheless imperfect and, perhaps, impure. Certainly, it is a misleading light: it paints the landscape in shades of silver and gray, bleaching out the colors and making everything seem different and strange. And that is the key to the meaning of The Moon in the Tarot as well: its light can obscure as much as it reveals. It is a tricky, shifting light and within its scope, things are not always as they appear. Navigating through the moonlit landscape, and circumventing the threat of lunacy – taking the wrong path and finding oneself mired in a swamp that seemed nothing more than an innocent field – is one last trial for the hero on the road to apotheosis.

The Moon gives way to The Sun, and here we have Apotheosis realized. In traditional depictions of this card, the Sun itself dominates the sky, and the main figure is a triumphant and smiling child astride a white horse: the hero has become a child again, renewed, reborn, and returned to a state of innocence. But, if Campbell's notion of "at-one-ment" holds true, the hero is also the Sun itself: in union with the perfected light of the Universe. Any mystic writing about such an experience of union, from St. Teresa of Avila to Jelal ad-Din Rumi, remarks upon the true challenge of such an experience: the challenge of ever wanting to return from it again. Once attained, this connection with the divine becomes seductive, and the idea of separating again in order to return to the mortal world is almost painful. And yet, the point of the journey as outlined by Campbell and reiterated in world myth time and again, is not to go and never come back. Rather, the hero is a hero because he or she engages in this entire process, burns away his or her imperfections through challenges and trials, and ultimately tastes the milk of paradise in order to come home – and to bring the vision, or the heavenly fire, or the Holy Grail *back* to those who could not make the journey for themselves. This is the selfless aspect of the hero's quest, the true cost of sacrifice. The hero, changed by these experiences, must return and change the world.

This brings us to the Return portion of Campbell's reading of the Monomyth, the first portion of which is identified as "the refusal to return." Having endured all the trials, having been laid low and broken and put back together again, and having had a taste of the ultimate truth that lies beyond it all, who would not hesitate at that door leading back to the hovel or farm or family business where it all began? And so the Powers of the Otherworld often have to force a return. In the Tarot, this is embodied by Judgment.

Traditional representations of the Judgment card depict a scene thick with Christian eschatological imagery: the angel Gabriel blows his trumpet, and on earth, the dead rise from their graves. Early versions of the card are called not Judgment, but The Angel. Many people new to the Tarot have trouble distinguishing between Judgment and Justice. But rather than viewing Judgment as a sentence passed, consider instead Judgment as a resolution. Within the context of the Monomyth, it is a resolution to the hero's dilemma of remaining versus returning. No matter how alluring the state of union with the divine might be, the hero cannot remain in suspended animation. The purpose of the journey is to be reborn, not simply return forever to the state of the womb. So here our angel of Judgment stands, brandishing his sword or his trumpet or whatever symbol of office provided him, and he marks the line between the two worlds. Furthermore, he demands that the hero complete the full cycle. If we follow the traditional depictions of the Tarot, that full cycle is resurrection: a return to the flesh, albeit different and purer flesh. And that takes us finally to The World.

The World, quite simply, is the completion of the journey. It is the end of the path – which leads inevitably to the beginning of another. It represents a change of states, and in the monomythic tale of the hero's journey, it represents the triumphant and enlightened return home. From The World, the last two sections of Campbell's outline logically follow: Master of the Two Worlds and The Freedom to Live. The "master of the two worlds" refers to the entire process of the hero's departure, initiation, and return. Having journeyed to the Otherworld, having been touched and changed by it, and subsequently returning to the world of mortals still bearing those changes and all the wisdom and insight that comes with them, the hero stands as a being between worlds, a living embodiment of the union of heaven and earth, spirit and flesh. The very act of carrying this wisdom back to the world gives not only the hero but all he or she comes into contact with the "freedom to live." The hero is now the spiritual healer or his or her age, sometimes literally initiating a golden age in the realm of humankind, and sometimes only doing so symbolically by restoring life to the fair maiden or the Fisher King.

In our Tarot, the full meaning of the World card is embodied in the figure of Enoch himself. Where the Watcher Angels are concerned, the main text that tells their story is known as the *Book of Enoch*. But the Watchers themselves can be so compelling in their actions and subsequent judgment that oftentimes the figure of Enoch himself is overlooked. But he plays as large a role – if not larger – within the course of the *Book of Enoch* as the Watchers themselves.

65

Where the Watcher Angels, at the start of the book, choose to leave Heaven and initiate an experience for themselves among mortals on earth, Enoch begins as a mortal man who ultimately makes the journey to the Throne of God. The book is not only a tale about the divine becoming human, but it also recounts the process of a human becoming divine. In Gnostic and some Jewish teachings, Enoch is not only carried up to Heaven to view the workings of the Universe and converse with God; in the end, he is transformed into an angel himself. This angel, called *Metatron,* is known in Jewish texts as the "little Yahweh," because he becomes the right-hand of God and is the go-to person for all the other angels called to deal with the Presence.

That cycle, the divine becoming human and the human becoming divine, is why I chose the Watcher Angel myth as the perfect myth to reveal the depth and power of the transformational journey encoded in the Tarot. I see it as a process that is integral to reality itself, not something that is linear but rather cyclical: as spirits, we descend to flesh in order to learn and experience the things that can only ideally be realized within the boundaries imposed by mortal, earthly existence, and once those insights have been obtained, we travel back from flesh to spirit, experience that for a while, only to choose to return to enlarge upon our understanding of the entire process, time and time again. It is the hero's journey, as read by Campbell, and it is the underlying journey of the Major Arcana, nothing less than the archetypal journey of the soul.

Mythos Part II: An Introduction to the Watchers

A fundamental concept behind the Watcher Angel Tarot is, of course, the integration of the Watchers themselves with the mythic cycles of the Tarot. The Watcher Angels are promethean figures whose story is told in a variety of Biblical and extra-Biblical texts, with the most complete narrative unfolding in the mysterious *Book of Enoch.* The *Book of Enoch* is an apocryphal book – meaning that it was labeled a secret or hidden part of the Biblical tradition by early Church Fathers. Straddling the time period between the rise of Messianic Judaism and fledgling Christianity, the *Book of Enoch* is a curious and compelling work lost to mainstream Christianity for over a thousand years. While it is hardly the only place where the story of the Watchers unfolds, it is nevertheless a text essential to the myth as we understand it today. The *Book of Enoch* serves as the primary resource for the Watcher Angel myth as it is expressed within the Tarot, but it's important to note that portions of the story – or at least fragments of it – exist in other works as well. One of these is the Hebrew Bible, which Christians know as the Old Testament.

Scattered throughout the Hebrew Bible, there are fragments of an unfinished tale. It is a tale of love, lust, betrayal, and divine retribution. These fragments hint at the existence of angelic beings who abandoned their place in Heaven in order to cohabit with the daughters of men. Often referred to as Watchers, or *Irin,* these "sons of God" are connected with the Flood story in Genesis. The story of these Watcher Angels is never fully elaborated in the Bible that we know. Instead, the lines that do exist merely hint at a much bigger story for which there is little context. Biblical scholars, ancient and modern alike, have had mixed feelings about these enigmatic passages, sometimes seeking to explain away what they really mean, and sometimes seeking to gloss over lines that are an uncomfortable reminder that the Bible does not always neatly make sense.

The main portion of these fragments appears in Genesis 6: 1-4. Because, in English, we are only reading the Bible in translation, it is interesting to compare more than one gloss of these lines. First, let us look at how the King James Bible tells the story:

(1)And it came to pass, when men began to multiply on the face of the earth, and daughters were born unto them, (2) that the sons of God saw the daughters of men that they *were* fair; and they took them wives of all which they chose. ... (4) There were giants in the earth in those days; and also after that, when the sons of God came in unto the daughters of men, and they bare *children* to them, the same *became* mighty men which *were* of old, men of renown.

(Genesis 6:1-4, King James Bible)

There are a few notable differences if we seek out a popular version of the Hebrew Bible and compare the same lines. In the Hebrew Bible, Genesis is called *Bereshit*, and the first five books of the Bible are called the *Tanakh*. Out of respect for the name of the divine, God is never fully spelled out, and is typically rendered "G-d." But despite these minor differences in format, the fragment of this story is nearly identical, with a few curious twists:

(1) And it came to pass, when men began to multiply on the face of the earth, and daughters were born unto them, (2) that the sons of G-d saw the daughters of men that they were fair; and they took them wives, whomsoever they chose. ... (4) The Nephilim were in the earth in those days, and also after that, when the sons of G-d came in unto the daughters of men, and they bore children to them; the same were the mighty men that were of old, the men of renown.

(Bereshit 6:1-4, the Tanakh)

The King James version talks about "sons of God," and, from the sense of the passage, these sons of God are somehow notably distinct from the "daughters of men." The same phrase is used in the Jewish translation. And yet, if we seek out other translations of the Bible, sometimes this passage only speaks of the "sons of the nobles" or the "sons of the judges." So the real question is, what is the root word here? What original phrase is being translated in some versions as the "sons of God" and in others the "sons of the nobles?"

The phrase in the original text is *bene ha elohim*. It means literally, "the sons of the gods" (Elohim is a plural, a textual issue far beyond the scope of this book). "Sons of God" is a phrase that has unsettled many a translator of the Hebrew Bible, for it does not fit neatly into the picture otherwise painted by the Book of Genesis. If the Bible is to be taken literally, word for word, this phrase throws something of a monkey wrench into the developing picture of Genesis. Prior to this point in the Biblical story, the only things created and living on the earth are animals, fish, plants, and birds, as well as the first human beings: Adam, Eve, and their descendants. So who are these sons of God? Clearly, they end up having relations with the "daughters of men," for the last line of this section tells how the children of this mixed union were the "mighty men of old, the men of renown." The Jewish translation throws an even bigger curveball at readers by overtly giving a name: *Nephilim.* This curious word appears only one other place in the Bible. In *Numbers* 13:33, spies are sent to scout the land of Canaan. They return rather frightened, for they encounter puissant fighters of imposing stature:

We saw the Nephilim there (the descendants of Anak come from the Nephilim). We seemed like grasshoppers in our own eyes, and we looked the same to them.
(New International Version)

Sometimes the term *Nephilim* is translated as "giants." From the description in *Numbers*, it would seem that they were a race who towered over ordinary men. This would probably explain why *Genesis* 6:4 tells us that "the same *became* mighty men which *were* of old, men of renown." Especially in the sort of tribal culture that seemed to flourish in the days of the Genesis story, if a child was bigger, and stronger, and in many ways superior to his fellows, he would naturally rise to the top. If he did not become a ruler outright, he would likely become a great hero, much like the Greek Heracles.

Yet the story is incomplete. Aside from these four lines in *Genesis,* and a few oblique references in later Biblical books, nothing more is said of the "sons of God" or the *Nephilim* or even the "men of renown." From the placement of this fragment at the start of *Genesis* 6, it is possible to infer that the actions of these sons of God and possibly the actions of their children somehow played a role in the wickedness of mankind that eventually culminated in God's judgment and the Flood. Yet, once more, nothing in the Bible as it has come down to us today, offers any further details that are overt. The story begins and ends at *Genesis* 6: 1-4.

Who are these mysterious "sons of God?" What makes them different from the "daughters of men?" How could there be "giants in the earth"—or "Nephilim in the earth," if we go with the Jewish translation? Who – or what – are these Nephilim? What does any of this really mean? In order to answer these questions, or at least to begin to answer them, we have to search beyond Genesis to a text that was cut from the Bible entirely. Lost to Western scholars for over a thousand years, the *Book of Enoch* (sometimes referred to as *I Enoch* or the *Ethiopic Enoch)* contains the most complete account of the rebel sons of God, also known as the Watcher Angels, and their illicit affair with the beautiful daughters of men.

I Enoch is one of several books that were originally viewed as Scripture, but which were then later cut from the Bible. Other books went through the same process, such as the Book of Tobit and the Book of Baruch. They are recognized as Apocrypha. This term means "hidden," and Apocryphal texts were originally removed from the main text of the Bible and reserved for only the most learned readers. In later years, these Apocryphal texts came under dispute and were removed entirely from the Biblical canon (although in some cases, different sects of Christianity rejected or retained different apocryphal texts). Despite this, many of them still find their way into certain versions of the Bible, sometimes reprinted at the very end, and sometimes worked in among the regular Scriptures without so much as a note about their debated status. Others Apocryphal texts, such as the Gnostic *Gospel of Thomas,* are so controversial that they are rarely reprinted at all in connection with any official version of the Bible.

In addition to being apocryphal. *I Enoch* is officially labeled a *pseudepigraphal* text. These often extra-Biblical writings are attributed to an ancient author, while their true authors remain anonymous. Generally, the name of a famous Patriarch was adopted in order to give the book more apparent authority. Such texts were often cut from the Biblical canon because their authorship was called into question or because they contained heterodox views later rejected by the Church. Typically, one reason engendered the other. In the case of the *Book of Enoch,* Church fathers were still referring to the text as divinely inspired Scripture in the first and second centuries of the Common Era. By around three hundred CE, however, the book had already fallen out of favor. We may eventually take a closer look at why *I Enoch* went from an accepted part of Biblical tradition to something which St. Augustine warned readers to avoid, but for now, we are simply going to explore the basics of this book and its fascinating story.

*It is important to note that there are at this time actually three books that bear the title, *The Book of Enoch.* These are numbered based upon the order in which it is believed they were written, with *1 Enoch* being by far the oldest. *2 Enoch,* a Slavonic text that further details Enoch's flight through the heavens, coming much later, and *3 Enoch,* which details a Rabbi's encounter with Enoch in his capacity as the Metatron and may be tied to the Merkaba tradition, coming even later still.

Mythos Part III: The Book of Enoch

The primary source for the Watcher Angel myth as it is expressed within our Tarot is the *Book of Enoch* as translated by R.H. Charles. This was the authoritative version of the *Book of Enoch* in the English-speaking world for over a hundred years. Although, at this time, several more complete translations have been produced by scholars (most notably Nickelsburg's *I Enoch*, integrating several recently discovered fragments, as well as the Enochic material from the Dead Sea Scrolls), the Charles *Enoch* continues to be in print and is the most widely accessible to readers outside of the circles of Biblical academia. For this reason, the version of the story – and in particular, the presentation of the angels' names – as they appear in the Charles translation are most familiar with the widest circle of readers. This widespread familiarity a main reason that the Charles translation was chosen as the primary basis for the deck despite its age and potential flaws.

The *Book of Enoch* is a curious text with a curious history. Lost for almost a millennia due to its hotly debated status within the Christian Church, the book was ultimately recovered by adventurer James Bruce in 1773 during his explorations of Ethiopia. The version presented in the Charles translation is based primarily upon this text, a copy of which was stored in the Bodleian Library. Written in Ge'ez, an old Ethiopic tongue, the *Book of Enoch* was still considered part of official Scripture by the Coptic Ethiopic church. They had kept copies the whole time that the rest of Europe was conjecturing about the nature and authenticity of the work.

Bruce was a curious figure and it is perhaps fitting that he was the one to retrieve the lost book. A massive red-headed Scot, Bruce proudly traced his lineage to Robert the Bruce, one of Scotland's most famous warrior-kings. According to some sources, Bruce (James, not Robert), was a Scottish Freemason in addition to being something of an errant adventurer. He recorded his epic journey down the course of the Blue Nile in a travelogue that might make Indiana Jones flush with jealousy, *Travels to Discover the Source of the Nile*, printed by J. Ruthven in London, 1790.

At the time of Bruce's journey, Ethiopia was still known as Abyssinia and was thought of by Westerners in romantic terms, as a fabled and exotic land (consider Coleridge's famous fragment of a poem, "Kubla Khan" and its references to an alluring "Abyssinian maid"). One of the biggest questions about Bruce's trip and his subsequent discovery of the *Book of Enoch* is how he came across the book in the first place. There are implications that Bruce was *not* exploring so much as he was searching for the *Book of Enoch* specifically. But could Bruce have even known about the book (and its possible Ethiopian connections) to go looking for it?

The *Book of Enoch* may have been lost to the Western world, but it was certainly not forgotten. Missing since perhaps the eighth or ninth century CE, it was attested to in writings by numerous Church Fathers. An inspired writer of the New Testament, Jude, references the book in verse 14 of his letter, identifying Enoch as a prophet in the same passage. Other Church Fathers, notably Justin Martyr, Clemens of Alexandria, Origen, Irenaeus, Tertullian, Eusebius, Jerome, Hilary, Epiphanius, Augustine, and others refer to and make use of the book in their own writings.

All of these, with the possible exception of Tertullian, viewed the book as Apocryphal – which is to say, secret and not a part of canonical Scripture. One of the latest references to the work occurs in the writings of the Patriarch Nicephorus, where it is referred to as an Apocryphon of the New Testament. Shortly before him, a learned monk of the eighth century, Georgius Syncellus, produced a *Chronographia,* including a few choice extracts of the *Book of Enoch.* Syncellus's work, although its presentation of *I Enoch* is fragmentary at best, contains perhaps the most complete reference to the work extant within the writings of Christendom once the book itself had been lost. Church Fathers differed in their opinions regarding the value and legitimacy of the work. Augustine, perhaps predictably, is the most heated in his criticisms of the book, based in large part because its portrayal of angels seriously diverged from his own stark dualism wherein beings of pure spirit could never be seen to mingle with the world of flesh.

With all of these references to the *Book of Enoch,* but no book to satisfy the curiosity the references inspired, many European scholars of both the sacred and the profane became intrigued with the work. In some ways, the *Book of Enoch* became the most influential book *never* read through Christian Europe in the Middle Ages and Renaissance. Perhaps its most famous influence was had upon astronomer and scholar Dr. John Dee. Court magician and possible master spy for Queen Elizabeth in England in the 16th century, Dee claimed to have a series of visions, through his work with medium Edward Kelley. These visions were with beings that Dee and Kelley claimed were nothing less than heavenly angels. The spirits communicated with Dee and Kelley through an elaborate language which Dee seems to have believed was the heavenly tongue (though it should be noted here that Dee was also a master cryptographer). He called the language *Enochian.* Although Dee's system of Enochian magic that resulted from his work with Kelley and the spirits with which they communicated has little else to do with the *Book of Enoch,* his choice in the name for this heavenly language shows that he had at least some familiarity with the work and its implications that Enoch became an angelic scribe following his Biblically-attested assumption into heaven.

Shortly after Dee's time, around the beginning of the seventeenth century, rumors began to circulate around Europe that copies of the book could be found in Abyssinia. One or two copies were retrieved by travelers, but these all proved either to be shams or to be very different books of Ethiopic folklore and religion (such as the *Book of the Mysteries of the Heavens and the Earth* acquired for the Peiresc collection). Enter explorer James Bruce. Bruce stayed at least two years in Abyssinia once he arrived in the country by way of Alexandria and the Blue Nile. The text that we now know as the *Book of Enoch* itself was in the hands of monks at a monastery in Gondar. As near as Bruce reports, he just happened to be in the neighborhood, and the good monks of Gondar offered to show off their collection of curious texts for their striking six foot one, red-headed European visitor.

Perhaps understandably, given the mystique that had grown up around the text during the years that it was missing, some conspiracy theories surround Bruce's exploration of this region and, in particular, his "discovery" of this text. As his travelogue states, ostensibly, he was traveling to discover the source of the Blue Nile, when in fact that source had already been discovered by two Portuguese priests earlier that century. This discovery was known to Bruce, leading most conspiracy theorists to imply that the exploration was merely a cover for the Scotsman's true purposes in Abyssinia – which range, depending upon the conspiracy theory, from garden variety espionage to a Freemason-sanction search for the *Book of Enoch* based on information regarding its whereabouts acquired by Templars fighting in the Third Crusade.

Of course, if Bruce's main motivation for traveling to Abyssinia was, for some reason, to retrieve the *Book of Enoch,* he never got to enjoy the fruits of his labors. Bruce brought three copies of the Ethiopic *Book of Enoch* back with him upon his return. One of these found its way into London's Bodleian Library, the other was presented to the Royal Library of France, and the third was kept by Bruce himself. Bruce died in 1794, four years after the publication of his travelogue, yet no one sought to translate these fabled texts for almost another twenty years. In the year 1800, Silvestre de Sacy, in his *"Notice sur le livre d'Enoch,"* in the *Magazin Encyclopedique, an.* VI., *tome* I., p. 382, gave examples of the book in the form of extracts from a Latin translation of chap. 1 and 2, chap. 5-16, and chap 22 and 32 (it should be noted that, with de Sacy, the book went from the Ethiopic Ge'ez tongue to Latin, having already gone from Hebrew and/or Aramaic, to Greek, and into Ge'ez. Talk about Babelfishing!). From De Sacy's work, in 1801, a German translation was made by Rink.

Despite the fact that the *Book of Enoch* had inspired so much intrigue and speculation throughout the near-millennia of its absence from the eyes of scholars, yet another twenty years passed before an English translation was attempted. Dr. Richard Laurence, an Oxford Hebrew professor and later the Archbishop of Cashel, Laurence produced the first English translation in 1821 under the wholly unwieldy title so typical of writers from his era: *The Book of Enoch, the Prophet: an apocryphal production, supposed to have been lost for ages; but discovered at the close of the last century in Abyssinia; now first translated from an Ethiopic MS. in the Bodleian Library, Oxford, 1821.*

At this time, many fragments of the *Book of Enoch* exist, but the Ethiopic version is the most complete. Because several very different texts are called the *Book of Enoch* (all of them concerned, to one extent or another, with the Patriarch Enoch, heavenly journeys, and angels), the Ge'ez text recovered by Bruce is sometimes referred to as *I Enoch* or the *Ethiopic Enoch* to distinguish it from the rest. As noted earlier, with the discovery of numerous versions of the *Book of the Watchers* among the Dead Sea Scrolls, new information has come to light since the Robert Henry Charles edition. The *Book of the Watchers* is the primary section of the *Book of Enoch* with which we are concerned, as this is the section that recounts the tale of the Watcher Angels as they came to earth.

Scholars agree that the *Book of Enoch* itself is comprised of several different books written over a wide period of time and then combined and redacted to make what appears to be a complete text. 21st century Enochic scholar Annette Yoshiko Reed, in her book *Fallen Angels and the History of Judaism and Christianity: The Reception of Enochic Literature* (Cambridge University Press, 2005) identifies no less than five originally independent units integrated into the framework of an apocalypse. As she notes on page 24 of her densely-written and exhaustively researched work, "Some of these units are themselves composite, constructed from threads of even more ancient texts and/or traditions."

What this means for us is that there is no one definitive version of the story. Although the *Book of Enoch* itself was lost for almost a thousand years, the story of the Watcher Angels lingered on in a variety of sources – mainly in Rabbinic tales and Jewish folklore. As is often the case with stories that began as oral traditions, each version of the Watcher Angel myth contains variations, and while the key characters are recognizable throughout, the names are often different, depending on the version one is referencing. The sometimes frustrating variation in names is a topic I'll tackle in another chapter, as it had a significant impact upon the presentation of the Major Arcana. For now, let us simply take a look at the passages of the *Book of Enoch* that are most significant for the Watcher Angel Tarot:

VI.-XI. The Fall of the Angels and Demoralization of Mankind

VI. 1. And it came to pass when the children of men had multiplied that in those days were born unto them beautiful and comely daughters. 2. And the angels, the children of heaven, saw and lusted after them, and said to one another: 'Come, let us choose wives from among the children of men and beget us children.' 3. And Shemyaza* [this is spelled *Semjâzâ* in the text], who was their leader, said unto them: 'I fear ye will not indeed agree to do this deed, and I alone shall have to pay the penalty of a great sin.' 4. And they all answered him and said: 'Let us all swear and oath, and all bind ourselves by mutual imprecations not to abandon this plan but to do this thing.' 5. Then sware they all together and bound themselves by mutual imprecations upon it. 6. And they were in all two hundred; who descended in the days of Jared on the summit of Mount Hermon, and they called it Mount Hermon because they had sworn and bound themselves by mutual imprecations upon it. 7. And these are the names of their leaders: Shemyaza [this is actually spelled *Sêmîazâz*, which differs from the prior spelling of Shemyaza, *Semjâzâ*, even though it is clear from the text that they are one and the same], their leader, Arâkîba, Râmêêl, Kôkabiêl, Tâmîêl, Râmîêl, Dânêl, Êzêqêêl, Barâqîjâl, Asâêl, Armârôs, Batârêl, Anânêl, Zaqîêl, Samsâpêêl, Satarêl, Tûrêl, Jômjâêl, Sariêl. 8. These are their chiefs of tens.*

VII. 1. And all the others together with them took unto themselves wives, and each chose for himself one, and they began to go in unto them and to defile themselves with them, and they taught them charms and enchantments, and the cutting of roots, and made them acquainted with plants. 2. And they became pregnant, and they bare great giants, whose height was three thousand ells: 3. Who consumed all the acquisitions of men. And when men could no longer sustain them, 4. The giants turned against them and devoured mankind. 5. And they began to sin against birds, and beasts, and reptiles, and fish, and to devour one another's flesh, and drink the blood. 6. Then the earth laid accusation against the lawless ones.

VIII. 1. And Azâzêl taught men to make swords, and knives, and shields, and breastplates, and made known to them the metals of the earth and the art of working them, and bracelets and ornaments, and the use of antimony, and the beautifying of the eyelids, and all kinds of costly stones, and all colouring tinctures. 2. And there arose much godlessness, and they committed fornication, and they were led astray, and became corrupt in all their ways. 3. Semjâzâ taught enchantments and root-cuttings, Armârôs taught the resolving of enchantments, Barâqîjâl taught astrology, Kôkabêl* [note the different spelling from VI. 7.] the constellations, Ezêqêêl the knowledge of the clouds, Araqiêl the signs of the earth, Shamsiêl the signs of the sun, and Sariêl the course of the moon. 4. And as men perished, they cried, and their cry went up to heaven...

*Note that, along with Shemyaza, only nineteen angels are named here, although earlier the text clearly states that the Watcher Angels numbered two hundred in all. If these are in fact their chiefs over groups of ten, there should be twenty names, all told. As the list of names varies from manuscript to manuscript, it is safe to say that someone got lost along the way.

As you can see from this snippet, one of the most challenging aspects of the *Book of Enoch* is the matter of names. Even within a short span of text, the names are not presented consistently. This led several scholars in the nineteenth century to dismiss the significance of the names entirely, deciding that they bore little relevance to the text and were little more than gibberish. I tend to disagree, largely on the basis that angel names traditionally are *very* significant. An angel's station – his very purpose – is written into his name. Basically, his job, his essence, and his identity are all the same, and these are expressed in the angel's name. Thus, Raphael, the angel of healing, has a name that marries the root *raph,* "healing," with the suffix "-el," meaning "lord" or "god," and usually taken to mean "of God." So Raphael's name means "healing of God" (or "God of healing," if you happen to side with the theory that the angels themselves are remnants of a polytheistic faith that pre-dated and perhaps evolved into Jewish monotheism). With the *Book of Enoch,* this poses a problem, because of all things to have gone through the repeated transcriptions from language to language, Hebrew, Aramaic, Greek, Latin, Ge'ez, and later, French and German and English, the names are the words that are most likely to become severely deformed along the way.

A word, like "God," is recognizable as such to a translator knowledgeable in a text's original language, and while sometimes there are two or three synonyms in the language of translation, the most a translator has to worry about is which of these seems to fit the root word best. For example, "God," "Lord," or perhaps, "Creator." A name doesn't generally have a synonym in another language. It's a proper name, and while it may have roots, it doesn't have the same clear meaning as a word. Thus, the best a translator can normally do is to translate it phonetically. Consider that the names of the angels in the above excerpt were so confused that you can have the same name spelled three different ways in the manuscript within the space of two paragraphs.

Now, to make matters even more confusing, the entire story of the descent of the Watchers and their intermingling with mankind repeats later in the *Book of Enoch.* Except this time, it presents a number of entirely new names – or radical variations on the names quoted above. Then, after providing a list of the chiefs of ten, this curious and somewhat incoherent chapter gives yet another list of names – entirely different from anything we have seen before. The section in question, numbered by Charles as chapter 69, repeats itself frequently, then trails off into some nearly unintelligible discussion about an oath, making a sudden divergence from fallen angels to heavenly dictates. The section connects the Watchers with Satan and the serpent who tempted Eve, connections that are not overtly stated in the earlier (and likely the primary, in terms of when it was recorded) account of the Watchers' tale. The garbled nature of the passage, together with its sudden and inexplicable diversions, suggests that the chapter itself is a fragment or later redaction, and almost certainly corrupt. Nevertheless, I'll present it here, because at least a few of the names appearing in it have become a part of the Watcher Angel canon – in particular, Penemuê:

LXIX. The Names and Functions of the Satans: the Secret Oath

LXIX. 1. After this judgment, they shall terrify and make them to tremble because they have shown this to those who dwell on earth.

2. And behold, the names of those angels and these are their names: the first of them is Samjâzâ, the second Artâqîfâ, and the third Armên, the fourth Kôkabêl, the fifth Tûrâêl, the sixth Rûmjâl, the seventh Dânjâl, the eight Nêqâêl, the ninth Barâqêl, the tenth Azâzêl, the eleventh Armârôs, the twelfth Batarjâl, the thirteenth Busasêjal, the fourteenth, Hanânêl, the fifteenth, Tûrêl, the sixteenth Sîmâpêsîêl, the seventeenth Jetrel, the eighteenth Tûmâêl, the nineteenth Tûrêl, the twentieth Rûmâêl, the twenty-first Azâzêl.* 3. And these are the chiefs of their angels and their names, their chief ones over hundreds and over fifties and over tens.

4. The name of the first is Jeqôn: that is, the one who led astray all the sons of God, and brought them down to the earth, and led them astray through the daughters of men. 5. And the second was names Asbeêl: he imparted to the holy sons of God evil counsel, and led them astray so that they defiled their bodies with the daughters of men. 6. And the third was named Gâdreêl: he it is who showed the children of men all the blows of death, and he led astray Eve, and showed the weapons of death to the sons of men, the shield and the coat of mail, and the sword for battle, and all the weapons of death to the children of men. 7. And from his hand they have proceeded against those who dwell on the earth from that day and for evermore. 8. And the fourth was named Pênêmûe: he taught the children of men the bitter and the sweet, and he taught them all the secrets of their wisdom. 9. And he instructed mankind in writing with ink and paper, and thereby many sinned from eternity to

---

*note that Azazel appears twice, giving us a total of twenty-one. The next line changes the traditional "chiefs of tens" to also include chiefs over "hundreds and over fifties." Line three is likely what is known as an *interpolation* in the text: a section that is added or redacted in order to explain an idea that has become corrupt through transcription errors or to insert new, more popular concepts into an older text.

eternity and until this day. 10. For men were not created for such a purpose, to give confirmation to their good faith with pen and ink. 11. For men were created exactly like the angels, to the intent that they should continue pure and righteous, and death, which destroys everything, could not have taken hold of them; but through this their knowledge they are perishing, and through this power it is consuming me. 12. And the fifth was named Kâsdejâ: this is he who showed the children of men all the wicked smitings of spirits and demons, and the smitings of the embryo in the womb, that it may pass away, and the smitings of the soul, the bites of the serpent, and the smitings which befall through noontide heat, the son of the serpent named Tabâ'êt.* 13. And this is the task of Kâsbeêl, the chief of the oath which he showed to the holy ones when he dwelt high above in glory, and its name is Bîqâ. 14. This angel requested Michael to show him the hidden name, that he might enunciate it in the oath, so that those might quake before that name and oath who revealed all that was in secret to the children of men. 15. And this is the power of this oath, for it is powerful and strong, and he placed this oath Akâe in the hands of Michael.

If the end of this excerpt becomes nearly unintelligible to you, you are not alone. This is a passage with multiple corruptions, redactions, and textual interpolations. However, it gives us a good example of what can happen to a text in the course of multiple copies and translations – even a text that its copyist viewed as sacred Scripture.

Even if you believe that sacred texts are divinely inspired, and thus originate from an infallible source of infinite wisdom, I think it's fair to admit that the human instruments of that inspiration are anything but perfect. If sacred texts are the words of God refracting as light into the world through the lens of the mind of humanity, our prism is cracked. Sections of a sacred work like this one are direct evidence of how human flaws and short-comings will twist the form of a text over time. Keep in mind that this section appears *within* the document we know as the *Book of Enoch*. It's presented merely as a later chapter within that work, even though it's clear when taken by itself that it is really a retelling of chapters six through eleven, probably recorded at a much later date.

The document we know as the *Book of Enoch* is not a story that moves smoothly from beginning to end. In fact, it is actually composed of multiple books, many written at different times, then collected together at a later point and streamlined with various interpolations in order to give it the appearance of a complete work.

Although attributed to the scribe Enoch, it was written by multiple individuals. Thus it earns its designation as a *pseudepigraphal* work.

The various books that make up the *Book of Enoch* include the *Book of the Watchers* (the core of this is chapters six through eleven), Noachic fragments, possibly from a lost *Book of Noah,* and the *Book of Giants,* related to and from the same tradition as the *Book of the Watchers* (both of which were apparently popular among the Essenes, as multiple copies of these books have been found within the Qumran manuscripts, otherwise known as the *Dead Sea Scrolls*). These are all added to what is most properly called the *Apocalypse of Enoch,* as its subject matter and the time period during which it was most likely written (that is, the last few centuries before the Common Era) make it a prime example of Apocalyptic literature. The *Book of the Luminaries* and the *Book of Parables* are also sections appearing within what we know as the *Book of Enoch* which are, strictly speaking, separate books in their own right connected thinly by the figure of Enoch and the key topics of heavenly journeys and angelophanies. Notably, the story of the Watchers appears yet again within the *Book of Enoch* in chapter 86, a section of the *Book of Parables.* Here, it takes on a wholly different format, omitting the names and symbolically representing the integration of angels among mankind as the intermingling of oxen and cows. Later in the *Book of Parables,* the fall and integration of angelic stock among humanity is represented through stars that fall from the sky.

Scholars have not always agreed upon when this book was compiled or (depending on the scholar's take) composed. The version of the *Book of Enoch* published in 1882 by Rev. George Henry Schodde of Capital University in Columbus, Ohio identifies it as a Christian work. Many of the nineteenth century scholars assumed it was Christian in origin due to certain key phrases, such as "Son of Man," which are also typical of New Testament writings. Later research places the book between the second and third centuries before the Common Era, making it definitively a Jewish text. It should be noted, however, that in one of the most recent translations, *I Enoch* by George Nickelsburg of the University of Iowa and James VanderKam of the University of Notre Dame, the book is described as "texts that were composed between the late fourth century BCE and the turn of the era." This is in their introduction to *I Enoch* on page *vii*. Their dating of the book is the oldest I have seen at this time.

Note that Nickelsburg and VanderKam use the word "composed," implying that the whole of it was written in the last few centuries before the Common Era. That is another point of contention among scholars: was this time period when the material we know as the *Book of Enoch* (including the tale of the Watchers) was written from scratch, or is it a time period during which versions of the story were compiled, recorded, or retold? Although the most popular scholarly opinion currently is that the *Book of Enoch* was *composed* during this time, the story of the Watchers in particular is nevertheless predated significantly by Genesis 6:1-9. These lines tell the by-now familiar story of the "sons of God" coming down to the daughters of men and begetting giants, or Nephilim. This fragment of a tale goes relatively unexplained in the Biblical Genesis, although it leads into references to Noah and the Flood. Currently, most Biblical scholars argue that the *Book of the Watchers* is a *later* attempt to expand upon and otherwise explain these mysterious passages. Nickelsburg and VanderKam, for example, specifically state: "Chapters 6-11 are an interpretation of Genesis 6-9 that identifies events of the primordial past with those of the author's time" (Nickelsburg, p. 2). The implication here is that, an author living in the last few centuries before the Common Era saw the fragments in Genesis 6: 1-9 and made up the story of the Watcher Angels to explain these otherwise incomplete sections – notably, this argument also requires that pseudepigraphal author to have also chosen to integrate the figure of Azazel, obliquely referenced in the *Book of Leviticus*, as a key figure within this tale.

Although it is not an opinion supported by current Biblical scholarship, I believe that the sections in Genesis 6:1-9 as well as the references to Azazel in Leviticus represent fragments an early story that was old when Genesis itself was compiled. This story is the myth of the Watchers, or Sons of God, who also make an appearance in the Book of Job. I believe the Sons of God, or Watcher Angels, are remnants of a mythic tradition that pre-dates Jewish monotheism, later demonized when their civilizing actions upon the world could no longer be reconciled with the accepted view of creation. Angels in general are likely lingering figures from a full-blown pantheon whose various members could not be stamped out but instead were recast as messengers or servants under the monolithic figure of Yahweh. Further evidence of this may lie in the fact that an alternate word for God, used interchangeably with Yahweh throughout the Book of Genesis is *Elohim* – a word, though translated repeatedly to indicate a singular deity is, in fact, a plural form.

The thing to take away from this first is that there is more to all Biblical writings than meets the eye. Reading these works in the modern era, it is easy to forget the sheer amount of time through which these stories have passed and the difficult process of transmission – both orally and textually – by which they have managed to survive at all. Even though we have texts to read, we must accept that these texts are incomplete and have come to us – if not flawed, then certainly altered from their original forms. All scholarship on these texts represents each scholar's best attempt at recreating the past and, ultimately, make an informed guess at the shape of the original. The texts themselves have gone through various permutations of language, and with each translation from one tongue to the next, alterations both large and small occur.

At this point, it is virtually impossible to recapture the original tale, let alone prove precisely when and under what circumstances that tale was created. Because of this, with the Watcher Angel Tarot, rather than attempt to approach the tale of the Watchers from a strictly scholarly perspective, I have opted instead to work more in the spirit of myth, retelling and in some cases reframing the familiar figures, places, and events. In this way, much like the anonymous writer (or writers) who penned the tales for the Essenes, we bring the story forward so the essence of it can live again – perhaps inspiring further retellings at a later date.

Mythos Part IV: The Myth of the Watchers

Although I think that the scholarship behind the *Book of Enoch* and related Enochic literature is important to understanding the roots of the myth, the focus of the Watcher Angel Tarot is less on the facts surrounding this work and more on the story as a whole. To this end, I have worked in the spirit of the same individual or group who collated *I Enoch* from the existing texts of his or her time period in order to present a cohesive myth that reflects all the fragments scattered throughout Christian and Jewish literature pertinent to the tale of our deck. While I have necessarily taken some creative liberties in choosing which themes to include and which to exclude, I think presenting a dramatic retelling of the Watchers' myth will be helpful overall for understanding the deck. I take a softer stance overall on the moral state of the Watchers. In the timeline of development for the Watcher myth, the Watchers become more thoroughly demonized as time passes until, by the Christian era, they become the prototypes for Satan and his fallen angels wreaking havoc on the earth – if not directly identified as Satans. However, in many of the earliest versions, although the Watchers receive judgment for their errors in judgment, they sometimes initially act with the blessings of God himself.

The following story has been compiled from various sources of Enochic literature. The base of the Watchers' tale is primarily drawn from Charles' translation of the Ethiopic Enoch as well as the Nickelsburg/VanderKam translation, which integrates Syncellus and the fragments from Qumran. Additional information is drawn from the *Chronicles of Jerahmeel* and Ginzberg's *Legends of the Jews*. Please remember that this is not a direct translation of the *Book of Enoch*. Rather it is a poetic retelling of the ancient tale of the Watchers. Whenever possible, I retain the language and style of the original sources throughout, often integrating whole lines into the text to retain the feel and sense of the originals.

Part One: The Watchers Conspire

And it came to pass in those days when the children of men had multiplied, there were born unto them beautiful sons and daughters. And the angels, children of heaven, looked down upon them and found them fair. And they said to one another, "Let us take lovers from among the children of men and beget our own children. For we have been set over them to watch them, and how better to watch than to walk among them?"

So they descended to the slopes of Mount Hermon, two hundred of them, where they could better watch the children of men. And Shemyaza the Strong, who was their leader, said to those gathered there, "I fear that you will not agree to do this deed, and I alone shall have to pay the penalty of a great sin."

And they answered him and said, "Let us all swear an oath, and bind ourselves by mutual imprecations so that none of us will turn back from this plan until we have fulfilled it and seen it through to the end."

Then they swore together and bound themselves with oaths. And they were, in all, two hundred Watcher Angels who descended in the days of Jared upon the slopes of Mount Hermon. And they called it Hermon because it was there that the angels swore and bound themselves with oaths.

And these are the names of their chiefs: Shemyaza, their leader. Arakiba, second to him; Ramthael, third to him; Kokabiel, fourth to him; Tamiel, fifth to him; Ramiel, sixth to him; Daneial, seventh to him; Zaquiel, eighth to him; Baraquiel, ninth to him; Azazel, tenth to him; Armaros, the eleventh; Amariel, the twelfth; Hananel, thirteenth; Sethiel, fourteenth; Shamsiel, fifteenth from him; Sariel, sixteenth from him; Toumiel, the seventeenth; Turiel, the eighteenth; Iomiel, the nineteenth; and Yehadiel, the twentieth. And these are their chiefs over tens.

All these and the others with them went among the children of men. And when they went among men, the lovely maiden Na'amah, sister of Tubal-Cain, greeted them with dancing and with song. And the Watchers chose among the daughters of men, taking to wive all of whom they pleased. And they began to go into the tents of the women and to couple with them as children of the earth.

To their wives and those with whom they joined, they taught forbidden knowledge: sorcery and charms, root-cutting, and the properties of plants:

Azazel taught the fashioning of swords and shields and all the tools of war. And he made known all the metals of the earth and the precious stones. And he taught how to fashion jewelry and ornaments for the women, dyes for their clothing and pigments for their eyes.

Shemyaza taught spells and root-cutting. Armaros taught sorcery for the loosing of spells and enchantments. Baraquiel taught the signs of the lightning flashes. Kokabiel taught the signs of the stars. Zaquiel taught the signs of comets and shooting stars. Arakiba taught the signs of the earth. Shamsiel taught the signs of the sun. And Sariel taught the courses of the moon. Of the others, Kasdeya taught smitings, even the stilling of the infant in the womb. Penemuê taught the bitter and the sweet and all the secrets of wisdom. And he instructed mankind in writing so that their works and the works of their children could be recorded for all time. And Kasbiel guarded the oath of the Secret Name.

And the women conceived to them and bore them great giants: Gibborim and Rephaim, Anakim and Zamzumim, and the Nephilim. These giants and half-breeds were earthly like their mothers but tall and mighty like their fathers. And they were called Nephilim because the women could not always bring them forth, and so the infant fell from the womb.

All these were the mighty ones of old, the heroes of renown. And each grew in accordance to their greatness. Their appetites were so fierce that the labors of men could not sustain them. So the giants began to kill men and to devour them. And they began to sin against the birds and the beasts, the creeping things and the fish, and to devour one another's flesh. And they drank the blood.

And Azazel led them all in war. And Shemyaza raised a mighty empire so their children could go forth and conquer all which they pleased. And the giants and the half-breeds spread across the earth. And everywhere, men perished.

Then the earth cried out against their lawlessness.

Part Two: The Archangels Intercede
Michael and Gabriel, Raphael and Uriel looked down from the sanctuary of heaven, and they saw much bloodshed. All the earth was filled with violence and death.

And they said to one another, "The voices of the slain raise their cries even to the gates of heaven. And now to us, the holy ones, the souls of men make suit, saying, 'Bring our judgment to the Most High and report our destruction to the Lord of Lords.'"

And the archangels approached the majesty of the Lord. And they said, "You are the Lord of Ages and the throne of your glory exists for every generation from old. You have created all things and you possess authority over them. All things are made manifest before you, and there is nothing you cannot see.

"You know what Azazel has done. He has taught iniquity upon the earth. He has revealed the mysteries of the heavens which the sons of earth were forbidden to learn. Likewise, you see Shemyaza, he whom you gave authority to rule over those who are with him. They have gone in to the daughters of men, and they have lain with them like creatures of the earth. And they have revealed to them all manner of sorcery and hate-inducing charms.

"And now look: the daughters of men have born children to them, giants and half-breeds. And they shed the blood of men upon the earth. And the souls of the men who have died make suit. Their cries reach even to the gates of heaven. It does not cease.

"You know all things before they happen. You see these things, and you permit them. Yet you do not tell us what we ought to do."

Part Three: God Passes Judgment

Then the Great Holy One spoke. And he sent Uriel to Noah, son of Lamech, saying, "Go to Noah and say to him in my name, 'Hide yourself!' And reveal to him that a flood is coming and it will destroy everything on the earth. Teach the righteous son of Lamech what he should do to preserve himself so that his seed may endure for all generations to come."

To Raphael, he said, "Go and find Azazel and bind him hand and foot. Make an opening in the desert, in that place called Dudael, and cast him into the darkness. Cause him to lie upon rough and jagged stones, and cover his face so he may not see the light. Leave him there to suffer. And on the day of great judgment, he will be called forth, and he will be cast into the fire.

"Then go ye forth and heal the earth, which the Watchers and their sons have devastated. And announce that the destruction will be healed, and all the sons of men will not perish on account of the mysteries that the Watchers taught to their children. And tell them Azazel is held accountable for the deeds which have desolated the earth."

To Gabriel, he said, "Go, Gabriel, to the bastards and the half-breeds and the sons of miscegenation. Destroy these sons of the Watchers from among the sons of men. Send them one against the other in a war of devastation. Length of days they shall not have.

"And to their fathers, the Watchers, let it be known that no petition will be heard on their behalf. They hope for these children to have a place in heaven, but that place is forbidden to them. For the spirits of heaven alone may seek heaven as their dwelling place. As for spirits born on earth, the earth alone shall receive them."

Then the Lord of Ages addressed Michael. And he said, "Go, Michael, and bind Shemyaza and all the others with him who have mated with the daughters of men. Suspend them between the heavens and the earth, for through their actions, they belong to neither. And bind them with their faces turned toward the earth so they may forever look upon the source of their temptation. As for heaven, they may never again turn their vision upon it. Such was their oath and such their punishment must be.

"And as their sons go forth and destroy one another, do not allow them to look away. But force them to look upon the destruction which through their actions they have brought upon the earth. Then, after seventy generations in the valleys of the earth, they will be led forth to the torment of the fiery abyss, and bound in a prison where they will be forever confined. And henceforth, anyone judged and condemned will be bound together with them until their judgment is consummated.

"When this is done, go forth and cleanse all their works from the face of the earth. Let every wicked deed come to an end. Plant the seed of righteousness so I may open the store chambers of blessings which are in heaven and send truth and peace to the works and labors of men."

Part Four: Enoch Commissioned by the Watchers

And there was among men the scribe Enoch, seventh from Adam. And he was a righteous man whose eyes were opened by God. And Enoch walked among the holy ones and was carried to the high heavens.

And before the judgment of the Watchers, Enoch was hidden, and no one among the children of men knew where he had gone. But his activities had to do with the Watchers and his days were spent with the holy ones in heaven.

And once the judgment had been passed, Enoch was called before the majesty of heaven. And he was told: "Enoch, righteous scribe, go to the Watchers who forsook their eternal station in the highest heaven and say, 'You will have neither peace nor forgiveness.' And concerning their sons, the mighty heroes in whom they rejoice, say also that they will see the slaughter of their beloved ones. They will lament over the destruction of their sons, and they will petition heaven on their behalf, but they will receive no mercy."

And Enoch was told: "Find Azazel and go to him. Tell him, 'A great sentence has been passed to bind you. And because of the forbidden things you have revealed to mankind and the destruction which these have wrought, you will receive neither relief nor mercy."

Then Enoch went forth and he spoke to all the Watchers together. And he told them of the judgment and of Azazel's sentence. And as they listened to him, great fear and trembling seized them. They did not wish to see their works on earth pass away. They did not wish to witness the destruction of their mighty sons. But judgment had been passed and heaven would hear no petition from them. And so they petitioned the scribe Enoch, so that he might go forth to heaven and speak on their behalf.

Part Five: The Dream-Vision of Enoch

Then Enoch wrote out the petition of the Watchers, their deeds individually and their request for forgiveness and length of days. And Enoch went and sat down by the waters of Dan, to the southwest of Hermon. And he read the petition until he fell asleep.

And Enoch dreamed. And a vision fell over him. And in the dream-vision, the clouds beckoned Enoch. And a mist came, and lightnings and stars sped and hastened his transit. And then the winds lifted him upward and bore him flying into heaven.

And in heaven, Enoch saw a wall built of crystal and surrounded by tongues of flame. When he passed through the fire, Enoch beheld a great mansion. It was built all of crystal. Its ceiling was like the path of the stars, clear as water, and between the lightnings and the stars were fiery cherubim. The walls and all the portals blazed with fire, and Enoch was afraid. Great trembling seized him. His limbs grew weak and he fell upon his face. For a moment, he could not move on.

Then a door opened to him, and Enoch beheld a second house, greater than the first. And this one was built entirely of tongues of flame. The splendor and majesty of the place surpassed anything Enoch had ever seen, and he found himself at a loss for words. And the ceiling here was fire and lightning flashes, and further on there was a great throne. And it seemed the throne was made of ice with wheels like the shining sun. And there was a great sound of cherubim, and rivers of fire issued forth from beneath the throne.

And the Great Glory of the generations was seated upon the throne, clothed in raiment so bright, Enoch could not see. And around Him were multitudes, holy ones who never left their appointed posts, day or night. And even the angels could not look upon the face of majesty for its splendor and glory.

Enoch, prostrate and trembling, lay on his face before the Lord. And then the Lord called to Enoch and said, "Come to me, Enoch, and hear my words." And one of the holy angels approached Enoch and raised him up. And he was conveyed to the throne, and he stood before the majesty with his head bowed and eyes cast down.

And the Lord addressed him again and said, "Fear not, Enoch, for you are a righteous man and a scribe of truth. You have come here to petition for the Watchers, but you must go to them and say, 'You should petition on behalf of humans, and not humans on behalf of you.' For me, you will ask them, 'Why have you forsaken the high heaven to take wives and do as the sons of earth do? Why have you lain with women and begotten giants? You were holy ones, and spirits living forever. Yet you have acted as flesh and blood, that die and pass away.

"'The sons of earth are fated to perish, and therefore I have given them women, so that they might beget children and nothing would be wanting to them on earth. But you were spirits, living forever, and you had no need of wives or children among you.

"'The spirits of heaven are meant to have heaven as their dwelling place. But these giants begotten of both the spirit and the flesh – they have no place in heaven. Their dwelling will be on earth, for they have come from the earth. And when the spirits go forth from the flesh of their bodies, they will become evil spirits on the earth.

"'And the spirits of the giants will afflict, do violence, make desolate, attack and wrestle and wreak destruction upon the earth. They will take no food, but nevertheless will they hunger and thirst and smite the living. And these spirits shall rise up against the children of men because they have proceeded from them.'

"And then say to the Watchers who sent you to petition on their behalf: 'Judgment has been consummated against you. From now on, you will not ascend into heaven nor will heaven hear your pleas. And you will be bound to the earth and you cannot leave. And before this judgment is carried out, you will see the destruction of everything you love. As you watch, your mighty sons will slay one another and fall by the sword. No petition will be heard on your behalf. You will have no peace.'"

And Enoch was sent forth to reprimand the Watchers. But before that time, he was carried by the holy ones through the seven heavens. And to him was revealed the mystery of the heavens, the courses of the luminaries, and the mansions of the moon. And he was given visions of the judgment and the world that was to come so that he might return to his people and instruct them in these things.

And the Watchers had no peace, for no petition would be heard on their behalf or on behalf of their sons. And their sons made war and each slew the other until all of them fell by the sword. And when it came time for the works of the Watchers to be washed away in the Flood, Enoch was called once more to the high heavens so he would not perish. And the Lord of Ages placed Enoch among the holy ones, where he took up the station of the Metatron, the righteous scribe of heaven.

And the Watchers remain bound to the earth they desired, and the spirits of their children linger still, born and reborn throughout the ages because the final day of judgment has yet to be consummated.

FIN

I've not pulled any punches here, even though some of the harsh language reserved for the Watchers by the denizens of Heaven goes against my overall vision for these beings. Within the Enochic tradition, the Watchers are the bad guys – or at least, by the time the tale comes down to the versions of the *Book of Enoch* we now possess, they are unsympathetic characters. The earliest fragments seem to suggest that this was an evolution of demonization, and the very root of the story was more Promethean – but remember that even Prometheus, father of humanity, was punished horribly for giving his favored creations the power to warm and protect themselves. No good deed goes unpunished, it would seem.

With the details of this epic tale fresh in mind, let us now turn to the Tarot itself so we can see how this story unfolds within the cycles of the cards.

Section III: Tarot

Tarot Part I: Tarot History

The Tarot stems from an ancient and mysterious tradition – if you consider something created within the last half dozen centuries or so ancient and if you consider trick-taking card games to be mysterious. The earliest surviving Tarot is dated approximately to 1441 and consists of a hand-painted set of the cards produced for the court of Filippo Maria Visconti, Duke of Milan. Textual references to the cards do not appear until around this time as well: a letter from 1450 written by Duke Francesco Sforza of Milan requests a pack of Tarot cards. Around the same time, edicts issued in Florence against gaming specifically exempt the game of Tarot. Although there is a long-standing claim that a pack of cards held in the Biblioteque Nationale of Paris was painted in 1392 by Jacquemin Gringonneur for King Charles VI of France, these cards are Italian in origin, dating back to the 1480s.

What we recognize as the Tarot – a set of numbered cards and court cards, together with a set of twenty-two additional trumps – was invented in Italy in the early 15th century. It was played as a game, and despite a great deal of later theory to the contrary, there is no written evidence to indicate that the Tarot was originally intended to be used as anything *but* a game (yes, there was a lot of weirdness going on in Florence and Milan at that time period, what with the Medici and their fascination for ancient magick. Arguments could certainly be made that someone, somehow, wove alchemical, Platonic, or hermetic symbolism into the cards. But as far as written, documentable evidence is concerned, the Tarot was just a game).

Originally called *trionfi* in Italy, which is related to the English word "triumph" and eventually the word "trump" itself, the name *tarocco* (plural *tarocchi*) did not develop until the 1500s. It became *tarock* in German, *taroky* in Czech, and *tarot* in French. According to Decker, Depaulis, and Dummett in their book, *A Wicked Pack of Cards,* Tarot came from playing cards and not the other way around. The kernel of these decks was transplanted to the Western world from Islamic sources at some point in the fourteenth century. While Decker, DePaulis, and Dummett adopt a superior and often acerbic tone that is openly condescending toward practitioners of the occult, what they lack in personality, they make up for in scholarship. Their research is solid and comprises one of the most complete histories of the Tarot available, shedding a great deal of light on the evolution of the deck.

The Tarot's use as an occult tool and a divinatory device was not firmly established until the 1700s. There is some textual evidence that playing cards, as well as the Bolognese version of the Tarot, were used by some for fortune-telling, but this was neither a common nor a widely reported usage of the cards. We owe almost everything we know today about the Tarot as an esoteric device to three men who lived, worked, and wrote in France in the second half of the 18th century: professional fortune-teller, Jean-Baptiste Alliette (who wrote under the pen-name Etteilla); Protestant pastor and state censor Court de Gébelin; and a far less well-known contributor to the occult tradition of the Tarot, an officer general by the name of Louis-Raphaël-Lucrèce de Fayolle, le comte de Mellet.

Etteilla invented the very word *cartonomancy* which achieved its more recognizable form, *cartomancy,* within his lifetime. Gébelin described a system of ancient meanings hidden in the allegorical figures of the Tarot Trumps – meanings which he claimed could be traced back to the ancient Egyptians. And de Mellet established the practice of tying the twenty-two Tarot Trumps to the twenty-two letters of the Hebrew alphabet. Etteilla later expounded on all of this, creating an elaborate system of divination that married Hebrew letters, astrological symbols, allegorical meanings, and a romanticized notion of a perfect, lost age, calling the whole the *Book of Thoth.* The individual cards of the Trumps were seen as pages to this book and were appropriately called *feuilles* (leaves) or *lames* (keys). The Hebrew letters, each of which has a corresponding numerical value, were married to the cards *starting from the World and counting backwards through the Trumps.*

I realize that I'm roasting some sacred cows here, but it's important to understand that, at the start, the Tarot had nothing to do with the Kabala. Astrological values also are absent originally from the cards. Both of these were artificial structures imposed upon the cards by occultists who repurposed the Tarot from a game to a magickal tool – and the most influential writer on the subject initially was Etteilla. Gébelin theorized. De Mellet seems to have been a gentleman occultist, but Etteilla was actively reading cards and instructing people in their use in Paris throughout the latter half of the 1700s. He tied the Tarot to the *Corpus Hermeticum* by way of the *Pimander,* and he ultimately founded a *Nouvelle Ecole de Magie* in Paris in 1790. He wrote multiple books and pamphlets on the subject, expounding upon his interpretations of the ancient, sacred, and enlightening *Book of Thoth.* The tradition that the game of Tarot somehow encodes the secrets of Thoth-Hermes by way of allegorical imagery is still echoed in some of the cards today: it lies at the heart of the choice to label the Crowley-Harris deck the *Thoth Deck.*

Etteilla, de Mellet, and Gébelin: all three men were steeped in the rich cultural milieu of occultism and illuminism that flourished in France during the latter half of the 18th century (Gébelin held membership in the same French Masonic lodge that also boasted such luminaries of the time as Benjamin Franklin and Voltaire). In his massive multi-volume work *Monde Primitif,* Gébelin claims to have been the very first person to intuit the true meanings encoded in the Tarot Trumps (and he may have gotten into a bit of a tiff with Etteilla concerning his use of the cards). However, given the way that Gébelin's, de Mellet's and Etteilla's notions and theories about the occult character of the Tarot cross and recross, sometimes converging and sometimes contradicting one another, it seems more likely that *Monde Primitif* merely gave voice to beliefs that had developed within the occult circles of the day, possibly among the Freemasons (particularly because of the interposition of trumps and Hebrew letters).

Gébelin's work, which contains de Mellet's own essay on the Tarot, became the source for later writers who lived and wrote within the next century's milieu of French occultism: Eliphas Lévi, Papus, and Paul Christian. These added their own interpretations to the devices of Egyptianism, Kabalism, astrology, and allegory attributed to the cards. Lévi, best known for his *Doctrine and Ritual of High Magic*, reiterates, among other things, de Mellet's assertion that the Tarot suits represent key items from Scripture: the cup of Joseph; the rod of Moses; the sword of David, and the talisman (*pentacle*) of Solomon (for Lévi and Christian both, this becomes the golden shekel, a type of currency from Biblical times).

Lévi continues (in fact, perpetuates) the tradition of approaching the Tarot Trumps as keys and viewing them as the source of ancient and secret knowledge. Christian, in his *History and Practice of*

Magic, ties the Tarot to rites of initiation supposedly held in ancient times in secret passages beneath the Sphinx, noting seventy-eight rungs on an iron ladder of descent and twenty-two steps on a spiraling staircase, all of which the initiate must climb in pursuit of his goal (pp. 89-93, Christian). Seventy-eight, of course, is the total number of cards in what has become a standard Tarot deck and twenty-two is the total number of Trumps within that deck.

Papus builds upon an oblique claim made by Gébelin that identified the Gypsies as the preservers and disseminators of the cards. Papus's book, *The Tarot of the Bohemians,* first published in 1889, is founded upon this very concept, drawing upon the Hebrew, astrological, and allegorical structures established by his predecessors and further elaborating upon his own interpretations and attributions. Papus's book presents reference images for the cards. These are drawn from the Tarot of Marseille. This is essentially the French version of the Tarot, derived from the Italian roots of the game. The same year that Papus released his influential book on the Tarot, Swiss occultist Oswald Wirth produced a set of the twenty-two Tarot Trumps based upon the Marseille deck. Both Papus and Wirth were influential to the development of the Rider-Waite-Smith deck, and many of Wirth's images are all but reproduced in the Major Arcana designed by Waite.

Attributions of Hebrew letters and astrological symbols figure significantly for all of these writers, and their teachings on the matter find the most influential expression in the Rider-Waite-Smith Tarot. The Rider-Waite-Smith, despite its reputation in the English-speaking world for being a veritable font of Tarot tradition, is actually a construct of the twentieth century: the deck did not come out until 1910. The Crowley-Harris Thoth Deck, based upon the same roots, was finished in 1943 (a scant four years before Crowley's death), but did not see publication until 1969.

I could write an entire book on the development of the Tarot and how the various attributions of Kabalism, astrology, and allegory came to be applied to the cards. Rather than get bogged down in retracing the steps of this development from its obvious roots in 18th century France, let me make a few key statements. First, it is unlikely that the Tarot was originally created with the intent of conveying hidden symbolism in the cards, either of the Major or the Minor Arcana. Its genesis can be firmly placed as a game developed in Italy in the 1400s. This does not, however, invalidate its use as either a tool for divination or personal insight. Rather, the repurposing of the Tarot for occult uses is simply a part of the fascinating evolution of the deck since its debut in the courts of Florence and Milan.

The Tarot Trumps are allegorical figures. At the time of the deck's creation, these were *exoteric* rather than *esoteric* symbols – which is to say that the symbols represented within the Tarot Trumps possessed widely recognizable meanings for the culture in which they were produced (including a good deal of undeniably Christian imagery). But their very identity as allegorical figures is what so readily opened to door to further interpretation, leading to the rich and highly nuanced meanings we have today. That development was spurred by the writings of Etteilla, Gébelin, and de Mellet, then elaborated upon by Lévi, Christian, and Papus, all of whom are French. The English-speaking world owes almost all of its initial exposure to the Tarot to the Hermetic Order of the Golden Dawn founded in London in 1889 (the same year Papus's book and Wirth's Tarot were published). Waite was a key member, and he founded his interpretation of the Tarot upon the teachings of the Golden Dawn, ultimately embodying them in the Rider-Waite-Smith deck.

The second important thing to note concerns the "traditional" astrological and Hebrew associations attributed to the cards. These traditions were established within the last two hundred and fifty years, and the attributions which are now widely viewed as authoritative really owe their provenance to Waite and the Golden Dawn. The whole affectation of associating Hebrew letters to each of the Trumps hinges upon the numerical progression of the Trumps themselves which was, in the course of the Tarot's development, not nearly as stable as one might like to think. The astrological associations are also not as firmly set as many Tarot fundamentalists may be comfortable acknowledging, mainly because these were interpretations imposed upon the cards, rather than information encoded within them (for the curious, charts comparing different attributions appear in Appendix II on page 307).

At this point, with revisioned decks like the Rider-Waite-Smith and Crowley-Harris, there is a significant amount of both exoteric and esoteric information encoded into the images, and these do form a tradition of their own. This is a tradition that has developed and evolved with each occult thinker who turned his (or her) mind toward the cards since the middle of the 1700s. But it is important to understand that, although these attributions have meaning now, they are relatively recent evolutions for the Tarot.

And this brings us to the final point that I feel must be noted: the Tarot is *still* evolving. As a rich and nuanced system with profound and evocative imagery, the Tarot in its occult application is not a static device. By the very nature of symbols, the symbolism can and must change with each viewer and with each new presentation of the cards. As an example, from the early portions of the twentieth century onward, notions of psychology – particularly the theories of analytic psychologist Carl Jung – have found fertile expression within the Tarot, even though such symbolism was not an overt nor an intentional part of the original Tarot. Many modern theorists, myself included, freely marry these interpretations to the cards, and this is done in much the same spirit that Kabalists like Lévi and Waite projected their preferential symbol structure onto the Tarot. These meanings are not invalidated because they are projected upon the cards. Rather, when the cards are used as tools for insight and intuition, they are even more meaningful *because* they are projected. This is the nature and use of symbol and allegory. They tell us stories, and while certain aspects of myth and symbol are culturally and temporally defined, our ultimate experience is necessarily subjective. This subjective aspect is what takes the symbol from universal to personal, so that each of us can take something useful and validating away from the experience: *as above, so below.*

Tarot Part II: Basic Terms and Concepts

Some of you coming to the Watcher Angel deck have a great deal of experience with the Tarot. However, we realize that for many of you, this may be your very first deck. The Tarot has a complicated history, and the cards are laden with traditions about what they mean and how they are read. For those who are new to the Tarot, this wealth of history and tradition may seem a little overwhelming. This section is intended to help ease the learning process. I've collected basic terms associated with the Tarot and supplied brief definitions here so when you encounter these terms later in the book, you'll have a firmer grasp on what they mean in relation to the Tarot. If you've been reading Tarot for any length of time, all of this will be familiar territory, but if you are new to the Tarot, this section will help give you the language necessary to understand the extended interpretations of the cards that follow.

Tarot Suits: Like traditional playing cards, the Tarot has four cycles of numbered cards ranging from ace through ten. These numbered cards are also called *pip cards*. A *pip* is a general term for each individual symbol used to mark or quantify the number of a specific card (thus, the Ten of Cups has ten individual pips in the form of cups which appear on the card to indicate its number). In the Tarot, the four suits are Cups, Swords, Pentacles (sometimes called Coins), and Wands. We correspond them to the suits in traditional playing cards as follows: Cups for Hearts; Swords for Spades; Pentacles for Diamonds; and Wands for Clubs. As an interesting note, the suits have been associated in the past with each level of society: Cups for priests and clergy; Swords for the nobility; Coins for the merchant class; and Clubs/Wands for the agricultural class or peasantry.

Major Arcana: The "Greater Mystery." The Major Arcana are twenty-two trump cards in the Tarot. They are numbered from zero to twenty-one, typically in Roman numerals to help distinguish them at a glance from the Minor Arcana, or pip cards. The cards in the Major Arcana represent sweeping cosmic forces at work in human fate and they are the most archetypal and symbolic of all the cards. Figures like The Hermit, The Chariot, and The World belong to the

Major Arcana. In a metaphysical sense, the Major Arcana represents the Macrocosm, or "that which is above."

Minor Arcana: The "Lesser Mystery." The Minor Arcana are the pip cards of the Tarot, numbered from ace (one) through ten. They are arranged in four suits: Cups, Swords, Pentacles, and Wands, with four court cards per suit: Page, Knight, Queen, and King. Some books on the Tarot separate the court cards from the Minor Arcana when presenting definitions. In the Watcher Angel Tarot, the court cards are included in their respective suits. In a metaphysical sense, the Minor Arcana represent Microcosmic forces or "that which is below." Accordingly in readings, these cards tend to address specific worldly experiences or issues, reflecting the flux and flow of daily life in contrast with the huge, sweeping forces represented in the Major Arcana.

Tarot Trumps: Sometimes also called Keys. This is another term for the cards in the Major Arcana. When Tarot was played as a game, the cards that we know as the Major Arcana were used as trump cards and the term has survived. The designation of these cards as keys arises from a belief, popular among 18th and 19th century occultists, that the cards of the Major Arcana represented literal keys to an encoded system of magick founded upon the Jewish Kabala and/or the *Book of Thoth.*.

Court Cards: Face cards that appear in each of the four Tarot suits. They correspond to the Jack, Queen, and King of traditional playing card decks. However, in the Tarot, there are four court cards, not three. They still represent positions traditionally associated with the royalty of Medieval Europe: Page, Knight, Queen, and King. Some Tarot books interpret the Court Cards as forces when they come up in readings, while others present them as people. In the Watcher Angel Deck, the Court Cards are read as people. The Court Cards are sometimes also referred to as "royals," as they each represent a member of the nobility (an interesting historical note: a hand-painted deck made for the Milanese court in the 1440s had male and female representatives of each of the royals).

Querent: A term used to denote the individual who is the focus of a Tarot reading. Typically, the querent is different from the person doing the reading, although it is possible to do readings for oneself (in which case, the reader is also the querent). The querent is the main focus of the actions, forces, and people represented within the reading by the various Tarot cards. The term "querent" is derived from the word "query," which means "to ask a question." Sometimes also called the seeker, I have stuck with querent throughout so as not to confuse the term with our Seeker Card.

Significator: A card chosen to represent the querent in a reading. Often, this is a court card selected to best represent the traits and qualities of the querent. The Rider-Waite-Smith Tarot has an elaborate system of correspondences linking each suit with specific eye and hair color combinations intended to help guide this selection process. Age and gender are traditionally reflected by the rank of the court cards themselves: pages are typically selected for young women; knights for young men, queens for mature women, and kings represent mature men. It should be noted that not every reader nor every deck adheres to these attributions.

One drawback to using a court card as a significator for the querent is the fact that this removes a card from the deck for the reading. The Watcher Angel Tarot has an optional Seeker card. This card can be used as a universal significator so all readings are done with a complete deck. It should be noted that not all readers make use of a significator. For those who are interested in the traditional coloring attributions associated with each court card, a chart follows. We do not hold to these strict definitions of appearance in the Watcher Angel Tarot but instead focus on the mental, spiritual, and emotional qualities associated with each court card.

Traditional Significator Chart*

Wands: blonde hair, blue eyes

Cups: light brown hair, hazel eyes

Swords: brown hair, brown eyes

Pentacles: black hair, black eyes

*from Eden Gray's *Mastering the Tarot,* 1971 Signet Publishing Group

Tarot Spread: A set pattern into which Tarot cards are dealt for the purpose of doing a reading. Each station or placement of a card has a specific association pertinent to the overall meaning of the reading such as "Romance" or "Family." Perhaps the simplest Tarot spread involves three cards representing Past, Present, and Future. The most popular Tarot spread is a pattern of ten cards known as the Celtic Cross. While there are a number of traditional Tarot spreads used by readers, it is possible to design or develop one's own unique spread. In addition to the Celtic Cross, twelve cards can be drawn (often arranged in a circle) to forecast the themes of each month for a coming year; three cards can be drawn to represent any number of triplicities, including Past, Present Future, Heaven, Earth and the Path Between, and Issue, Basis, Outcome.

Reversed: Upside-down. A card which is dealt into a reading upside-down is considered reversed. The reversed state alters the card's meaning, essentially turning the traditional meaning of the card on its head. This often results in a darker, more ominous meaning for a reversed card, although this is not strictly the case. Not every deck, nor every Tarot reader, acknowledges reversed meanings. When first beginning to master the Tarot, many readers find it useful to ignore reversals, instead integrating this additional layer of meaning once they are more comfortable with the Tarot as a whole. Another approach to reversed cards is to see them as the negative aspects of that particular card *brought down upon* the querent – i.e., the querent has brought these qualities or consequences upon him or herself.

Tarot Part III: Beliefs and Traditions

As soon as you declare that you are interested in picking up a Tarot deck, you'll likely get unsolicited advice from family and friends on where to buy it, how to store it, and the best way to keep it "charged." This section addresses some of the most common modern folk traditions concerning the Tarot. Some have practical value. Others, less so. A few actually qualify more as superstitions. I've described them here as "modern folk traditions" because few have any basis in hard facts, and the value for most of them comes down to what you, the Tarot owner, personally believe.

Buying Your Own Tarot: As soon as we started promoting the deck online, I received messages from people wanting to know whether or not it was advisable for them to buy their own deck. I've always bought my own Tarot, so this was a new one on me. I've not been able to track down the source of the belief, but many people currently hold that a Tarot deck should be received as a gift. Buying the deck yourself is thought to jinx it somehow. If this tradition is a fundamental part of your personal belief about the Tarot, I do not want to belittle it. However, I believe that the most important thing about selecting a Tarot deck for one's own use involves the appeal of the deck's symbolism and images. For best results with the Tarot, you should pick a deck that speaks to you. The art should be appealing. The symbolism should be appealing. The overall concept and feel of the deck should be something that resonates deeply with you. In my experience, the only way to be certain that a deck is right for you is to pick that deck out yourself. That tends to be easier when you are the one purchasing the deck, although I suppose it could be feasible to bring a friend along and have them buy it for you.

In my opinion, it is not strictly necessary that your deck be gifted to you. I have always bought my own decks, and I have noticed no negative repercussions from this practice. Do not feel obligated to adhere to this Tarot tradition unless it has a great deal of personal meaning for you.

Handling Your Tarot: Some Tarot owners are very picky about who they let handle their decks, while others can be very casual about this. You may have heard that it is considered impolite to touch someone's deck without asking them first, and you may also have heard that you should never let people casually handle your deck outside of readings. Some traditionalists refuse to allow anyone to handle their Tarot but themselves – even when doing readings. I come from the school of thought where it is helpful to a reading to have the querent shuffle the deck at least once while focusing on his or her question.

Does this mean that people should play around with your Tarot willynilly? Because the Tarot is a tool and not a toy, it should be accorded a certain amount of respect, and some of this respect comes in the form of handling it only with intent. That is not to say that you cannot pick up your deck and sort through it just to look at the pretty pictures. That is part of familiarizing yourself with the deck and, ultimately, it serves a purpose in your ownership of the deck. Having other people handle your deck is not strictly forbidden, but it is polite to ask to handle a deck. This is less because casually picking up someone else's Tarot deck is going to somehow magically destroy its mojo and more because Tarot decks tend to be very personal to the people who own them. As their personal property, one shouldn't simply pick a deck up and thumb through it without permission. Encouraging others to treat your deck with respect also serves to remind you that it is a tool and not a toy.

A lot of the beliefs about how a Tarot deck should be properly handled stem from the notion that Tarot decks are magickal tools that can be imprinted with and influenced by psychic energies. We will delve more completely into the connection between the Tarot and psychic energies a little further on. For now, just know that the influence of psychic energy on a deck is a very real consideration for some readers.

The most important consideration when addressing the proper handling of a tarot deck is the fact that your Tarot is not a game. Although Tarot cards and regular playing cards are related to one another (and games are still played using the Tarot), if your primary purpose in owning a Tarot is to use the deck for divination and insight, then you should treat the deck with a certain amount of respect. Consider keeping your Tarot in a location where it is not likely to be casually picked up by visitors or children in your home. Children, especially, are bad news for a Tarot deck because they often become enamored with all the pretty pictures, and they have a high tendency of losing, damaging, or destroying some of the cards. To help protect it and to acknowledge the deck's identity as more than a toy, give the deck a little bit of its own space. Many Pagans and magickal practitioners actually set aside some space for their decks on their altars. But you don't need an altar to maintain a small section of dedicated space. A little corner of your bedroom dresser or a specific nook on your favorite bookcase works just as well.

If you have children, let them know that your deck is not a game to be played with. You may not want to make the deck forbidden to them, however, as this tends to only increase the appeal of any object to a child. Rather, you may find it helpful both to your child and your deck to sit down and look at all the pretty pictures with the child, at the same time letting them know that the pictures tell a story, and that story is special to you. How or if you want to address the divinatory potential of the Tarot with a child will really depend on two main factors: how much of these beliefs you can safely share with the child and how capable the child is of approaching those beliefs in a mature and responsible fashion. Sometimes letting them know that the deck in the corner is yours and not theirs to play around with has to suffice.

Charging Tarot Decks: Many people who work with Tarot believe that a deck can hold a "charge" of magickal or psychic energies. This is especially true among practitioners of magick, but one does not have to practice magick in order to appreciate the energy that goes into a treasured deck. There are two main ways in which a deck is charged. First there is the way in which a reader charges his or her deck. For some, this can involve elaborate rituals, but it can be as simple as holding the deck in one's hands and concentrating on the meaning and utility of the cards. The second way in which the cards are charged occurs during a reading – or more properly, just before the cards are laid out. Many readers give their deck to the querent to shuffle, asking the querent to concentrate on his or her question while doing so. The idea behind this is that the querent's touch and concentration, plus the act of shuffling the cards, helps to imprint the deck with that person's energy, therefore facilitating a reading that is tuned to the needs of the querent.

All of the concepts involving "charging" one's Tarot deck are founded upon a belief in psychic energy and how this can be conveyed consciously or unconsciously through physical touch. If you don't believe in psychic energy, you can approach this process in terms of psychology (in the end, what we call magick and psychology are so intertwined that they're virtually the same thing anyway). As a reader charging your cards, consider that intentional, ritualized actions help you to focus on the meaning of the deck. By handling the deck differently from an ordinary object, you are priming your subconscious to view the cards as a valid method of expression. Essentially, ritual actions remind us that the focus of those actions is important. You can even look at this in terms of quantum physics: you are making a conscious choice to interact with and thus observe the action of your Tarot. The very act of observation will influence the outcome of shuffling and randomly distributing the cards.

To charge your deck when you first get it, I recommend taking some time to go through the cards, looking at the words and the images, and allowing your mind to wander over what these mean to you. Go through the whole deck like this several times, simply allowing the cards to "speak" to you and make the experience tactile as well, holding them, shuffling them, and getting the feel of them familiar in your hands. You can go a step further and, once you have gone through the whole deck like this, take a few moments to hold the cards in your hands while you close your eyes and concentrate on the purpose you desire for this deck. You can state this purpose out loud or silently to yourself, or you can leave it as an unspoken feeling, expressed beyond words. When this is done, set the deck aside somewhere. Make sure that it has its own space that is separate and distinct (I'll go into this further under "storage").

Some practitioners feel that no one but the person to whom a deck belongs should ever touch that deck, for fear that another person's energies might interfere with this charge. I've never felt that having another person handle my decks was that much of an issue, so long as they handled them with respect – but how or if you give permission for others to interact with your deck will be entirely up to you and your comfort levels. One casual interaction on the part of another is not, in my opinion, enough to interfere with the charge of a deck – or if it is, you did a lousy job of charging that deck in the first place. A few Tarot workers don't even like querents to handle their decks for a reading. They may not have the querent shuffle the cards at all (though I feel this makes the querent feel unnecessarily passive and distanced from the reading. Some interaction helps them connect with the work just as much as it helps the deck "connect" with the querent). Some limit the querent's contact with the deck by merely having the querent cut the cards once the reader him or herself has shuffled them and is satisfied that the deck is ready for the reading.

One other note on charging a deck that applies to readings: there is a widespread belief that by shuffling the cards, one is essentially shuffling the question into the deck. Whether it's a matter of magick or psychology, I have certainly found that it helps to have a question firmly in mind prior to laying the cards out for a reading. Think of it again as priming your subconscious, this time to approach the language of the cards with a certain perspective or goal in mind.

Tarot Deck Storage
Once you have bought your deck, where and how do you best store it? A Tarot deck is quite different from a deck of playing cards. It is not a game but a tool. Many practicing Pagans view their Tarot decks as ritual objects. Decks are often given a special place upon a practicing Pagan's altar. Because of the special nature of the Tarot, there are a number of different approaches to storage that seek to acknowledge the Tarot's magickal potential.

Tarot Wraps: Tarot traditionalists will tell you that once you acquire a deck, you will need to also procure a wrap or a cloth for that deck. The Tarot is wrapped in the cloth for storage and, ostensibly, to protect the energies of the Tarot from degradation and outside influences. Most traditionalists will tell you that you need a cloth that is 100% silk, preferably in a single, solid color. Within some belief systems, the color of the cloth can affect the character of the deck. White, black, red, green – they all have different (and sometimes conflicting!) magickal associations and not all systems agree with the specific associations of each color. Personally, I believe that the color or pattern of a cloth is more an expression of individual preference than a magickal obligation, but if colors speak to you, they can add to the process of personalizing your deck.

Silk is recommended because it is a natural fiber. A lot of magickal systems express a preference for natural fibers and other components in their ritual and sacred items. Generally, it is thought that magickal and/or psychic energies flow better through natural as opposed to man-made substances. As natural substances are seen as "purer" than man-made substances, they are also thought to interfere less with the magick or energy of the item or ritual tool. For Pagan systems, the added connection to and reverence for the earth implicit in natural substances also has significance. But, the operative question for your Tarot deck is: does it work?

On a practical level, a Tarot wrap is a good idea because it helps keep the deck clean. It keeps all the cards together and it protects them from physical damage. While you may opt to keep your Tarot deck in its original box, over time the box sees enough wear and tear that it will begin to fall apart. A Tarot wrap is a good substitute for the original box because it makes the deck quite portable, the wrap can easily be cleaned, and it doubles as a reading cloth. If you find yourself doing a spontaneous reading with no better place to lay the cards out than on the ground, in the grass, or on your college buddy's questionably vacuumed carpet, you can unwrap your Tarot, lay down the cloth, and do your reading right there.

So, does it have to be silk? Does it have to be a specific color? Is there a set size specification for a proper Tarot cloth? In my experience, these are questions best answered by you, the Tarot owner. Almost all of these considerations come down to personal preference and belief. Just as your deck and its symbolism should speak to you and appeal to you, so too should the traditions you adopt for maintaining and storing that deck speak and appeal to you. Notably, my favorite Tarot cloth for many years was a head scarf that my mother used to wear when I was very little. It was black silk with a pattern in gold and autumn colors in the center. I preferred it to more traditional wraps specifically because of its associations with the early years of childhood before my mother moved away.

Now, I said that *almost* all of the considerations come down to personal preference and belief. Here's the exception: *size does matter*. You don't need to cut your Tarot cloth to the specifications of the golden ratio, but you do need to make sure that you have enough cloth to cover and completely wrap your Tarot – but not so much that you drown your deck. If you want your Tarot wrap to double as a reading cloth (and I highly recommend this very practical usage), then you want to consider how much space you may need to lay out cards for a reading. Cloths cut into squares work best from a utilitarian stand-point, and something that is more than two feet on either side is excessive. If you can barely find the Tarot deck within the voluminous folds of your Tarot wrap, then you need to consider trimming it down to a more manageable size.

Tarot Boxes: Slightly more permanent (and often more ostentatious) than a Tarot wrap is a Tarot box. This is exactly what the name implies: a small box, typically of wood, of a size and shape to comfortably store your Tarot deck. I've seen people store their decks by first wrapping them in cloth and then placing the wrapped deck inside a special Tarot box, and I've seen people put the deck, original box and all, within a larger and more ornate box. A lot of how you go about storage is a matter of personal style and taste, and so is the character of your Tarot box – should you choose to have one. The box can come pre-made, or you can craft it yourself, decorating the exterior with symbols or images that you feel are appropriate. A box does give you a specific and special place to store your deck, which helps subconsciously to reinforce the special quality of the deck. It can be pretty and practical, and the act of creating or decorating a Tarot box can be integrated into your process of charging and personalizing your deck. A hand-sewn (or knitted!) pouch can take the place of a tarot box and is even more portable.

The Bottom Line: When you read the Tarot, it speaks to you in the language of visions and dreams. That communication occurs in your head (all magick, like all psychology, begins in your head). It follows that your mental state has a significant impact upon how receptive you are to the meanings and interpretations of your Tarot. Anything that puts you in a comfortable, open, and receptive mental state is helpful to working with your Tarot. Anything that makes you uncomfortable, shuts you down, or clouds your mind with unrelated associations will negatively impact your work with the Tarot. This is why the tools, items, and objects you use in conjunction with your Tarot should encourage the former and avoid the latter. The meaning to you is tantamount and trumps any and all traditions.

Tarot Part IV: Stories in the Suits

There are stories that unfold in each of our suits within the Watcher Angel Tarot. These stories are married to the concept of the suits as a whole as well as to the primary element traditionally associated with that suit. Briefly stated, Pentacles embody the element of earth. Cups are water. Wands are fire. Swords are air. Earth is traditionally associated with wealth, fertility, production, and material stability. Water is associated with emotions, creative expression, psychic experiences, and the unconscious mind. Fire is passion, energy, potential, and the vital spark of both illumination and inspiration. Finally, air is connected to the mind, communication, ideas and words – and the conflicts which inevitably arise when any of these things work at cross-purposes to one another.

It should be noted that the Tarot suits are usually presented in a different order than in our deck. Wands, as fire, almost always come first in other Tarot decks for they are seen to represent the first spark of creation. For our deck, however, the first suit is Pentacles. This is in keeping with the mythos of the Watcher Angels, and it allows their story to unfold more fully within the deck. Pentacles represent the element of earth. Because earth was the goal of the Watchers – and through it, access to earthly experiences – the Pentacles are the opening suit of our deck. The Pentacles represent the age of establishment, where the Watchers first come down to the world of flesh and begin to build families and homesteads, cities, and eventually empires. From Pentacles, it moves to Cups. The Cups represent the Golden Age of art, architecture, and personal refinement that follows the Age of Establishment. The Wands are that restless fire in the soul which leads to invention and experimentation. Thus Wands tell the tale of an Age of Discovery during which the Watchers instruct competitive mortal students in the magick of the spheres. Finally, the Swords tell the tragic tale of an Age of Civil War where the children of the Watchers rise up against one another, bringing all their strength to bear in bitter battle.

Here is a little more insight into each of the suits:

Pentacles: In their rustic figures and rich autumnal tones, Pentacles represent earth, material possessions, and crafted works. In the Watcher Angel Tarot, the Pentacles also represent the period of time during which the Watchers first establish themselves on the Earth, joining with mortals, making cities, and starting families of their own. The Pentacles themselves represent in a visual manner the marriage of Heaven and Earth implicit in the Watchers' tale. On each pentacle, a blue pentagram points up, representing a quest toward spirit. A red pentacle points down, representing a quest toward flesh. The two intertwined indicates these yearnings conjoined in the human condition, in balance yet always pulling against one another.

Cups: The blues, whites, and subtle grays of this suit visually connect the cups to the element of water. The sensual, elegant curves of the drapery in the Ace establish a theme which reaches its most complete expression in the neo-Classical and Renaissance designs of the costumes and architecture found throughout the suit. Within the narrative of the Watchers, the Cups represent a dream-like age of art and beauty that blossoms following the early establishment of civilization witnessed in the Pentacles.

Wands: Wands are fire. More than that, they represent energy, both potential and realized. In the Watcher Tarot, this is expressed most poignantly by releasing that energy from the wands themselves so the pips of each card become swirling balls of force that power magick, creation, and change. Thus, the wands themselves are the stolen fire from Heaven that the Promethean Watchers give to humanity in the form of forbidden knowledge – especially knowledge about magick. Accordingly, the Wands are set in a time when mortals compete to master the Watchers' forbidden arts at a Hermetic school of magick. Releasing the energy from the wands to manifest as balls of force represents externalized potential: this is the underlying meaning of all of the wands – channeling potential power into form through the direction and application of the magickal Will.

Swords: Gray and cold, with a desolate winter landscape in many of the cards, the Swords are the final suit of the Watcher Angel Tarot. This suit is tied to air and represents a devolvement of society into warfare and struggle due to conflicting ideologies. The Ace of Swords represents the crafting of the first weapon and thus the introduction of warfare to a previously peaceful society.

Tarot Part V: The Court Cards

Some Tarot theorists approach the Court Cards as personifications of cosmic forces, much like the trumps of the Major Arcana. In our deck, however, the Court Cards definitively represent people and their roles or qualities. These can be individuals in the querent's life, or they can appear more like mirrors, embodying different aspects or faces of the querent. Either way, the Court Cards are characters in the story that unfolds within each suit and, more broadly, throughout the Tarot as a whole.

Each of the four Court Cards represents a role: Page, Knight, Queen, and King. These roles are drawn from the traditional social structure of feudal Europe, particularly that of the British Isles. Some of these roles are more clearly gendered than others: Kings are definitively masculine; Queens are definitively feminine. Most other Tarot decks cast Knights as masculine as well, leaving Pages as either girls (in both the Golden Dawn system and in Crowley's Thoth deck, they are called "Princesses") or as adolescents whose gender identity has not fully blossomed and therefore can remain ambiguous or set to a default of "youth" (still generally implying a boy). Thus, when the Court Cards come up in a reading, most traditional interpretations cast Queens as women – and usually older women who are well-established in their lives. Kings are mature men. Knights are younger men, still spurred on by the fire of youth, and Pages are allowed to be either male or female, but almost universally are perceived as young and just starting out on the journey of life.

In our deck, because we perceive gender as something that exists more along a continuum, two of our Knights are distinctly female while the other two are male. Two of our Pages are feminine, while the other two are left ambiguous and could be taken either way. One of the goals behind these representations is to make the identities of the Court Cards more universally applicable – especially in a world where gender is not always black and white. When reading the Court Cards, be flexible in your interpretations, even when it comes to the apparently clearly gendered cards, such as Kings and Queens. Note that earlier I described them as "distinctly feminine" and "distinctly masculine." This does not necessarily mean that a Queen will always represent a woman, or that a King will always represent a man. Rather, the masculine and feminine aspects embody, in my opinion, different personalities and interior qualities which can exist separate and distinct from a person's physical sex.

To best understand the qualities represented by the Court Cards, it may be helpful to place less focus on gender and instead consider the *role* embodied by each of the four subsets. These four roles bring the feudal concept of the Court Cards forward to archetypes that a modern person is better able to relate with and understand. They are as follow: Pages are messengers; Knights are challengers; Queens are nurturers; and Kings are directors. There are still shades of our socially constructed concepts of gender inherent in this approach, and thus it does not deviate completely from the traditional approach to the Court Cards (as best embodied by the Rider-Waite-Smith system). A nurturing personality is linked to the archetype of the Mother and is thus perceived as feminine (note: not necessarily *female*). These are our Queens. Directing-types, who dictate and enforce structure tend to fall into our collective perception of the Father, and are thus seen as masculine. These are the Kings. As challengers, Knights tend to be perceived as male because of collective assumptions about strength, daring, and innovation. But we no longer live in a society where raw physical strength is the best measure of a successful challenger: cunning, intelligence, insight, and a whole host other qualities can allow a person – male, female, or otherwise – to establish themselves in that role. Thus, Knights can go either way and should be read based upon the input of the cards around them, as well as the intuitive sense of the reader. Pages, as messengers, are even more versatile. It is their very function to exist in transition. Their job is to move from the message-giver to message-receiver, and therefore they are always in a state somewhere between the two. This transitional nature of Pages allows them also to best represent people who exist between or beyond standard concepts of gender, persons in transit and walkers-between.

Court Cards and Myers-Briggs
Another approach to the Court Cards that removes the issue of gender entirely involves wedding the sixteen royals of the Tarot to the sixteen personality types defined by the Myers-Briggs system. This system is very eloquently outlined in Jana Riley's *Tarot Book* and is most popular among people who take a Jungian approach to

the Tarot. An influential psychologist of the 20th century, Carl Jung helped to define the personality types that serve as the basis for the MBTI, or Myers-Briggs Type Indicator. First, he split people into two broad categories based upon their preferential interactions with others. Those who tend to prefer their own company and are more focused on their own interior world, Jung labeled *introverts*. Those who prefer the company of others and are more focused on experiencing the world outside of themselves are *extraverts*.

Jung further defined people by their main psychological function: thinking, feeling, intuitive, and sensing. He linked thinking people with air, intuitive with fire, feeling with water, and those whose focus lay more on sensation he linked to earth. Notably, Jung also studied the symbolism of medieval alchemy, finding key points that he felt were expressive of human psychology – thus his connection between psychological types and the four elements of Western magick. For the Tarot, this nicely links these four approaches to the four suits, each of which is also linked to one of the four elements. Initially, Jung constructed eight basic psychological types through combinations of these above qualities. Myers and Briggs then added two more categories: judging and perceptive, which represent the way in which people tend to process their experiences with others, themselves, and their world. Their approach to personality is defined in *Gifts Differing* by Isobel Briggs-Myers and Peter B. Myers.

The Myers-Briggs Type Indicator gives us sixteen different personality types, starting from whether a person is an introvert or an extravert, their dominant psychological function, their auxiliary (secondary) psychological function, and their attitude: judging or perceiving. These categories are each represented by their initial letter and encoded in four-letter acronyms such as ENFP or INTJ. The first letter of these acronyms is either E for Extravert or I for Introvert. The next two letters are a combination of N for Intuitive (because I is already taken for introvert), F for Feeling, T for Thinking, and S for Sensation. The first of these two indicates the dominant type and the second is the auxiliary. Finally, the last letter is either J for Judging or P for Perceiving. Interestingly, the Golden Dawn's approach to the Court Cards in terms of the elements lines up very nicely with the Myers-Briggs index, even though the two systems are separated by forty years and rather different approaches to reality. But the Page, or Princess of Wands, is defined by the Golden Dawn system as Earth of Fire. Fire – intuition – is her dominant type, and Earth – sensation – is her auxiliary. Thus, within the Myers-Briggs system, the Page of Wands would be ENFP.

Myers-Briggs Personality Types

ENFP	Extraverted Intuitive Feeling Perceptive
ESFJ	Extraverted Sensing Feeling Judgmental
ESTP	Extraverted Sensing Thinking Perceptive
ESFP	Extraverted Sensing Feeling Perceptive
INFJ	Introverted Intuitive Feeling Judgmental
INFP	Introverted Intuitive Feeling Perceptive
ISTJ	Introverted Sensing Thinking Judgmental
ISFP	Introverted Sensing Feeling Perceptive
ENTP	Extraverted Intuitive Thinking Perceptive
ENFJ	Extraverted Intuitive Feeling Judgmental
ENTJ	Extraverted Intuitive Thinking Judgmental
ESTJ	Extraverted Sensing Thinking Judgmental
INTP	Introverted Intuitive Thinking Perceptive
ISFJ	Introverted Sensing Feeling Judgmental
INTJ	Introverted Intuitive Thinking Judgmental
ISTP	Introverted Sensing Thinking Perceptive

Although it may carry with it some unsavory connotations, I personally feel that the Sensing type would be better represented with the word *Sensual*. Sensing types prefer sensations, experiencing their world through touch, taste, sight, hearing, and smell.

In Jana Riley's approach, introvert and extravert qualities alternate from King to Queen and Knight to Page. She associates Knights and Kings with extravert qualities, assigning Queens and Pages introvert qualities. Notably, she distributes Introvert and Extravert along gender lines throughout, renaming Knights as Princes and Pages and Princesses. Her logic seems to stem from the notion that Knights and Kings are active forces within the Court Cards, while Queens and Pages are receptive.

While I agree on the distribution of active and receptive qualities, I don't agree in all cases with the introvert and extravert associations. Actually, Riley's identification of the Queen of Wands as an INTJ inspired me to attempt to create my own distribution of the Myers-Briggs personality types throughout the Court Cards because I found that attribution so intellectually jarring. One thing I learned from this exercise is that several of the Court cards are extremely obvious in the type they represent. Several others have some wiggle room, largely depending on one's attitude toward that particular card. If you are familiar with the MBTI, I strongly recommend that you take a look at the Court Cards yourself and try to determine your own associations across these types. I've included a chart below with my attributions as well as those of Riley so you can compare and draw your own conclusions.

This method of reading the Court Cards will be highly enlightening for some and confusingly abstruse to others. Although a Myers-Briggs interpretation of the Court Cards will not be for everyone. The elemental designations in the chart below are drawn from the teachings of the Golden Dawn:

Court Card	Element	Riley	Belanger
Page of Pentacles	Earth of Earth	ISFJ	ISTP
Knight of Pentacles	Air of Earth	ESFP	ESTP
Queen of Pentacles	Water of Earth	ISTJ	ESFJ
King of Pentacles	Fire of Earth	ESTP	ISFJ
Page of Cups	Earth of Water	INFP	INFP
Knight of Cups	Air of Water	ENFJ	ESFP
Queen of Cups	Water of Water	ISFP	ENFJ
King of Cups	Fire of Water	ESFJ	ISFP
Page of Wands	Earth of Fire	INFJ	ENFP
Knight of Wands	Air of Fire	ENFP	INFJ
Queen of Wands	Water of Fire	INTJ	INTP
King of Wands	Fire of Fire	ENTP	ENTP
Page of Swords	Earth of Air	INTP	ESTJ
Knight of Swords	Air of Air	ENTJ	ISTJ
Queen of Swords	Water of Air	ISTP	ENTJ
King of Swords	Fire of Air	ESTJ	INTJ

Tarot VI: Reclaiming the Names

One of my original concepts with the Watcher Angel Tarot was to assign a different Watcher to each of the Trumps in the Major Arcana. Because there is a wide cast of characters mentioned in the *Book of Enoch,* and many of them are described as having a connection with some subject of magickal or forbidden knowledge, this seemed like it would add great depth of meaning to the Major Arcana, tying it definitively to the mythic narrative. However, this idea proved easier in theory than in practice. On the surface, it seems like it should be simple: within the *Book of Enoch,* there are several sections that list the names of the Watchers. These sections, mainly in *I Enoch* 6-9 and 69: 1-14, describe their stations and, in several cases, explain the different types of knowledge these Watchers revealed to humanity. Several of these names repeat throughout Enochic literature (as we've seen, the *Book of Enoch,* while arguably the most complete, is not the only source for the Watchers' tale). The two most prominent are, of course, their leaders: Shemyaza and Azazel. Shemyaza is repeatedly referred to as the "chief" or "leader" of the Watchers, and Azazel seems to be his second-in-command. Both of them are in positions of authority, and both are held accountable for the actions of the Watchers as the story unfolds. The problem with picking names to assign to each of the Major Arcana will become clear as we consider the issue of Shemyaza and Azazel. These are the two most frequently named Watchers throughout Enochic literature, within the *Book of Enoch* and beyond, yet their names are rarely spelled the same way twice – sometimes with noticeable deviations even within the same manuscript.

Anyone who is familiar with my work on the *Dictionary of Demons* knows that I get a little intense when it comes to the issue of names. I feel that names have power, and it's important to get powerful names right. In a number of systems, the nature of a being is expressed within the sound and meaning of its name, and this is especially true with angel names. But the deeper I delved into the surviving Enochic literature, the more complex the issue of the Watchers' names became.

The angel whose name I learned first as Shemyaza appears in the Charles translation of the Ethiopic Enoch as *Semjâzâ.* In the Laurence edition of 1821, one of the earliest English renderings of the Ethiopic Enoch, the name appears instead as *Samyaza*. And in Hoffman's German edition, translated by John Baty in 1839, the name is *Samiaza*. All of these editions, it should be noted, are working from essentially the same manuscript. The differences are slight, and it's clear they're all evoking essentially the same sounds, but which one is the *most* right? For that, I tried digging deeper.

If we go back to the *Chronographia* of Syncellus, written at the second half of the 8th century CE, we see the name as *Semiazas*. The source of Syncellus's synopsis of the Watcher Angel tale is uncertain, although similarities evident in some of the names suggests that he may have been working from one of the versions of the *Book of Enoch* kept by the Essenes among what are widely known as the Dead Sea Scrolls – or at least they shared similar sources. If that wasn't confusing enough, in the Jewish literature concerned with the Watchers, such as the *Chronicles of Jerahmeel,* the name of the chief of the Watchers is rendered *Shemhazai*, while his partner-in-crime is *Asael* – even though this angel is linked directly in the text with the Azazel mentioned in Leviticus. Finally, to complicate matters even further, there are instances in Jewish literature where these two figures are referred to simply as *Uzza* and *Azza* – both of which are from a root word meaning "strong."*

Shemyaza and Azazel aren't the only Watchers whose true names – if ever there were such a thing – are difficult to pin down. *I Enoch* 6:7 contains a list of the chiefs of the Watchers. They're generally referred to as the "chiefs of tens," suggesting that there should be a total of twenty names in the list, since earlier it's stated that a total of two hundred Watchers came down to the slopes of Mount Hermon. However, the most current Charles edition lists only nineteen, including Shemyaza and Azazel. Earlier versions have only eighteen, due to an error where the name of Urakiba (or Arakiba) was conjoined with that of Ramiel – and this error repeats in multiple translations of the Ethiopic Enoch throughout the nineteenth century. Later in the same book, the list of names reappears in Chapter 69 –

* These names also appear in the Quran and were known to have once been worshipped as a god or gods: "Al-'Ozza was the special idol of the Kinanah tribe who dwelt near Chaibar, on the mercantile road to Syria. Its name, 'Ozza or 'Uzza, signifies "the Mighty One," from the root 'azza, to be strong." p. 115 from Abram Smythe Palmer's *Studies in Biblical Subjects Series, issue 2: Jacob at Bethel,* London: 1899.

only now there are twenty-one "chiefs of tens," and Azazel is named twice. It's enough to make one tear out their hair.

The list of the chiefs of tens is not the only section where names appear – along with significant variations and inconsistencies between manuscripts (not to mention the different translations). Chapters 6-9 of the Ethiopic Enoch also contain the primary source that tells us which Watchers taught which subject of forbidden knowledge – from weaponsmithing to divination – and there are difficulties here as well. Not all source manuscripts give the same list of names, and not all translators render these names (let alone the subjects which they're supposedly teaching) exactly the same. Furthermore, Chapter 69 in the same book introduces an entirely new cast of characters when it comes to the matter of forbidden teachings, appending several new categories of knowledge to the list.

The textual issues make sense if you stop to think about it (although this makes them no less frustrating). What we know as the *Book of Enoch* is really a compilation of a number of different manuscripts. Many of these manuscripts are fragments at best. They span a number of different languages, from Greek to Ge'ez, and some of them were themselves originally compiled from what may have been an old and fragmented story in the time of the Essenes. Most scholars postulate that the original source of the tale was written in Hebrew or Aramaic, but this remains an educated guess. If we assume the story of the Watchers originated in Hebrew, one thing we know for certain is that the surviving versions have undergone a number of permutations of language. The Ethiopic Enoch alone had to go from Hebrew to Greek, from Greek to Ge'ez, from Ge'ez to German and then to English in the course of its journey through time and translations to arrive at the influential Charles edition of the nineteenth and early twentieth century. A difficult prospect when producing any translation is the matter of symbolic words for which there is no clear translatable meaning. Names are perhaps the worst for this, and the best a translator can really do is to attempt to render the name phonetically. As different languages contain different sounds, oftentimes this means that the overall character of the name changes – however slightly – from one language to another. Now consider the build up of even slight changes through a progression of not one, not two, but at least *four* different languages. No wonder there's some confusion!

Of course, knowing that it's nigh impossible to arrive at the "true" character of the original names never really dissuades me from the attempt. Despite the difficulties, I really liked the idea of assigning a Watcher to each of the Major Arcana, and I pressed ahead with the project. The first challenge to be surmounted was the matter of the names themselves: which spellings should I use? For this, I compared as many different translations and editions of the *Book of Enoch* that I could get my hands on. The ease of access for digitalized books on the Internet made this much easier than it might have been five or ten years ago (I even tracked down a copy of the original Ge'ez and contemplated finding someone to translate this). Ultimately, I gathered nearly a dozen variations, including a number of nineteenth century sources, the Charles translation, the 2004 Nickelsburg translation, and Syncellus's work.

Focusing on the paragraph that lists the "chiefs of ten," I created a chart for comparison. Then I picked the names – or versions of names – that appeared with the greatest consistency. In a few cases, I made adjustments of my own based on what we have come to recognize as traditional angel names. Turêl becomes Turiel, for example. When I was in doubt, I compared the results against Gustav Davidson's *Dictionary of Angels,* also using this resource to help guide me in the matter of the meanings of the names. I think it's important to note that my goal here was less about a strict academic rendering of the linguistic roots of these names and more a matter of capturing the spirit or feel of the Watchers as characters in what I feel is a vibrant and compelling myth. In a few cases, as much as I wanted to make changes to a name (I'm convinced that the angel *Penemuê* should really be rendered *Penemuel,* but I can't find adequate textual evidence to support this), I stuck with what would be most recognizable to anyone familiar with the *Book of Enoch*, defaulting to the Charles edition not because it is the most current academically, but because it is the most widely accessible.

Casting the Characters
After the matter of names had been settled, the next hurdle was to determine which Watcher found its way to which Trump. In a few cases – such as that of Azazel – the decision was easy. Although later representations of Azazel as a desert-dwelling demon connected with the rite of the scapegoat in Leviticus might lead toward some

associations with The Devil, I felt Azazel was better served as The Emperor. After all, it was Azazel who taught humanity all the arts of war, and through warfare, empire-building. For the Watchers specifically (and consistently) named in connection with some aspect of knowledge or power, the associations came easily: Shamsiel taught the signs of the sun; Sariel taught the signs of the Moon; Kokabiel revealed knowledge of the stars. For a number of the so-called "chiefs of tens," however, it was difficult to choose. Very little information is offered about these angels, save for their rank in relation to Shemyaza, their leader. Davidson's resource was invaluable in this case, as his *Dictionary of Angels* provides the meaning behind some of these names. Turiel means "rock of God," and rocks imply strength (it really is curious to me how many of these angels' names ultimately mean "strength"). Thus, I felt it would further underscore the meaning of Strength to see such a rock-solid angel laid low by the subtle charms of a mortal woman, playing beast to her beauty. Davidson was particularly useful in arriving at the association with Justice. Satariel (whose name is one of the least consistent among the various versions of the "chiefs of ten" section, also appearing as Samsipiel and Samipisiel) is closest in character to *Sathariel.* According to Gustav Davidson, the name of this angel means "concealment of God." He further adds that Sathariel is the angel "who hides the face of mercy," from a source by Waite. The variant phrase, "the veil which conceals the face of mercy" was the inspiration for Jackie's rendering of card XI., Justice.

No one was harder to narrow down than Shemyaza. In chapter six of *I Enoch*, Shemyaza is identified as the leader of the Watcher Angels. He is the first among them to decide upon a plan for going down among the daughters of men in order to take wives and establish families. He is also the one who leads the two hundred rebel Watchers to the slopes of Mount Hermon and encourages them to swear an oath to commit themselves to their planned course. As the Watchers gather on the mountain, Shemyaza tells them, "…and I alone will pay the penalty of a great sin." This makes him an excellent candidate for The Fool, but as The Tower is intended to depict the fateful decision made on Mount Hermon, he also seemed a good choice for that card. Later, in Chapter 8:3 of the *Book of Enoch*, Shemyaza is attributed with teaching enchantments, an area of knowledge that seemed to make him an excellent candidate for The

119

Magician. In Rabbinical stories about the Watchers, Shemyaza is described as being punished (or choosing to punish himself) by hanging suspended head-down between Heaven and Earth, a state very evocative of The Hanged Man. There are several references where Shemyaza repents his transgressions, working to redeem himself, while in contrast, Azazel rebels and actively works to sow discord, fighting, and wickedness throughout the mortal world.

In the Jewish tale of the Star Maiden, Shemyaza could also fit neatly into either Strength or The Lovers. The Star Maiden is known variously as Estrahai and Istahar and may be a reference to the ancient goddess Ishtar. She is depicted in Jewish legend (such as the *Bet Ha-Midrash* 5:156) as a virtuous maiden who rebuffed the advances of Shemyaza. More than that, she tricked the lusty angel either into revealing the ineffable name of God or into giving her his wings – depending on the version of the story. Ultimately, because the maiden refused to have sex with the angel, God raised her into the heavens, placing her among the stars. There she became the constellation of the Pleiades. After being snubbed by Istahar, Shemyaza approached the voluptuous maiden Na'amah, sister of Tubal-Cain (and therefore a daughter of Cain himself). Na'amah, as a dedicated Cainite was more than happy to explore the pleasures of the flesh with the chief of the Watchers (in Apocryphal books like the *Testament of the Twelve Patriarchs* and the *Book of Adam and Eve,* we see the tensions unfold between the children of Cain's branch of humanity – invariably indulgent, voluptuous, and wicked – and those of the righteous Sethian branch). Finally, because Shemyaza's main transgression is one of sensual indulgence and sexual temptation, he could also easily become our Devil.

As the Watcher most frequently named, along with his cohort Azazel, throughout the many permutations of Enochic literature, Shemyaza gains the most associations. Pinning him down was a real chore. Admittedly, I went back and forth between The Tower, The Devil, and The Fool for Shemyaza. I even considered naming him more than once within the Major Arcana, and simply using the many variants of his name (Semiaza, Semjaza, Shemhazai, etc.,) in order to distinguish between the Shemyaza of say, The Devil, and the Shemyaza of The Tower. In the end, however, I knew this would be confusing for readers, and especially for those new to the Watcher Angel myth. And a primary reason for pairing the Tarot with the

Watcher myth in the first place was to facilitate association with a solid storyline, thereby making it easier to read the Tarot overall.

After waffling for weeks on the matter, I stopped and asked myself, "What is Shemyaza's most fundamental role in the Watcher tale?" And that role, quite definitively, is the role of The Fool. As much as Shemyaza is clearly a being possessed of great magick and power, as much as he is also carnally-inclined, ultimately expressing his love for humanity in a very earthly, very sexual way, his most significant act is to inspire the conspiracy of the Watchers. Shemyaza, as the Watcher appointed to lead the rest, is the one who urges the others to leave heaven for earth. It is through his words in I Enoch 6: 1-7 that the other two hundred Watchers agree to bind themselves and take the leap, as it were.

Shemyaza gets the others to act because he does not want to be the only one who pays the price for what they have all discussed – and this is really the key that makes him a natural for The Fool. The verbal exchange depicted between Shemyaza and the Watchers in *I Enoch* 6: 1-7 shows us that they have all discussed the lure of humanity prior to convening on Mount Hermon. They have all "looked down on the daughters of men and found them fair," and they have all thought about what they would like to do with those lovely ladies of the earthly realm. Yet Shemyaza is the only one willing to commit himself to the act – at least at first. He may not foresee all of the consequences, but he knows that these decisions will spark an inevitable chain of events, and not everything that comes from that chain will be desirable. Even so, he is still willing to take the plunge, to risk the wrath of heaven and act upon his desire.

This is The Fool through and through: The Fool stands at the edge of the cliff and leaps off, because sometimes it is better to leap into the abyss under your own power than to allow time or circumstances to push you over against your will. Whether you feel ready for what might wait at the bottom or not, whether you feel that you can predict the full outcome of the action, The Fool's best and worst quality is that he turns his thoughts into actions – come what may. Shemyaza leads the other Watchers to leap from their comfortable place in heaven to an uncertain future among the children of men. And even if the others fail to act and come with him, he's already made up his mind to do the deed. Shemyaza has jumped into the abyss the moment he sets foot on the slopes of

Mount Hermon. Just like The Fool, who starts the whole cycle of self-discovery and transformation that underpins the Major Arcana, ready or not, there he goes.

With Shemyaza's leaping off into the character of The Fool, the rest of the Major Arcana seemed to fall into place. One of the other decisions that helped with this involved important side characters and locations like Na'amah and Mount Hermon. Since it presented such difficulty, rather than limiting the Trumps of the Major Arcana exclusively to angels named as Watchers within the *Book of Enoch,* I opted instead to be true to the mythic character of our deck and include a variety of characters pivotal to the Watchers' tale. Thus, we have Na'amah depicted in The Lovers. Mount Hermon is the location depicted in The Tower, and thus its name appears upon the card. Michael, as one of the archangels specifically named and sent in judgment of the Watchers, appears in all his intimidating glory in Judgment. Uriel and Raphael, who reveal the workings of the heavenly luminaries to the Patriarch Enoch, appear on that pivotal card, The Wheel. And then there is the character of Enoch himself. His role in the myth of the Watchers as it unfolds in the *Book of Enoch* is sometimes eclipsed by the flamboyant activities of the Watchers themselves, but with his inclusion into the Major Arcana, the cycle of the entire deck was complete.

Enoch, the pseudepigraphal author of the *Book of Enoch,* plays a curious role in the story of the Watchers. A Biblical Patriarch, seventh from Adam, he was revered as one of the first – if not the very first – human beings to write a testament. He is, essentially, the very first scribe. In addition to that, within the Bible, Enoch has the distinction of being one of the few individuals who does not die, but seems to be bodily assumed into heaven. In Genesis 5:24, Enoch "walked faithfully with God; then he was no more, because God took him away." The *Book of Enoch* elaborates on this rather enigmatic passage, telling the tale of Enoch's passage into Heaven. In the *Book of Enoch,* the Patriarch actually travels the heavens more than once, returning to the earth to pass his learning on before being taken away a final time for good. Enoch is chosen in part because of his identity as a scribe, and his ability to faithfully report and record all that is revealed to him is clearly valued by both God and the heavenly angels who serve as Enoch's guides. Curiously, once judgment has been passed upon the Watchers, they approach Enoch, a mortal man, to intercede for them with the divine, since by their choices, they are no longer allowed an audience themselves. That a mortal man has greater access to the godhead than the angels themselves is remarkable – and is further accentuated in a scene where Enoch is conveyed directly to the foot of God's throne for a direct interview with the Almighty himself. While all of the experiences of the Watchers are unfolding on the earth, Enoch is undergoing his own transformation. While it is not directly expressed within the *Book of Enoch* itself, elsewhere in related Jewish literature, Enoch is described as not only being given a place in Heaven as a sort of divine scribe, but he is transfigured into an angel himself. He becomes the Metatron, sometimes known as the "little Yahweh," so great is his influence in the heavens.

This transformation of the divine becoming human and the human becoming divine cinched my storyline within the Major Arcana. Thus, we see the experiences of the Watchers unfold through the Trumps, but woven among them, we see Enoch's tale unfold as well. This includes his journey into Heaven courtesy of an angelic guide in The Chariot, to his instruction in the secret machinery of the Universe in The Wheel, to his final transfiguration as the Metatron in The World. Here he (and possibly even the Watchers) has the option to leave behind the most recent cycle with all its beauty and destruction in order to venture into another state of being entirely.

It's a wild ride. Let's take a look at how it unfolds.

Tarot Part VII a:

Extended Interpretations

The Minor Arcana

"True it is, certain and most true, true and without falsehood: that which is below is like that which is above, and that which is above is like that which is below, working the miracles of the One."

--from *the Emerald Tablet of Hermes Trismegistus*

Ace of Pentacles: *Production*

Image: A crafted pentacle featuring two interwoven stars: the blue star points up, the red star points down. The pentacle is displayed upon a rough wooden table with a tool in the foreground. The dominant colors are rusts and browns, lending an earthy, autumnal tone.

Meaning: *Production.* The start of a new project. A beginning related to money, work, and/or physical creation. A new job; entering into a period of material gain. Establishing creature comforts, hearth and home.

Reversed: Material wealth and related concerns become a source of anxiety or obsession. There is a danger of succumbing to greed or gluttony. Immersion in material things may lead to stagnation or complacency.

Interpretation: Aces of any sort represent beginnings, and the Ace of Pentacles marks the beginning of a material phase. Within the story of the Watcher Angels, this material beginning is quite literal: with the Ace of Pentacles, the Watchers initiate their lives among mortals in the physical world, choosing spouses, starting families, and ultimately building an earthly empire. In this sense, the Ace of Pentacles represents the establishment of family, hearth, and home – as well as all of the work that must go into supporting oneself and one's chosen family unit. The tool in the foreground and the hand-crafted pentacle both suggest that this is a hands-on phase. Most cloth represented in this suit is homespun; rugs are hand-woven. Arts and crafts play a significant role in this process of building and establishment: everything of value is being built from the ground up, but despite the primitivism, there is still a wholesome, earthy beauty in it all. This Ace is the spark of all that work.

It is important to remember, however, that the Ace of Pentacles (and the suit as a whole) is not merely about subsistence living. Rather, it represents the first blossoming of earthly riches. In some Tarot decks, the suit of Pentacles is recast as Coins, and this is entirely in keeping with the spirit of the suit.

When this card comes up in a reading, reflect upon all the different ways that material wealth and development can manifest in a person's life. This card does not automatically guarantee stability and riches, but it certainly indicates a time wherein such things move to center stage in the querent's life. As an Ace, the card represents potential, and thus it rests upon the shoulders of the querent to properly respond to and harness this potential as it moves into his or her life.

Two of Pentacles: *Integration*

Image: An angel holds a distaff as his mortal wife spins thread. Two pentacles hang from the bottom of the apparatus, serving as weights. The angel's gaze is on the woman as she works. The woman's attention is focused on the task at hand as she twines separate strands of wool together to make the thread.

Meaning: *Integration.* Decisions. The combination of two disparate things into something new. A partnership or working relationship. Opposites that compliment one another or work well together, as forces, ideas, or people.

Reversed: Too many details to juggle at once. The querent is overwhelmed by choices or is trying to take on too many projects. Unexpected complications frustrate plans.

Interpretation: In keeping with the arts and crafts theme of the Pentacles, we see an angel and a mortal woman, presumably his wife, spinning yarn for weaving. This process takes many different strands of fiber, such as wool, and combines them into something that is stronger and more cohesive than the strands are individually. Two pentacles serve as weights, assisting with the process. The Two of Pentacles, perhaps as part of its inherent "two-ness," has two widely recognized meanings: decisions and integration. Many Rider-Waite-Smith inspired decks favor the meaning of "decisions," typically depicting a figure who must choose between two things. These two things are usually represented by the two pentacles that serve as pips for the card. In some decks, like Karen Kuykendall's *Tarot of the Cat People*, they are depicted as being similar, yet with

129

notable shades of difference. In other decks, the pentacles are more or less identical, and the main figure holds them in balance, indicating that the real distinctions are a matter of personal preference. However, when presented with a choice between taking one thing or another, this interpretation of the card overlooks the third option that is usually available: combining the preferred qualities of both. Rather than exclusion, this approach favors integration. Given the nature of our deck and the story of the Watchers that threads through it, we opted to take the route of Integration with our Two. Of course, the additional meaning of "decisions" is hardly lost from the card: implicit in the process of integration is the decision of what to integrate and how best to go about it.

When this card comes up in a reading, it indicates that the querent is faced with choices and decisions that must be integrated into his or her life. These choices will be relevant to some aspect of the querent's material identity: career, home, family, and/or financial concerns. Given the nature of the Watcher Angel Tarot, there is almost always a hands-on aspect to this integration. The process facing the querent requires not only a decision but also real work to achieve the best possible marriage of forces, ideas, or resources.

Behind the Cards: The female model in this card is our friend Jessica Crutchfield. She owns Ties that Bynde, a company that produces custom corsets and other costuming pieces. She is the wife of Kheprian elder Jason Crutchfield, who appears on the Emperor card. We chose Jessica to model for this card because of her background as a seamstress. In corseting, she is always combining the hard and the soft, supple cloth and sturdy stays, to create a strong yet attractive end result.

Three of Pentacles: *Craftsmanship*

Image: A young man stands near a forge, pounding metal upon an anvil. He is wholly focused on his labor. Ranged around the anvil are three crafted pentacles. Their outer circles echo the bronze piece being worked into a crescent. The three finished works stand in testament to the crafter's skill.

Meaning: *Craftsmanship.* Labor that bears fruit. Hard work made enjoyable through strength of purpose. Production. Focus. The development of skill. Sometimes, a rigidity and/or reluctance to innovate on or deviate from established patterns.

Reversed: Sloppy workmanship. Cutting corners to save time and money, at the expense of quality. The skill is present for a desired project, but resources or funds are lacking to see it through to its optimal completion.

Interpretation: Work, and the products of work, are an underlying theme of the Pentacles. The theme builds upon imagery suggested by the Ace, taking the tool portrayed in the foreground of that card, which represented the *potential* for creation, and putting it (as well as other tools) into the hands of an active creator. In the Three of Pentacles, the decision of what and how to create has been made, and now we enter into the phase of creation itself. The backdrop of this card is a sooty workshop – and while we see many tools of the blacksmith's art, our artisan is not engaged in crafting a weapon. The crafter – intentionally gender ambiguous – has instead turned his or her knowledge, strength, and skill to creating a thing of beauty. Artful pentacles are pounded out upon the anvil, a laborious process that also implies the amount of physical effort required to bring forth these attractive works.

The fact that the artisan is crafting with metal – mainly bronze – is another nod to the earthy nature of this suit. In many early mythologies, metals are seen as the bones of the earth. Accordingly, deities with ties to the deep places of the earth are usually also the keepers and revealers of this hidden wealth, sometimes jealously guarding metals and precious stones, and sometimes teaching the art of extracting, refining, and working with these earthly treasures to a chosen few. Within the Watcher Angel mythos, the Lord of the Forge is Azazel, who not only teaches weaponsmithing but also reveals finer arts, such as jewelry-making and the use of metals and gems for decoration and beautification. Although he does not appear on this card, the artisan we see is certainly a disciple of Azazel, someone who has been given the knowledge and understanding of metals and has chosen to refine that skill. The end result of this process may be practical or merely decorative, but in either case, the objects are a testament to the crafter's work and skill.

When this card shows up in a reading, it is concerned with skilled labor and the end results of such labor. When the card is directed at the querent, it is an indication that his or her hard work will be acknowledged and rewarded. The querent has put great effort into learning, honing, and refining a skill, and others are in a position to appreciate it. Financial gain as a result of this skill is a likelihood, but this card often indicates more than simply getting paid for a job well-done. The work may earn an award or other distinction, or perhaps pave the way for a promotion or a raise. If the card is directed at forces around the querent, it indicates a project or undertaking that requires skilled labor to complete. The querent shouldn't settle for merely getting it done, but should look for and value the extra effort that goes into a truly accomplished work.

Four of Pentacles: *Stability*

Image: A city gate surmounted by stone lions. The architecture is primitive but sturdy. An armed man with a massive shield stands guard. Beyond him, rough-hewn stone steps wind up and out of sight, leading into the city he is guarding. Three pentacles adorn the gate and the fourth is emblazoned on the man's shield.

Meaning: *Stability.* Wealth which demands protection. A desire to keep what one has. Sometimes: miserliness. An unwillingness to yield or relinquish established assets, objects, or patterns. Comfort in one's familiar things.

Reversed: One fails to protect assets wisely, losing them to mishaps or spending too freely. The walls will be erected too late for adequate protection. Difficulties are encountered in a job or project that prevent adequate establishment.

Interpretation: In the Rider-Waite-Smith and related decks, the Four of Pentacles fixates on acquisitive and miserly tendencies. The card depicts a richly-appointed man surrounded by wealth and greedily clasping the discs of large pentacles. I've always felt this overlooked the potential positive qualities of the four. There are many symbolic associations with fours: the four elements, the four cardinal directions, and the four corners of a square – which itself can represent a foundation, such as that of a building. In a suit concerned with earth and earthly possession, the four should reflect this foundation and stability. Building upon this quite literally, our Four of Pentacles depicts the gate to a walled city.

In keeping with the storyline of the Watchers, the Pentacles depict the time of establishment: the Watchers first build families, then homesteads, and finally cities and an empire. In this card, we see the first city – or at least its primary defenses. The process of civilization and city-building, establishing a safe and comfortable place in which people can live, grow, and thrive, implies a need to gather and protect wealth and resources. And here is where the traditional meaning of the Four of Pentacles comes through, married to the notion of four as a stable and solid number. Gated cities mean that there are things outside the walls which potentially threaten one's wealth and way of life. The comfort and stability afforded by such a well-protected location can lead to greed and miserliness, where citizens are driven to hoard their little luxuries from any who exist outside the walls. We see this expressed directly in the card: with walls, there are gates, and with gates, there must be guards whose purpose it is to protect what lies within the walls. That need for protection can take on a positive or very negative spin, depending on various circumstances.

When this card comes up in a reading, it can mean that the walls are already in place for the querent, and these issues of protection or an unwillingness to let go of what one has may be at the forefront. The card represents stability, but stability can also lead to stagnation, especially if one becomes complacent behind the protection of the walls. It can warn of hoarding tendencies or an unwillingness to yield to outside forces that might otherwise allow for change and growth. However, the card can also indicate a need to establish stability in one's life, either in work or in the home. It then falls to the querent to address the necessary balance between wisely protecting one's assets and devolving into unyielding greed once the stability has been firmly established.

Behind the Cards: Jackie based this card upon the famous Lion's Gate at Mykonos, ancient Mycenea. The actual Lion's Gate is damaged, so we no longer can see the heads of the lions that stand over the gate. Jackie decided to recreate how she felt the lions would have appeared in ages past.

Five of Pentacles: *Poverty*

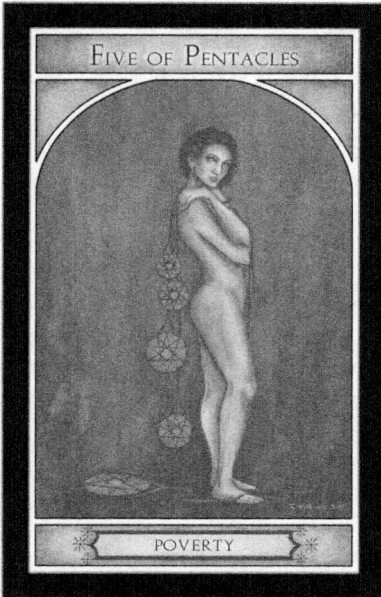

Image: A naked woman seeks to cover herself. Over her shoulder hangs a string with four pentacles. The fifth has torn loose and fallen to the ground. The background is an empty expanse of browns and greens. Shadows prevail.

Meaning: *Poverty.* Instability in one's assets or home. Anxiety over losses, either real, potential, or perceived. A feeling of being vulnerable and unable to adequately provide.

Reversed: Courage in the face of adversity. A destitute physical state leads one to better appreciate emotional or spiritual wealth. A time to count your blessings and appreciate what you have rather than fixating on what you don't.

Interpretation: Most of our suit cards progress with an internal storyline, each number within the suit building upon the one previous to it. The Five of Pentacles is an example of this: the impoverished figure depicted in this card bears relation to the walled city seen in the Four of Pentacles. For every "have," there is a "have-not," and for every cozy hearth inside the protected walls, there is someone on the outside, shivering in the dark. And that is what the figure in the Five of Pentacles represents. She stands before us, stripped and naked, her hair in disarray, and her body streaked with dirt. She clasps a string of pentacles, but the way they dangle, it is clear that she is in danger of losing these last vestiges of wealth as well. In fact, one of the decorated discs has already come loose and fallen to the ground behind her. The card itself is empty, and we have no idea how she got to this sorry state. But despite her obvious poverty, the figure turns to face the viewer, something like a challenge in her eyes. She covers her nakedness and does not bow her head: she has refused to lose her dignity along with everything else.

This figure is someone who stands on the other side of the walls in the bright city depicted in the Four of Pentacles. Either that, or she is someone living within the city whom the walls failed to protect. This is an important lesson and a cautionary tale for anyone who seeks to hoard and guard their wealth: just because walls are erected to protect material possessions does not mean that everyone enjoys either the protection or the wealth equally.

When doing a reading where this card appears, it indicates that the querent is in a precarious financial or material situation – or that the querent is overwrought with anxiety over the *possibility* of such a situation. It is important to note that poverty does not always have to mean raw monetary wealth, but can also indicate general material possessions, creature comforts, physical health, as well as hearth and home. Whether we're talking money or things or one's comfortable space in their home, this card warns of potential loss – as well as the feelings of vulnerability that goes with it.

Six of Pentacles: *Generosity*

SIX OF PENTACLES

GENEROSITY

Image: The naked woman from the five now stands clothed. Another woman, well-dressed, gifts her with a brightly colored shawl. Pentacles hang as decorations from both women's belts. The background is light, warm and inviting. The many colors of the women's clothing lend an almost festive feel.

Meaning: *Generosity.* Charity. The desire and ability to provide for others. Gift-giving. Abundance that leads to philanthropy. Paying things forward.

Reversed: Charity is doled out, but not in a genuine spirit of altruism. Gifts given to salve the gift-giver's ego. Pay-offs. Bribes. Money, food, or shelter that comes with strings attached. Generosity used to impress or control.

Interpretation: Here we have a recurring character traveling through the themes of a Tarot suit – something you will see throughout this deck. The destitute woman of the Five of Pentacles has encountered someone with fortune to spare. Suddenly, she finds herself sheltered, given clothing, and making a friend. There is still a tentative, somber expression on the dark-haired woman's face, perhaps because she is thinking back to her impoverished situation in the Five. Her new friend not only has placed a warm shawl around her shoulders, but she also seeks to comfort her by laying a hand on her arm. Concern is clear on the rich woman's face. The gesture of comfort suggests that the generosity of the card is not merely material in nature: there is an emotional element as well, and a genuine sentiment of altruism behind the gift-giving.

One of the things that artist Jackie Williams brings to the deck is the subtle meaning worked into her backgrounds and shading. As is probably clear from this card, the backgrounds for the suit of Pentacles are all done in rich, autumnal earth tones, as is befitting a suit tied to the element of earth. But the shades aren't simply a passive aspect of the cards. The swirls of color, their shade, and density speak a language of their own. In the Six of Pentacles, the dark and brooding colors of the Five brighten, matching the mood of the card. Adding to this are the festive colors of the women's clothing. Although their garb is simple homespun, it is richly dyed and accented – in the case of the rich woman – with attractive jewelry. The action of the card shows us that the generosity of one person easily becomes the good fortune of another. The shades of the card reinforce this, visually capturing the bright emotions connected with gift-giving.

When this card comes up in a reading, the querent may identify with either one of the two central figures depending upon their situation and the story told by the rest of the cards. For someone in need, the card can indicate a stroke of good fortune wherein a generous gift helps the querent out of a tough spot. But it is equally possible that the card is a suggestion for gift-giving and generosity on the part of the querent, especially if he or she is in a good position to give. Either way, this is the card of "pay it forward," reminding us that wealth is enjoyed best when it is shared.

138

Seven of Pentacles: *Expectation*

Image: A pensive angel holds his pregnant wife, his wings spread protectively around her. Both of them wrap their hands about her gravid belly. Seven pentacles dangle from strings gathered about their wrists.

Meaning: *Expectation.* The wait for work to come to fruition. The need for patience in the current endeavor. Labor that may produce results, but only after time and/or struggle. Also: uncertainty. There are no guarantees that the waiting will pay off. The time invested may fail to produce fruit. Risk. Potential loss.

Reversed: The work is wasted. Investments do not pay off. False or unreasonable expectations. Anxiety regarding the project at hand. A fear of inadequacy or of being unable to see a project through to completion.

Interpretation: This is often seen as the card of "you reap what you sow." Of course, in most traditional representations of this card, this is indicated through literal sowing and reaping: the main figure of the card is often shown standing in a newly planted garden, leaning on a hoe and dreaming of the crops to come. It is a card of manual labor, cultivation, and expectation of harvest. Wedded to the story of the Watcher Angels, this card takes on a very interesting twist. As we know, the Watchers came to the earthly realm with the stated intent of marrying and starting families. Things went wrong because of this forbidden comingling of heavenly and earthly forces, but before they did, the Watchers fathered strong children: giants who were conquerors, empire-builders, and mighty heroes (in Genesis, one reference calls them "men of renown"). However, mating humans and angels was apparently no easy task. One of the words for the children of the Watchers is *Nephilim,* and one meaning for this word often given is "miscarriage" from "to fall" – either from heaven or from the womb. The implication, of course, is that the Watchers' mortal wives did not always carry to term. As the children are described as "giants," one can also assume that births were risky to the mother as well as the child.

In keeping with the Watchers' tale, our Seven of Pentacles depicts a very fleshly variation of "casting seed." The fertile ground is a womb, and the expectation is for a healthy child rather than a fruitful harvest. The angelic father stands behind his gravid bride, arms clasped protectively around her pregnant belly. Both figures are contemplative, perhaps ruminating on the child they both hope to bring into the world. But there is a somber note to the father's expression: the infant is not yet born, and much can go wrong. Due to the difficulty of the labor, he has taken a massive risk: he could lose both mother and child. The card reminds us that no labor is without risk, and the higher the expectations placed upon a harvest, the more devastating its loss can be.

When this card appears in a reading, it does not automatically indicate that the querent is expecting – or hoping for – a child. Pregnancy is one possible meaning, but the card can also refer to projects in the workplace, the purchase of a home, or any situation that calls for hard work, dedication, and patience regarding the outcome. Whatever the querent has undertaken, he or she is now in a waiting game, and the results are not guaranteed. In this, the card itself is rather neutral: although it reminds us that expectations can be frustrated and things do not always come out as we expected, it does not promise either success or failure. It merely says, "Wait and see."

Eight of Pentacles: *Apprenticeship*

Image: An angelic tutor reads to a mortal child. Upon his lap is a thick book with many place markers. The girl smiles up from the floor, surrounded by stylus and papers. A pentacle lies before the child. Further pentacles hang from the place markers in the book and others decorate the wall.

Meaning: *Apprenticeship.* A period of learning. Applied knowledge. The development of skill for future reward. Honing existing skills or returning to learn a new trade.

Reversed: The proper focus and attention are lacking in learning and work. Skills are poorly managed or poorly applied. A talent or gift is going to waste, ignored or underdeveloped. The querent has a mistaken notion of his or her expertise in a talent, subject, or skill.

Interpretation: A baby is promised in the Seven of Pentacles, but there are concerns about a successful birth. In the Eight of Pentacles, we see a child in the hands of a teacher. The implication, of course, is that this is the same child whose birth was expected in the Seven. Her story carries forward to the Eight, where she is now in a stage of apprenticeship, learning the many secrets to which she is entitled as a child of the Watchers. Although it occurs further along in the progression of the suit, the Eight of Pentacles is a card that addresses the development of skills, but not mastery. Accordingly, the little girl has paper and a stylus for note-taking, but instead, her attention wanders. The stylus lays abandoned and she smiles off into the distance, simply listening to her teacher. The rich colors of the chamber, the child's jewelry and brightly-colored dress, together with the presence of both books and paper imply a life of comfort

141

and relative luxury in this early age of establishment. Although the child has much progress ahead of her, the card indicates that she has a good support structure and every opportunity to hone and develop her skills.

When this card shows up in a reading, it means that a learning process is coming into the querent's life. This often involves a trade or a skill specific to a career. The idea of apprencticeship involves applied knowledge: apprentices learn practical trades that can support them later in their lives. If the querent is young, the card is often a reference to the first meaningful tradeskill to be learned. If the querent is older, it may indicate that he or she is in the process of continuing education, either learning a new trade or going back to school in order to enlarge upon previous knowledge. Mastery, however, is a long way off, and the querent may feel like a child again in the sense of starting from the ground up with the knowledge. The card may also be a warning for the querent to pay better attention and focus on developing skills when opportunities for learning present themselves. The Eight of Pentacles is not a card of guaranteed success or money-making but rather the potential for such things – if the proper time and effort are dedicated to the development of that potential.

Nine of Pentacles: *Inheritance*

Image: A woman stands in a brightly-lit chamber surrounded by luxuries. She holds richly dyed fabrics and more are visible in a nearby hope chest. Pentacles decorate the room, hanging from drapery, from the chest, and from her belt. One pentacle adorns a vase brimming with peacock feathers.

Meaning: *Inheritance.* Luxury. Enjoyment of the fruits of shared labors. Creativity given its richest expression. Bringing to fruition projects that are not only successful but also elegant and beautiful. Inspiration to create or an inherited productive skill.

Reversed: Others covet what the querent has, and this leads to bad feelings. A threat of theft or legal entanglements regarding money. The loss of a valued friend or family member. A loss of comfort. Threats to the home.

Interpretation: There is an intentional echo between the face, hair color, and clothing from the little girl in the Eight of Pentacles to the grown woman in the Nine. As the story progresses from the Seven of Pentacles onward, the child of the Watchers has grown into a beautiful woman in her own right. As she has grown and blossomed, so too do we see a blossoming of the Watchers' world. In the Ace through the Four of Pentacles, there is only simple industry. The Watchers are still establishing themselves and building their ideal home in the earthly realm. As they become more involved with the mortal sphere, conceiving and raising children, they also become more invested in creating an ideal place in which to raise their families. In the Nine of Pentacles, we come to the card of

143

inheritance, where the heir to the Watchers' legacy is surrounded by comfort and beauty. Rich gifts surround her, but in her aspect and her bearing, we can see that she enjoys more than mere material wealth: there is also refinement, learning, and peace of mind. The hope chest behind her may represent a rich dowry as she moves into the stage of her life where she seeks to build a family of her own.

When this card comes up in a reading, it often indicates good fortune or an unexpected windfall. As a card of wealth and inheritance, its appearance generally means that the querent's needs will be provided for by outside forces or people. However, wealth and luxury can be double-edged blades, because implicit in having these things is the threat that they can be taken away. Thus, this card may also be a warning to guard one's inheritance – either literally from the threat of theft or through careful investments to nurture the family fortune. The card does not always have to indicate physical wealth, however. It may also suggest an inheritance of talent or skill which, when properly nurtured, will enable the querent to lead a rich and fulfilling life. The card is also a reminder to appreciate the treasure of family and friends and to acknowledge the ways in which other people enrich our lives.

Ten of Pentacles: *Prosperity*

Image: A field before harvest, rich with ripe grain. Through it, a path leads to a homestead where an angel warmly clasps his mortal wife. Hills rise in the background against a lushly colored evening sky. The start of the path is marked with two decorative poles, each festooned with pentacles and ribbons.

Meaning: *Prosperity.* Security. Creature comforts. The fullness of material things. A family well provided for. Abundance brought about through dedicated work. Richness. Fertility. The answer to one's material needs.

Reversed: Problems in the home. A sudden upset in fortunes. Stability has led to complacency or stagnation. Falling prey to sloth, greed, or gluttony. Taking one's good fortune for granted and being unable to adapt when it is disrupted.

Interpretation: From the Seven of Pentacles onward, we have followed the story of one woman's life: from her hopeful parents, to her young education, to a point in her adult life where she enjoys a rich inheritance. Now, in the Ten of Pentacles, the story comes full circle, because she has a home and is starting a family of her own. The focus of this card is no longer simply the woman, but everything she has gained in her life: land, a homestead, a rich, fruitful harvest, and a life-partner. As is fitting for this suit, the card is brimming with rich earth tones, from the ripening wheat in the field to the crested mountains in the distance. The homestead is simple, but the two figures, husband and wife, clasp one another warmly, content with what they have achieved. The focus is less on the figures and more on the fields and surrounding land. Here are the true riches of the suit of Pentacles: fertile earth and the majesty of the land.

Tens are numbers of completion, particularly in the Tarot. The potential promised in the one (ace) develops through the other cards, achieving its fullest realization in the ten. For every suit, the ten represents the fullness and completion of all things associated with that suit. In the case of the Ten of Pentacles, that means the fullness of material things: wealth, stability, comfort, and family.

When it appears in a reading, this card often indicates that the querent has achieved (or is soon to achieve) material success in life. This may be the pinnacle of a career, renown as an artisan or craftsperson, a happy family, or pure, raw wealth. If it takes a darker cast in the reading due to other cards, the Ten of Pentacles may indicate that the querent feels trapped or stifled by these things. The career has grown oppressive. The wealth has become a burden. The family has ceased to grow together in a healthy way. The most important thing to keep in mind with any ten is that the completion of one cycle begets the beginning of another. We see this implied in the husband and wife who clasp one another as they gaze upon their land: the daughter has become a wife, and will likely have children of her own. Those children will carry on their own cycle of growth. Whether the card shows up in a wholly positive or somewhat negative light, the querent who has reached this stage of development in their material life should be asking the most important question: *"What's next?"*

Page of Pentacles: *The Student*

Image: A young scribe sits at a desk copying well into the night. He (or she) pauses to contemplate the work. Candles shed pools of light about the workspace, yet the room is full of shadow. A convex bronze pentacle rests against the bottom of the scribe's desk.

Meaning: *The Student.* Someone in a learning process. An individual working toward mastery of a skill or an art, with progress yet to be made. A quiet, introverted person often focused on study, reading, or work. Someone who conveys messages concerning work, money, health, or projects.

Reversed: The student gets caught up in theory, abstracts, or impractical applications of knowledge and skill. Someone who harbors rebellion against or an inability to work within a structured learning environment. An individual who needlessly wastes time and resources related to learning and development.

Interpretation: The first and foremost message that this Page brings to the querent is "Learning is also work." This Page is a person in progress, and their dedication (or lack thereof) to the learning process can serve as an example to the querent. The Page of Pentacles may show up when the querent has some learning to do, and the message here is that education, even though it may cost more money than it earns, should nevertheless be approached with all the gravity and diligence of a full-time job. The influence of earth from the Pentacles implies practicality and dedication, but may mean that these qualities must be cultivated and brought to bear on the task at hand. This Page may also emerge when a student is coming into the querent's life in search of instruction. In this case, there will be learning experiences on both sides of the relationship, and the querent will need to assess and encourage the student's focus and diligence. Whether the card is indicative of the querent or of someone in the querent's life, the most important message here is that there is yet room to grow in this learning process, and many distractions exist that can hamper the end result. The card can serve as a warning to the querent to keep his or her feet on the ground when engaged in studies and to remember to consider the practical application of any current projects or endeavors.

Behind the Cards: The scribe's work station represented in this card is actually Jackie's art desk, dressed up with some candles and drapery. The modified scribe table is something Jackie herself owns and uses when producing her illuminated manuscripts. It angles the parchment up for easier work and opens to store inks, brushes, and pens.

Knight of Pentacles: *The Artisan*

Image: A young woman in lushly colored clothes puts the finishing touches on a pentacle on the side of a vase. Other pieces of pottery stand around the workspace, presumably also the work of her hands. The vases are bright splashes of color against the rusty earth tones of the card.

Meaning: *The Artisan.* A person learning skill with their hands. Someone who creates tangible and practical items. Someone focused on both form and function, creating things for profit and for show. Someone who challenges others to justify the time and effort invested in their work.

Reversed: A person who is irresponsible in his or her use of time and/or money, encouraging this in others. A troublesome co-worker who repeatedly blocks or sabotages the querent's progress in a career. A friend or family member who criticizes the querent's choices in job, family, or finances, but does so in a dysfunctional and non-constructive way.

Interpretation: Within the Court Cards, if Pages are messengers, then Knights are challengers. They take the fundamental meanings of the suit and bring challenging issues and considerations into the querent's life. For the Knight of Pentacles, this means raising issues about practicality: justifying the time, effort, and expense invested in any project. Is the work really worth it? Are you getting what you really want out of that job? What about that relationship you've been laboring to cultivate? It is the job of the Knight of Pentacles to raise these hard questions and to demand an answer from the querent. As such, the Knight may represent a friend or family member in the

149

querent's life who needles them (gently or otherwise) about practicality and wasted effort. Knights are bellicose in nature, however, so they are not often fun and games. More typically, the Knight is not a friend who drops subtle hints to the querent but is instead someone who brings direct conflict into the querent's life. This could be a boss or co-worker whose troubles with the querent serve as a wake-up call about stagnation in a current career. It could be a family member whose issues with the querent's use of time and resources inspire the querent to reconsider what he or she really values at home. Or it can be a client who makes the querent wonder how much his or her time is really worth. How – or if – the querent resolves these issues is the real question posed by this card. The Knight itself serves as a crux or flashpoint. The rest of the reading should shed light on how best the querent should respond.

Behind the Cards: This is our friend Rhiannon Levine, known online as Pink Spider. She is a very versatile model, and as such, she appears in a number of the cards in different guises. You can find her in the Page of Pentacles and the Knight of Cups in addition to the Knight of Pentacles. We feel the suit of earth fits her best, considering her career as a paleontologist.

Queen of Pentacles: *The Nurturer*

Image: A woman with sensual lips gazes into the petals of a lotus. She wears a pentacle on a black ribbon at her throat. Her hair is loose, her shoulders bare. The card is awash in greens fading to blue, lending an almost underwater feel to the card.

Meaning: *The Nurturer.* Someone with poise and confidence who uses these in support of others. A caregiver. Someone who provides the financial security or material stability necessary for another to flourish. Someone who supports and encourages growth in those around them.

Reversed: Someone who coddles or stunts the development of others by refusing to allow them to look after themselves. Someone who provides shelter and financial security at the cost of independence. A person who promotes co-dependency, enabling sloth, stagnation, or impractical endeavors.

Interpretation: Queens are guides who come into our lives to lead us to an expression of the qualities embodied in their suits. In the case of the Queen of Pentacles, these qualities are creation, practicality, and fertility. The Queen of Pentacles is fertile in mind, body, and spirit, nurturing and encouraging growth in everything she turns her attention to. This can manifest as mental or physical creativity, as well as abundance and growth in the home, industry, finances, and family. Queens guide by example, so the Queen of Pentacles is someone who has manifested these qualities in her (or his) own life and, in sharing this bounty with others, also shares knowledge and experience of how best to attain these things and to hold onto them.

151

With this in mind, the Queen of Pentacles is usually a mature person, well-established in his or her life. The Queen is not necessarily a woman, but certainly someone with a feminine and/or nurturing outlook. Earthy, well-established, the Queen of Pentacles is a scion of abundance: abundance of wealth; abundance of family; abundance of creative drive. There is a motherly feel to this card (and to some extent, to all of the Queens), but equating the card with the querent's mother or a significant mother figure in his or her life can over-simplify the figure of the Queen. Although Queens often represent mature adults, this does not always mean that the Queen is someone who is older than the querent. Instead, the person represented by the Queen may merely be someone with more life experience than the querent, who is further along in the process of establishing a healthy and productive home, family, business, or career. If the Queen shows up in a reading and seems to represent an aspect of the querent him or herself, then it is a call to the querent to use this greater establishment in his or her life to the benefit of others.

Of course, Queens do not always come into the querent's life as beneficent guides. Although they are by no means as challenging as the Knights, the Queens of the Tarot can be harsh and manipulative. They may teach their lessons and set their examples by working in opposition to the querent. In the case of the Queen of Pentacles, this might take the form of a boss or supervisor, a literal teacher, or an influential family member who has some control over the querent's choices in his or her projects, family, or career. In this case, the real work the querent must accomplish with the Queen is to learn from the experience, with the ultimate goal of breaking away from the Queen's direct influence so as to better take control of his or her own wealth, home issues, or material concerns.

King of Pentacles: *The Provider*

Image: A king, robed and crowned, stands amidst a bountiful harvest. His hands are outstretched in a gesture of both giving and of blessing. The fruits of many labors surround him in the form of wheat, fruit, and loaves. A woven pentacle stands in the forefront of the card. Autumn colors riot in the background.

Meaning: *The Provider.* An organized person who helps labors to bear fruit. Someone who takes charge of projects and material gains, guiding them toward their optimal conclusion. A stable and secure individual who can serve as the lynch-pin for financial, practical, and material development. Someone who oversees labor and growth.

Reversed: Successful and dedicated, yet lacking in vision. A leader firmly entrenched at the top, yet slow to adapt to changing times or views. Overly conservative, acquisitive, or controlling. Someone prone to nepotism or the taking of bribes. Old money that preserves wealth only for a favored few.

Interpretation: Kings represent individuals with strong personalities who lead and take charge, directing others and telling them what to do. Our King of Pentacles is a provider who not only oversees abundance, making certain that everyone he's in charge of gets what they need, but he is also a skilled manager who has helped to lead his team to successful production in the first place. In many ways, this King is the living embodiment of the old Chinese proverb, "Give a man a fish, and you feed him for a day. Teach a man to fish, and you feed him for a lifetime." Under his direction, his people have

153

prospered, and now he stands surrounded by worldly wealth, sharing his largesse with others.

When this card comes up in a reading, it generally represents a helpful, solid, and reliable person who has come into the querent's life to offer direction and support in issues of family, business, industry, or finances. This person is mature and well-established in his or her life, and is in charge of prosperous ventures of his or her own. A person of experience and authority, the King of Pentacles may be a business owner, the head of a large and organized social network or family, a chief of staff, or a CEO. Whatever the title, the King of Pentacles is someone in a position of respect and authority, and this position is well-earned. The role of the King of Pentacles is to "share the wealth" through careful instruction and management. The King may appear to help the querent hone his or her skills, to offer an internship, or to offer advice in matters of family or business. If the King of Pentacles emerges in a reading as a projection of the querent him or herself, it is an acknowledgment of the querent's position of successful authority, but should also serve as a reminder that the well-being of others relies upon the querent's dedication and responsible use of resources. Depending on the rest of the reading, the querent may find the support and direction of this King plodding or overbearing, and a proper understanding of the relationship should be cultivated in order to best take advantage of the shared prosperity this card can represent.

Behind the Cards: This is our friend and ally Matthew, a very grounded individual who provides for others in many ways.

Ace of Cups: *Inspiration*

Image: A golden chalice against a background of blue. The foot of the goblet rests against folds of cloth. The sinuous curves of drapery echo flowing water. Soft rays of light illumine the cup, suggesting inspiration from a spiritual power.

Meaning: *Inspiration.* New feelings and/or visions. The start of a new emotional experience. The spark of creativity. Art. Beauty. Sensuality beginning to unfold.

Reversed: Fear of relaxing and going with the flow of emotion or inspiration. Hesitancy or trust issues in love. Excessive materialism or over-intellectualization stifling or obscuring insight, intuition, spiritual or emotional growth. An unwillingness to yield to non-rational experiences.

Interpretation: The Ace of Cups is about the first blush of love, the beginning of poetic, creative, or spiritual inspiration, and the blossoming of experiences related to the heart and soul. The Cups are a suit concerned with creativity, but unlike the Pentacles which demand a practical and utilitarian application to arts and crafts, the Cups embody a sense of art for art's sake. Within the context of the Watcher Angel myth, the Cups represent that point in a society's development where all basic needs have been met. People are safely housed; food, clothing, and other necessities are in abundance, and there is free time for people to devote to art, romance, and spiritual pursuits. The Ace of Cups heralds this new stage of development, where practical concerns are no longer at the forefront and focus can shift to indulging the needs of one's heart and soul.

In addition to emotion, sensuality, and creativity, the Cups also embody all of the other classic associations with the element of water: mutability, shifting tides, psychic visions, and the deep realm of the unconscious mind. Consider that the chalice depicted in the Ace of Cups may be a celebratory goblet of wine, but it can just as easily represent the Holy Grail, the Cauldron of Inspiration, or the scrying vessel of a seer. The Cups are many-layered in their meanings and in keeping with their watery nature, those layers are fluid and prone to shift, even within a reading. The Cups also contain deep, still waters: the first meaning that appears when any of the Cups emerge is likely not the only message those cards seek to convey. Plunging past the appearance dancing on the surface is something a reader – as well as the querent – must be willing to do in order to fully plumb the depths contained within this suit.

With the Ace of Cups, the querent moves into a new phase of life where art and beauty, dreams and romance take enter stage. This can be a wholly interior period of reflection, where most of the action occurs within the querent's own thoughts and emotions, or it can involve exterior connections with family, lovers, and friends. In the flux and flow of this watery suit, rational thoughts and practical applications are rarely a consideration: emotion, inspiration, and intuition all rule the day. When this card appears in a reading, it generally heralds the beginning of such a phase, but it can also appear as a reminder to the querent to develop or shift focus to these aspects of experience. The Ace of Cups presents itself almost as a vision – a flash of insight or inspiration – and the card should be considered as such within the greater context of the reading. It can be a gentle reminder for the querent to relax and stop worrying about a particular outcome or relationship and instead to just "go with the flow" so that things will naturally blossom, or it can demand that the querent take some time to reflect on his or her emotional or spiritual needs and how best to begin to meet them.

Two of Cups: *Union*

Image: A young couple, clad in Renaissance garb, stand at the edge of a lake. His arm is around her shoulder. She clasps a goblet in her free hand. His sits abandoned in the grass. Above them, five stars shoot across the heavens. He raises a hand to this celestial phenomenon in surprise or salutation.

Meaning: *Union.* An engagement or marriage. The blossoming of a new romance. Embarking on a creative or artistic endeavor with a new partner. The start of a deep and emotionally rewarding friendship.

Reversed: A relationship falls out of balance. Misunderstandings create a schism between partners, lovers, or friends. Passion that burns hotly but quickly burns out. Circumstances twist love into hate, friendship into discord.

Interpretation: The Two of Cups is sometimes called the Marriage Card, so strong are its associations with engagement and matrimony. However – especially in the current age where many traditions are open to re-interpretation and personalization – it's important to keep in mind that this does not have to be a literal marriage. It can be a marriage of hearts, but it can also be a marriage of vision. In either case, it is a joining or a coming together of two things: romantic partners, Platonic friends, co-authors, dance partners, or any union between two people engaged in a shared artistic endeavor or dream.

When the Two of Cups appears in a reading, consider all possibilities before jumping to the easy conclusion of a marriage or engagement. Many people seek out Tarot (and other forms of psychic readings) for advice on their love lives, but the cards don't

157

always oblige people with what they *want* to know. When read properly, the cards are much more likely to tell the querent what he or she *needs* to know. The Two of Cups may indicate a romance that has progressed to an earnest partnership, but it may simply reflect the querent's fervent desire for such a relationship. Depending on where it appears in the reading and the other cards around it, the Two of Cups can also take on a darker spin, reflecting the querent's fear of never achieving such a balanced relationship. However, the card may be more concerned with art or friendship, and in this case it is likely speaking of the combination of talents between two people on a creative project or the joining of two fast friends who will become best friends for life.

Perhaps tellingly, I think of the Two of Cups as the card representative of my involvement with artist Jackie Williams in creating this deck: partnerships that come together around the production of something like a book or a Tarot deck function very like marriages. There is that same push-pull of personalities and, ultimately, the same blending of vision and talent that makes the end result something greater for having a partnership produce it rather than either of the partners singly could have achieved. Romance is but one aspect of the unions people build in their lives.

Behind the Cards: If you are a SCAdian, this card might remind you of Cooper's Lake, the Pennsylvania site of the Society for Creative Anachronism's annual Pennsic War. Artist Jackie Williams has fond memories of her days in the SCA, and nights watching the Perseid Meteor Shower at Cooper's Lake was in fact the inspiration for the setting of this card.

Three of Cups: *Pleasure*

Image: Three women bathe together near a hot spring. Three cups stand at the edge of the marble tub. All three women turn their gazes toward the viewer, as if in invitation, asking them to join the fun.

Meaning: *Pleasure.* Friendship. Enjoyment in the company of others. Expanding on previous connections. The deepening or development of feelings. Notably, some older systems equate this card with the three graces.

Reversed: Excess in pleasure. Over-indulgence. Fiddling while Rome burns. Pleasure sours or turns to pain, possibly due to social strife or gossip. A loss of enjoyment in the things one once found fulfilling. False pleasures and false friends.

Interpretation: The young woman from the Two of Cups reappears here, this time with friends. The three figures in the card are having something of a "girls' night out" at the baths, perhaps in celebration of the partnership depicted in the Two. If we take the most literal interpretation of the Marriage card, we may even suppose that the Three of Cups depicts the equivalent of a bachelorette party – or a beautifying session intended to prepare the young woman for a more intimate ceremony. However we spin it for the tales of love and pleasure that unfold within the Cups, we are witnessing a moment of easy revelry and sensuality shared between friends. This is an indulgent card where the main figures pamper themselves and put their cares aside in favor of camaraderie and joy.

When the Three of Cups appears in a reading, it typically heralds a time of enjoyment in the querent's life. There will be a

159

chance to stop and smell the roses and perhaps even find the time to cultivate some roses of one's own. Implicit in this opportunity is the promise that the querent will find these activities healing and rejuvenating. Joy and pleasure soothe a weary heart and soul. Standing as a bright counterpoint to the mournful Three of Swords, the Three of Cups is about pleasure for its own sake, and it reminds us that it's not bad to indulge once in a while. The card's appearance in a reading may also be a gentle nudge to a stoic or hard-working querent that he or she needs to take a break and relax, perhaps having an evening out with friends. All work and no play will give Jack (or Jill) an ulcer.

The three women traditionally depicted in this card are sometimes also equated with the Three Graces. They may also be seen as one of the three sets of muses (nine in all) who were revered as demi-goddesses of art and inspiration in ancient Greek myth. These muses brought gifts of art, poetry, music, dance, and other joyful inspiration to mortals. Taken in this sense, the Three of Cups does not have to represent pleasures strictly of the flesh, but may indicate artistic, emotional, or spiritual pleasures. These luxuries of heart, mind, and soul are no less rejuvenating than a day at the spa and in many cases, they are far more fulfilling in the long run.

Four of Cups: *Introspection*

Image: A young woman gazes wistfully out of an ornate window. Her image is reflected in the glass. Two cups stand on the sill and are also mirrored in the glass. The room is cloaked in shadow; the window provides the only source of light.

Meaning: *Introspection*. A period of reflection brought about by a surfeit of emotion. A need to detach and reassess. Boredom or apathy, potentially brought on by overstimulation. A time to withdraw and look within.

Reversed: The withdrawal heralds a new phase of pleasure, emotion, or connection. Seeking new friends or new attachments. A need to get out in the world or to let others in emotionally.

Interpretation: Our young lady from the Two and Three of Cups appears again in the Four. From the other cards, she has had some intense emotional adventures – but even when all the emotions are positive, intensity can still be exhausting. The Four of Cups is an expression of this emotional exhaustion: we see the young woman taking some time to herself, relaxing away from the crowds. She sits in a darkened room, gazing out through her window – but although her eyes are focused outward, rather than seeing the world beyond, she is gazing upon her own reflection in the glass. With all of her recent emotional experiences, she has become caught within her own interior world, reflecting upon what it all means and how she really feels.

A surfeit of emotion – any emotion – inspires the need for detachment and reflection. Otherwise, it is too easy to be caught up and carried along by the vicissitudes of the heart. When the Four of

Cups arises in a reading, it indicates a need for some quiet time – or it suggests that the querent has withdrawn already and is struggling to make sense of everything he or she is feeling. Intense, positive, but overwhelming emotional experiences can inspire such a need for withdrawal, but the card may also reflect a recent painful experience that has caused the querent to detach from others and cocoon. Whether they are inspired by good or bad experiences, introspective moments like the one depicted in this card can be lonely, perhaps even leading to depression. This card tells us that it's not always bad to withdraw and reassess – so long as the querent actually uses the time to better understand the landscape of his or her interior world rather than wallowing in melancholy, anxiety, or confusion.

If the card presents itself in a negative light within the reading (even if it is not specifically reversed), it means that the period of withdrawal has gone on too long or has ceased to be functional for the querent. It may indicate a dysfunctional detachment from the people and pleasures of the world, such that the querent is in danger of becoming a recluse or a shut-in. Taken in this light, the Four of Cups is a sign to stop merely looking out at the world and instead to start experiencing – even though such experience also comes with emotional risk.

Five of Cups: *Loss*

Image: A woman huddles on the floor, wrapped in a blanket. Four cups are overturned before her. The fifth is still upright, but barely. Her fingers lightly touch its rim. It is unclear whether she is trying to knock this last cup over or save it from toppling over.

Meaning: *Loss.* Disappointment. Miscarriage. A relationship that seems to be bearing fruit is suddenly cut short. Frustrated expectations. Some hope remains but the sense of despair may be overwhelming.

Reversed: Hope in the face of despair. A terrible experience reveals inner strength. Someone thought lost in the querent's life unexpectedly returns. What is perceived at first to be a loss turns out to be a boon.

Interpretation: Although the suit of Cups have associations with art, beauty, sensuality, visions, and the unconscious mind, their main thrust of their narrative within the Watcher Angel Tarot is concerned with emotion: positive emotions like love and delight or negative emotions like sorrow and despair. Although the type and tenor of the emotions change from card to card, the one constant is intensity. The Five of Cups is an emotionally intense card, but the emotions it represents are not pleasant. Although we see a new main character, the story arc of the Cups has not changed: we have gone from love and pleasure in the Two and Three to introspection, withdrawal, and possible anxiety in the Four. The Five of Cups completes the downward spiral, dragging us to the pits of despair. Alone in a darkened room, the woman in this card kneels before four overturned goblets. She reaches to save the last – or she may be knocking this final goblet over herself. We've all been in that mood where so many things have gone wrong, we find ourselves tempted to sabotage those few things still untouched by disaster.

In readings, the Five of Cups often indicates a time of disappointment on loss in the querent's life. Something – a person, a state of being, or even a situation – that once brought joy and pleasure to the querent's life has been taken away, and the querent feels hollowed out by its loss. This can represent a loss in the immediate future, or it can represent a loss that the querent is currently struggling through. It has every potential to be emotionally devastating. This card can herald a dark night of the soul – especially for individuals who place a lot of value on their emotions and on the people and things to which those emotions are tied.

An important detail about this card lies with the cups themselves. Note that, although four out of five of the cups have spilled, the last remains standing. It teeters, and the woman herself may be the force that finally topples it. But for the moment, not all is lost. The trick for the querent who gets this card is to understand that surrender to the dark emotions will complete the sense of loss. There is a chance to pick up and carry on, but it requires the querent to allow for hope and to work to see past all the dark visions clouding his or her path.

Behind the Cards: This Five of Cups was a redo: the original version of the card was painted very early on in the process of the developing the deck, and the artistic style did not mesh well with the other cards by the end. Our friend Sarah (also mentioned in my book *Haunting Experiences)* was around when we needed someone to model for the card. We wanted a sense of hopelessness and despair in the figure, the kind of thing one feels after a great loss, where everything else subsequently loses its appeal. Sarah, who has modeled before, knelt down and thought about the greatest loss in her life: the miscarriage of a child she had wanted to bear very much. Chalices often represent female creative power, and they can be symbols of the womb. Knowing Sarah's story, all the overturned cups in the card took on a new meaning for us. The energy brought to the figure by the model has woven the additional meaning of "miscarriage" very firmly into the fabric of this card.

Six of Cups: *Nostalgia*

Image: An elegant older woman sits on the edge of an ornate fountain, gazing into its waters. One cup sits before her on the fountain, another sits behind. The remaining four cups are part of the fountain itself. The colors of the card have a washed-out, ethereal quality, as if observed through a dream.

Meaning: *Nostalgia.* A return to something familiar and enjoyable. Happy memories. Gazing backwards to pleasant times. Joys that have come and gone, but may return in a new form.

Reversed: Clinging needlessly to outworn habits, morals, or attitudes. Something from the past re-emerges but fails to live up to its remembered form. A disappointing inheritance. The querent is unable to move beyond a traumatic experience and is essentially living emotionally in the past.

Interpretation: The Six of Cups is all about gazing backwards into the past. The memories thus encountered may be happy ones, warmly perceived through the lens of time. However, they may also be troublesome memories, reflected upon at a time when sufficient emotional distance allows one to view them with new eyes, reframing the experience. Even memories of unhappy times may trigger the sentiment of nostalgia that lies at the heart of this card. In looking back into the past, most tend to romanticize or idealize people, places, and experiences – especially when these things are now lost to the present. Thus, the Six of Cups is a very Proustian card, where *"remembrance of things past is not necessarily remembrance of things as they were."*

165

When this card appears in a reading, it is related to memory and sometimes also to inheritance – as in the things that come forward to us from our past, monetary or otherwise. In some circumstances, the Six of Cups is a suggestion to the querent to re-examine memories – especially emotionally-laden ones. It can also represent reminders of the past that are moving into the querent's life such that the querent will have no choice but to think about people, places, attitudes, or even concepts of self long-since abandoned. Note that the figure on this card is a mature woman. This stands in contrast to more traditional representations of the Six of Cups which feature children. Rather than simply implying "happy childhood memories" with an image of young ones at play, we wanted to capture a sense of nostalgic remembrance – which may be happy, but is more often bittersweet. Thus the card is not only about recollection, but also re-evaluation. Note that she gazes into a fountain. Water is a symbol of the unconscious mind, so in gazing into the waters, she is also gazing within, plumbing the depths of her recollections. With this in mind, the Six of Cups may be concerned with the querent's immediate past, but the card may also refer to memories of past lives or the process of memory work for past life recollection.

Depending on its placement in the spread, the Six of Cups may be a suggestion that time allows us to gain perspective, especially with regards to situations and experiences heavily laden with emotion. The card may also represent maudlin sentiment: the querent is getting lost in memories of an idealized past, rather than living functionally in the present. This warning can apply to memories of the current life but may also refer to past life work. The key issues of this card are memory, emotion, and perspective, whether that perspective has been gained, need to be striven toward, or has been lost entirely through some error on the part of the querent.

Behind the Cards: To get the soft and dream-like quality of this card, Jackie experimented with a different water-color technique. This involves pre-treating the paper with gum Arabic. This caused the paper to resist some of the pigments, giving the resulting image a washed-out, ethereal quality, intended to represent the misty veil of time through which we view all memories.

Seven of Cups: *Illusions*

Image: A woman in white surrounded by six cups, each with light streaming upwards from their bowls. She holds a seventh, spilling light down as if to catch it in her cupped hand. Her hand, however, is empty.

Meaning: *Illusions.* Visions and dreams which have import but may also mislead. The need for discernment in the present matter. Shifting through superficial or tempting appearances. Choosing what to believe.

Reversed: The manifestation of dreams in reality. Projecting the will to bring about one's desires. Visualizing goals to bring them about. Decisions should be made. Hopes and ideas should be carried through.

Interpretation: The standard Rider-Waite-Smith illustration for this card shows a young man faced with visions of seven chalices. Each contains something desirable, mysterious, or nightmarish; it is up to the dreamer himself to choose which he ultimately receives. Implicit in this series of visions is the Arthurian legend of the Grail. There are many false visions of the Grail, but only the worthiest knight, pure in mind, body, and spirit, is able to see beyond appearances to the true Grail. In our card, the young man is replaced with a young woman. The figure in this card wears robes suggestive of a priestess or seer. The white often implies innocence or purity, but in this case, it is more representative of a new beginning. From her face and hair, she may be a younger version of the woman in the Six of Cups and she stands at a moment of decision in her life, contemplating the ethereal contents of seven glowing chalices. All of the cups contain what appears to be the same thing: light or energy streaming forth into

167

reality. Yet when she seeks to grasp this, she comes away empty-handed. The light is illusory – or she has misunderstood its true nature by assuming that it is material in nature and can be captured in any physical sense.

Substantial versus insubstantial experiences or qualities as well as discernment versus illusion are a key issues at the heart of the Seven of Cups. This card in readings can be a warning that things are not always what they seem – and that the querent should carefully examine what is presented before making any decisions. But the card can also warn the querent that he or she is spending too much time dreaming about what may be and not enough time working to bring those dreams into reality. Building castles in the sky is all well and good, but those castles have a tendency to melt away by morning. Finally, the card is also about perception and appearances: the querent may be presented with an opportunity that must be carefully scrutinized in order to be properly understood or utilized to its fullest potential. In this case, the card warns against assumptions, encouraging analysis beyond first impressions. Overall, the Seven of Cups demands that we carefully examine the substance of our hopes and dreams rather than allow ourselves to be blinded to their true nature by our expectations or emotional investment. This is the card of rose-colored glasses, but its primary message is to take them off so you can see things for what they really are before making any significant decisions.

Eight of Cups: *Departure*

Image: A grand white city dominates the background. In the foreground, a woman robed and cowled walks away. She is somber and pensive. Behind her, scattered over the countryside, four overturned cups spill their contents into rivulets and streams. Four cups remain upright nearby.

Meaning: *Departure.* Leaving home. Abandoning one way of life for something new. Becoming restless with the familiar and striking out for the unknown. A sense of loss, uncertainty, or dissatisfaction while being in transition.

Reversed: Living in the moment. Great joy in worldly pleasures. A celebratory mood where time or progress is of little consequence. A moment of pleasure, inspiration, or spiritual vision which seems to exist outside of time, with no real ending of beginning.

Interpretation: The central figure from the Seven of Cups has made a decision by the Eight – and that decision is to leave her familiar life behind to strike out for something new. A beautiful white city rises in the distance behind her, but she is walking away along a pathless track. Inherent in this choice is a sense of melancholy and loss, represented by the cups spilling out over the countryside that stretches behind her. But four cups remain upright, and even those cups that have overturned are adding their contents to the life-giving stream that winds through the landscape. The woman covers her head, possibly in mourning, possibly as an added protection on the journey ahead. She bears a pensive expression, eyes cast down and focused more inward than on what lies ahead. The city behind her is hardly in ruins: this is not a forced abandonment, but a conscious

169

choice to move into a new phase of life. As she carries nothing with her on this journey, this may mean that she has chosen to leave worldly attachments behind in favor of less substantial things: visions, an emotional journey, or spiritual pursuits.

The Eight of Cups is a card of making changes. It can also show that the querent is leaving behind emotional baggage – or that he or she should seriously consider doing so. This is not exactly a happy card, but it is nevertheless a card of potential and transition. Here the querent is faced with a choice: be passive about the change from one thing to the next, mutely enduring whatever emotional rollercoaster may result or take charge of the experience and view the departure as less of a loss and more of an opportunity to begin anew. A lot of things may trigger this departure for the querent. The card may represent the decision to leave a friend, a relationship, or living situation. It may represent a less physical departure: changing attitudes, redefining one's sense of self, moving into a different and untested phase of life. Whatever the situation, there is a lot of emotional investment in what is being left behind as well as mixed feelings about the impending transition. The real crux of the card is how the querent is prepared to handle these endings and beginnings. Leaving something behind can sometimes be liberating, but it is also bittersweet.

When it comes up in a reading, the Eight of Cups may be a comment on a life change the querent is currently making, but it can also be a suggestion that change is needed. Whether that change will come easily or will feel emotionally costly to the querent is a matter that will likely play out in the other cards. However, the bottom line here is that change – even when it is difficult – is necessary for further growth.

Nine of Cups: *Wishes*

Image: A young woman leans over a large cup used as a cauldron or scrying bowl. Three upright cups are set alongside it. Five more cups, ethereal in nature, swirl up from the main chalice. The girl meets eyes with the viewer, a smile of satisfaction on her lips.

Meaning: *Wishes.* The fulfillment of desire. Getting what you want (though perhaps not always what you need). Magick as an act of Will. Manifesting desire.

Reversed: Overindulgence of desires, especially in food or drink. Wishes go unfulfilled. Desires are unrequited. Magick done selfishly or without forethought. The querent is drawing experiences, consequences or people into his or her life, but unconsciously and without proper control.

Interpretation: In this card, we see a daughter of one of the Watchers engaged in an act of magick, harnessing the otherworldly knowledge and power that is her birthright. She gazes at the viewer with an expression of pride, confidence, and satiation: she has no doubt that she will get what she wants.

The Nine of Cups is often known as the "Wish Card," which is to say, when this card comes up in a reading, it is often seen as an indication that the querent will get his or her wish. As the Nine of Cups is generally depicted as a sensual card, the wish is usually interpreted as something tied to the sensual world: luxury, riches, romance, or the like. Implicit in this is the idea that the wish, although titillating, is somewhat superficial. This is not a "wish for world peace" card but rather a "wish for what I think will make me happy" card. In many decks, the main character depicted on this card is rosy-cheeked and pleasantly plump to further underscore the essentially carnal nature of the good fortune embodied by the Nine of Cups. In our deck, we take a slightly different spin. Sensual pleasure and worldly delight are still fundamental meanings of the card, but in our Nine, the central character is not merely sitting in the midst of her riches: she is actively working magick to bring about her heart's desire. Of the four physical cups which adorn this card, one is much larger than the rest and takes on the function of a scrying bowl or cauldron. The other five cups are ethereal in nature, wishes or visions that emerge from the cauldron as a consequence of her magickal act.

Oftentimes, when a reader presents the Nine of Cups as the Wish Card, the next statement to follow is, *"Be careful what you wish for."* What you want is not always what you need. With the magickal aspect directly expressed within our card, this caveat becomes even more essential. When wishing is a dedicated act of drawing one's desires forth from the world, then no wish should be casual or superficial in nature. In a magickal reality – especially in the world of the Cups – desires can be made manifest whether or not we are wholly conscious of the role we play in the process. With this in mind, the Nine of Cups can emerge in readings to herald good fortune, but it can also take on a cautionary note. The card is a reminder of our potential to make our desires a reality – but this may include fears as well as hopes, nightmares as well as dreams. The card is an acknowledgement of this magickal potential, but also a suggestion that such abilities are best performed consciously and with informed intent.

Behind the Cards: The model for this card is Becca Kirschbaum, a student of magick with a particular gift for manifesting her desires. As a professional writer, she also engages in this manifestation as a part of her art, weaving worlds and building characters that take on a reality of their own.

Ten of Cups: *Fulfillment*

Image: A seated woman smiles warmly, surrounded by four friends (or family members). A little dog sits at her feet. There is an abundance of cups raised in celebration.

Meaning: *Fulfillment.* Getting not only what one desires, but also what one needs to flourish. Joy shared among friends and/or family. Love in its perfected state. A fullness of emotion.

Reversed: Disruption in the happiness of one's family or close circle of friends. Family quarrels and schisms, especially among parents and children. Debauchery and hedonism which drown or obscure finer emotional or spiritual pleasures.

Interpretation: The Nine of Cups may be about wishes, but the Ten of Cups is about genuine fulfillment. Here is the culmination of the suit of Cups. It is not merely about love, beauty, art, sensual pleasure, or dreams but about sharing all of these among family and friends. Implicit in the jovial camaraderie depicted in this card is a profound sense of psychic connection, a rapport which manifests as a tightly knit bond among the revelers. They are not simply partying for the sake of sensual bliss; they all raise a glass together in celebration of their very identity as family or close friends – the family of the heart. To underscore this sense of unity and shared bonds, an animal companion sits dutifully at the feet of the seated central figure. The dog is a symbol of loyalty, companionship, and unconditional love – all of the truly good things in life, at least from a Cups perspective.

173

When this card comes up in a reading, it can mean that the querent has the potential to achieve not only what he or she *thinks* is desired but what is truly needed to thrive in heart, mind, and soul. There is a spiritual undercurrent to this card which stands in contrast to the sensuality traditionally associated with the Nine of Cups. Thus, the many blessings represented by the card tend toward spiritual and emotional connections, inspiration, creativity, and states of mind rather than material pleasures. The rather blissful state suggested by this card may exist for the querent as a possibility in the very near future or it may already have come to pass – in which case, the card has emerged as a commentary upon how the querent is reacting to this state of good fortune. The querent may not even fully realize his or her position: the Ten of Cups can also appear as a reminder to the querent to stop searching so hard for fulfillment and instead appreciate the spiritual and emotional riches already present in his or her life. As a Ten, the card represents the fullness of the Cups suit, and is thus a completion of the cycle – which in turn suggests that once this phase has been enjoyed, the querent will move into a new stage of their emotional or spiritual journey.

Behind the Cards: The models for this card are all associated with House Kheperu's Counselor caste – the role in our magickal society dedicated to connection, emotion, and heart. The dog is Jackie's rat terrier, Penny. The only living animal depicted in the deck, Jackie included Penny in this card because to her the dog's loyalty and love, as well as the way pets in general enrich our lives, best embody the sense of emotional fulfillment represented by this card.

Page of Cups: *The Dreamer*

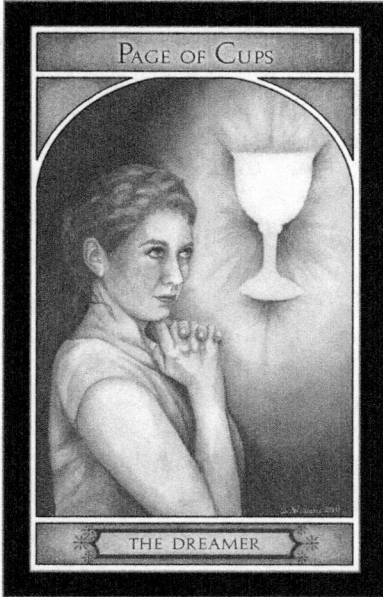

Image: A young girl clasps her hands as if in prayer. The figure's huge blue eyes hold a dreamy, faraway gaze. A cup of light appears like a vision of the grail.

Meaning: *The Dreamer.* Someone easily overtaken by visions and/or emotions. A delicate heart, yearning for love but with a potential to be deeply wounded by the same. An idealist, perhaps unprepared for reality. Someone who brings messages about love, emotion, visions, and the psychic realm.

Reversed: The visions stem from madness or delusion. Someone who fakes or improperly uses their psychic gifts. A person lacking in imagination, emotionally closed off. Someone whose emotional vision is turned inward to the point of narcissism.

Interpretation: Cups, as a suit, possess a number of mythic associations. In modern Pagan traditions, the chalice represents feminine creative power, while the blade represents masculine power. The cup can also be related to the Cauldron of Inspiration belonging to the Welsh goddess Cerridwen. This was a potent symbol of transformation and rebirth from whence derived the mystic draught of wisdom and poetry. And of course, the chalice also holds profound Christian symbolism as the cup of the Last Supper. Taken altogether, Cups simultaneously embody the chalice of the wine of life, the scrying vessel of the seer, the cup of Dionysus, and the sacred well of memory.

Both Pagan and Christian associations found expression in the legends of the *Sangraal*, or Holy Grail, popularized in Arthurian myth. Here was a sacred cup that held a mystic draught capable of healing, granting visions, and inspiring insights into spiritual truths. In our deck, the Grail associations achieve their fullest expression in the Page of Cups. Here the Grail imagery is overt: the Page achieves a vision of the symbol of the suit, hands clasped and face enraptured.

The main function of the Page of Cups is to relay messages of visions, emotions, and dreams. This also means that the Page is a person who must experience these things to their fullest extent. Thus, the Page of Cups is someone immersed in the essence of the suit, for whom the boundaries of reality are fluid because he or she is not grounded in the practical, physical world. Rather, this Page exists in the very well of imagination, communicating to the querent what is perceived through direct personal gnosis and non-rational experience. However, the wine of inspiration is intoxicating and can lead easily to madness. There is a danger for the Page of Cups of becoming too dream-saturated, lost in visions, feelings, or interior perceptions. With eyes so focused inward – or on the worlds beyond – the Page may be in danger of losing touch with the physical and/or rational world. Similarly, the Page may find the experiences so immersing that there is no adequate control over them, thus turning the gift of vision into an affliction.

When this card comes up in a reading, it can represent a person with these qualities coming into the querent's life in order to share visions and dreams. This is a delicate individual who may need the querent's help, guidance, or protection. If the Page of Cups emerges as a face of the querent, this may mean that the querent has a raw psychic gift, powerful but undisciplined. It may also indicate a tender-hearted emotional idealism that could lead the querent to heartbreak if left untempered by realism. The Page of Cups can also represent a bright-eyed creative person involved in one of the fine arts who is still naïve about the practical considerations of sharing that art with the world. In this case, the Page of Cups needs to be careful with his or her sources of inspiration, guarding things like copyright and intellectual property rights.

Behind the Cards: The model for this card is our friend Stephanie Bingham, scholar, academic, and former ballet dancer.

Knight of Cups: *The Lover*

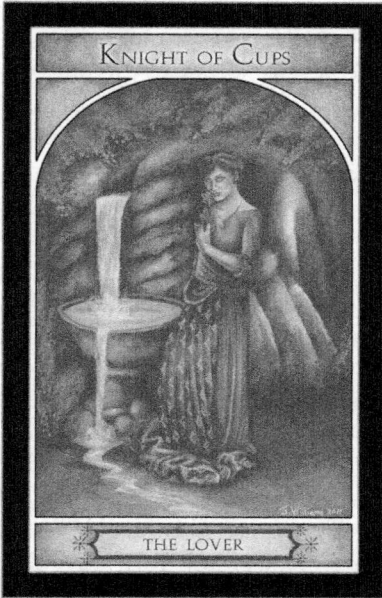

Image: A young woman with smoldering eyes stands beside a flowing fountain. She clasps a rose in one hand, lightly brushing the petals against her cheek. The background is earthy, like a garden that has begun to go wild.

Meaning: *The Lover.* An individual focused on romance and seduction. Passion and/or loyalty that is fierce yet fickle. A love for falling into love, but the ability to grow beyond the initial eruption of emotion may be lost.

Reversed: Everything you don't want in a lover: the person is fickle, with changeable affections. They lie freely or mislead to get what they desire. They let their imagination, heart, or loins get the better of them. The person is too in love with sensuality and may encourage the querent to indulge to the point of loss of self.

Interpretation: "I'm a lover, not a fighter," is a statement one might expect to hear from the figure in this card. Our Knight of Cups stands in a lush but wild garden, tucked away in what may be a sacred grotto. The cup on the card is a fountain, but its source is a natural spring, suggesting that the power of this card is something primal, arising from a place deep within. The waters of the fountain brim over, further suggesting the effusive power of the card: the forces embodied by this knight can be tempestuous, overwhelming, and difficult to contain.

The Knight of Cups is an instigator of emotion and inspiration, someone who brings action into the querent's life on these fronts – for good or for bad. Implicit in the Knight is a certain amount of struggle and conflict, but this is not necessarily a bad thing. Knights

177

challenge us to deal with the qualities and forces embodied by their suits. In the case of the Knight of Cups, these challenges often involve affairs of the heart, but they may also manifest as conflicts in the psychic or creative realms. When it appears in a reading, the Knight of Cups often represents a person coming into the querent's life as a romantic interest, or someone who raises questions about love and romance. This may also be a rival in affairs of the heart who, through his or her interference, inspires the querent to decide what he or she really wants out of a relationship – and how far the querent is willing to go in order to achieve this. Taken as a facet of the querent him- or herself, the Knight of Cups represents a passionate streak, sometimes difficult to tame, and a love for being in love. This is someone who pursues what they love with a kind of hungry determination that may seem excessive to some and may leave the querent pining when the sought-after prize escapes or resists their grasp.

Of course, despite the seductive and decadent qualities of the figure on this card, the Knight of Cups does not always have to be a lover or a potential suitor. The Knight of Cups can also be an artist, a poet, a dancer, or another purveyor of beauty and creativity who seduces the querent's imagination or senses in a more figurative manner. The love being taught does not have to be a romantic affair but may also be the love of an experience, an art form, a style of personal expression, or even an imaginative state that exists only in one's internal world. Whatever form the love takes, our Knight invites us to explore it without reservation, indulging freely and drinking deep the proffered cup of experience – possibly to the exclusion of all else.

Behind the Cards: Say hello again to our friend Pink Spider, aka Rhiannon Levine, this time with sultry, smoky eyes and a rose taken from my collection odd props and decorations kept from the days of Live Action Role-Play. And yes, for those who know the game *Vampire: the Masquerade,* the rose was used as a prop for a Toreador (the clan of artists). It seemed exceptionally fitting for the card.

Queen of Cups: *The Seer*

Image: A woman in a flowing blue gown cups a chalice in her hands. Her hair is twined with ivy. The chalice is also adorned with ivy and a mist-like energy rises from its bowl. A single star shines from within the mist.

Meaning: *The Seer.* A woman of vision, in touch with her intuition and/or feelings. Someone who nurtures psychic perception and/or creative inspiration. A muse. A guide who teaches from the heart, encouraging insight and reflection.

Reversed: The guidance is false. Reason has been eclipsed by irrational visions or emotions. The person's inspiration risks crossing into the realm of madness. Someone who seeks a position of mentor or teacher with ulterior motives, particularly those that serve his or her own sensual and/or carnal desires.

Interpretation: The Queen of Cups is the guide to the psychic and interior realm. Ivy wreathes her head and her cup to indicate the vibrant, life-affirming qualities of the gifts she bears. Her hair is loose, implying sensuality, but also an easy and unrestrained attitude: in order to master her abilities, she has learned not to impose structure but to simply go with the flow, being open and receptive when visions present themselves. These may be visions of the future, psychic impressions, flashes of creative inspiration, or insights into emotional states, for our Queen of Cups is a seer, gazing deeply into the mystic waters contained within her chalice. In this, she is related to the Page of Cups, but with the Page, there is an implication of passive reception or a lack of control. For the Queen, the visionary facility is fully developed and she is its master. The Queen actively pursues her visions and has the wisdom and experience necessary to know how to direct them and interpret them – as well as when to disengage. As a seer in control of her inner vision, the Queen of Cups is in a position to teach others how to do the same.

When the Queen of Cups appears in a reading, she may represent a literal or figurative guide who enters the querent's life to lead they way down the path of inspiration. She is a teacher, a mentor, or an initiator into the mysteries represented by the suit of Cups. She may present herself to help the querent become more in touch with and in control of his or her emotions, or she may appear to help the querent more fully develop and realize an artistic talent. A perceptive and a psychic card, the Queen of Cups is also someone who has learned how to listen to that still, small voice that guides us to intuitions, and either by direct instruction or by example, she has the capacity to lead the querent to the same awareness. The Queen is someone who may be older than the querent, but the maturity implied by the Queen may merely be a reflection of greater mastery and experience.

Taken as an aspect of the querent, this initiation and/or instruction may come from within: the Queen is a manifestation of the querent's *anima,* or inner soul, reaching out through dreams or visions to lead the way to greater understanding. The Queen of Cups may also indicate that the querent has achieved a level of personal mastery in artistic, emotional or psychic realms such that he or she is now in a position to guide others, and should seriously consider taking up this responsibility. In some cases, the Queen of Cups may represent a call to the take up the mantle of priest/priestess, medium, or seer, showing the querent an image of what they could and should become.

King of Cups: *The Dilettante*

Image: A well-built man with a crown of golden laurel leaves. Draped in minimal clothing, he poses beside a massive chalice of stone.

Meaning: *The Dilettante.* A sensitive man, in touch with or ruled by his feelings. An artist, actor, or performer, charismatic but potentially superficial. Someone who is attractive and well-loved but can be pretentious. Someone adept at presenting one face to the world while still keeping his secrets.

Reversed: Scandalous, shifty, and violent, he is ruled by his emotions rather than ruling them. He uses his charisma to manipulate others for his own benefit. He is a con-man, pretender or false prophet. In love, he is promiscuous and unfaithful, saying or doing anything to get what he wants.

Interpretation: Flamboyant and showy, this King can be a bit of a peacock. He is attractive and refined, and he knows it. He poses before an almost monolithic statue of his suit, proclaiming his mastery over all that the cup represents. His crown of laurel leaves is a traditional symbol of victory and accolades. He is accomplished, charismatic, and self-assured – as he should be, because the King of Cups is the Lord of the Heart. He rules the emotions intrinsic to his suit by seeming to be in control of them. In controlling them, he may also maintain a certain emotional distance from people, using his mantle of authority to avoid true intimacy in part because his own emotions can be so overpowering.

The greatest gift possessed by the King of Cups lies in harnessing and/or manipulating emotions – his own or the emotions of others. His empathic nature allows him to better understand what people want, and he maintains his position of superiority by showing it to them. The person represented by the King of Cups is often a showman, involved in acting, oration, or some other type of performance that allows him to make the best use of his magnetic personality and intuitive grasp of peoples' hopes and desires. He may also be a member of the clergy, utilizing his charisma and insight to inspire a spiritual following.

When the King of Cups comes up in a reading and he is working on behalf of the querent, he is a powerful ally. He is an inspirational figure, educated and refined, who can help open doors for the querent in the arts, in social, magickal, or spiritual circles, as well as affairs of the heart. He can share the secrets to his charisma and social adaptability, helping the querent become more in touch with his or her emotions and desires with the intent of better harnessing them. If the King of Cups is set against the querent, he is an equally powerful foe: slippery, manipulative, and given to shifting through many different guises to suit his needs at any given time. The person represented by the King of Cups is often a figure of authority in the querent's life, or someone with enough power and influence to easily be perceived as such. This power can be used to the benefit of the querent or it may be turned against the querent in some manner of manipulation or control, depending on the input from the rest of the cards in the spread.

An important thing to note about this king is the old saying that "still waters run deep." The King of Cups can have a tempestuous personality, and even when his exterior seems calm and placid, a maelstrom of potentially conflicting emotion surges just beneath the surface. He loves and hates with equal ferocity, and if he looses control, he can be difficult. In this respect, the King of Cups may emerge as a cautionary tale for the querent, showing the cost and potential consequence of seeking to control and direct the protean element of water.

Ace of Wands: *Energy*

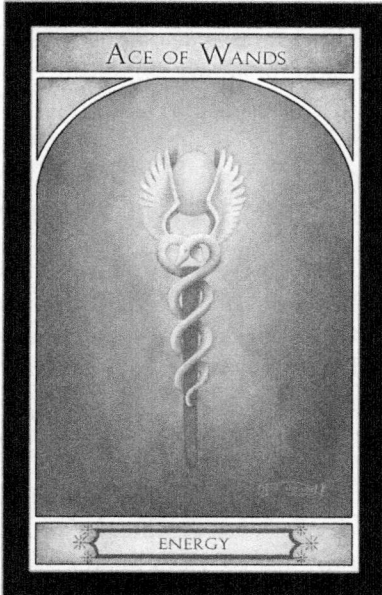

Image: A wand entwined with two serpents. An egg or solar disc emerges between their wings. The wand hangs against a vibrant background rich in the glowing shades of flame. The wand itself seems to be the source of this warm light.

Meaning: *Energy.* Kinesthetic, magickal, or creative potential. The magickal spark which awaits awakening, harnessing, and/or direction. A volatile process in the moment prior to the introduction of a catalyst. Spirit and/or form on the verge of transformation.

Reversed: Opportunity presents itself, but remains undeveloped due to a lack of passion or determination. The vital spark remains buried or unrealized, typically due to a lack of effort on the querent's part. The desire to start something new is frustrated due to circumstances or a lack of proper chemistry between the constituent parts.

Interpretation: The wand chosen to represent this suit is intentionally Hermetic in nature and is variation on the Greek caduceus. This is the symbol of station borne by the Greek Hermes, messenger of the gods. Hermes was a psychopomp – someone with the freedom to move betwixt and between, traversing heaven and earth as well as the realms of the living and the dead. Through the syncretic process that occurred as Greco-Roman, Egyptian, and Oriental systems met and merged in the cultural athanor that was Hellenized Egypt, Hermes also became equated with the Egyptian god Thoth. Eventually his name was bequeathed also to a legendary mortal sage, Hermes Trismegistus (the name means "Thrice-Greatest Hermes). This mythic sage is credited with having written the

Corpus Hermeticum, a book of wisdom and divine revelation produced in early Christian times that serves as the basis of Hermetic knowledge in the Western world.

The wand is unapologetically phallic in nature, representing vital force, energy, and the potential for creation. Similarly, the serpents twined around the central rod are traditional symbols of male fertility, as well as being symbols of transformation, rejuvenation and rebirth (largely on account of a snake's capacity to shed its skin, appearing reborn and renewed). The two serpents represent the primal, dual forces of reality and creation: the microcosm and macrocosm, humanity and divinity, masculine and feminine, flesh and spirit, heaven and earth, light and dark, and virtually all other pairs of dynamic opposites. In our wand, the egg or solar disc held up or emerging from behind the two wings is a further symbol of rebirth, promise, and vital potential.

When this card appears in a reading, it represents potential: the potential for growth, the potential for change, the potential for awakening and personal transformation. It is the vital spark which, if properly cultivated, can be fanned into a light-giving blaze. In this sense, the card is an embodiment of the Biblical act of creation: *Fiat lux,* or "Let there be light." This is simultaneously the light of knowledge, revelation, and creation. The card typically heralds the beginning of a period of growth and determination in the life of the querent, accompanied by a blossoming of opportunities for creation and expansion. This may be the literal creation of life or it may refer to the inception of inspired works, new passions, journeys (literal or figurative), or even business ventures. The card can also represent a catalyst or flashpoint in the querent's life. This can be an influential person, situation, or experience that sparks a new idea, goal, or direction for the querent. In the context of the Watcher Angel myth, the Ace of Wands is also a card of magickal inspiration: it represents the first awareness of the vital principle within humanity which can be cultivated and harnessed to enact change in the exterior world. In this, it is tied also to the divine spark within all beings, the "stolen" fire from Heaven which is, in truth, merely the birthright of the soul. It is the card of new beginnings and initiation.

Two of Wands: *Inception*

Image: An angel, in darkness, holds two unfinished wands. The power channeled through them is the only source of light.

Meaning: *Inception.* The beginning of realized power. Awakening one's magickal and/or creative potential. The release of latent energy. Exerting one's Will upon the visible world.

Reversed: The spark is missing. Focus, effort and dedication go unfulfilled. Stagnation, especially in the realms of personal or magickal development. Pushing boundaries without caution or forethought.

Interpretation: In the mythos of our deck, the Watchers left their place in Heaven to live like mortals in the physical world. In doing so, they chose to abandon a state of pure spirit and instead to take up bodies as mortals might take up garments – to become spirits merely robed in flesh. Consequently, the Watchers retained the full force of spiritual fire enjoyed in Heaven. This fire is at once their essence, their knowledge, and the source of their power: the Watchers themselves are the fire stolen from Heaven. In their original state, with bodies of energy rather than flesh, magick was as simple as thinking about it. There was no barrier to manifestation. However, the physical world places limitations upon the expression of this heavenly fire, so even the Watchers had to learn a new set of rules. The vital force of spirit slumbers within flesh and must be actively evoked in order to harness it for magickal acts. The Two of Wands illustrates this moment: a Watcher concentrates on two crossed wands, channeling his power beyond the flesh. This power emerges around the wands as a nimbus of light. This act of evocation –

channeling inner fire to the outer world in order to make manifest the essence of will – is the basis of all magick in the physical realm.

Aside from the Ace, the Two of Wands is the only card in the suit where the number is represented by the physical wands themselves. The significance of this lies in the very essence of the card. The Two of Wands represents the first scission, the splitting of the atom, that initial moment wherein the evocation of spirit is first achieved. In the posture of the angel and the crossing of the wands there is a conscious echo of primitive fire-making, where the friction of two sticks would eventually produce a spark. The only source of light in the card is that which is evoked from the wands themselves. All else is shrouded in darkness.

When this card comes up in a reading, it suggests that a catalyst has entered the querent's life that will enable the potential promised in the Ace of Wands to be realized in a manifest form. With the Two of Wands, a great deal of energy is released in the querent's world, but it's still up to the querent to recognize this and properly harness it. This energy can be used to fuel a number of things, from personal growth and transformation to the growth of ideas, knowledge, and even travel or business ventures. The card represents raw energy that has yet to be fully harnessed, so when this card appears, the querent should consider what he or she is most passionate about. At this stage, the querent still has some say in how this energy will ultimately be given direction, so they should reflect upon what they truly desire to see come forth in themselves or in their world.

In addition to its promise of manifest desire, the Two of Wands is also a volatile card. The raw power unleashed may be overwhelming. Like a blaze of fire itself, it could result in disaster or miracle, depending on how the end result is handled. How fully the querent is prepared to manage this release will determine the amount of finesse and control that can be maintained to guide the raw energy to its most ideal form. For devil-may-care querents who like to push buttons regardless of the potential consequences, this card can come as a reminder that, even if the querent doesn't mind getting burned once in a while, others they care about may also find themselves in the blast radius of their experiments. Thus the card can also manifest as a warning: *Danger, Explosives! High Voltage! Handle With Care.*

Three of Wands: *Development*

Image: An angel in Greco-Roman attire stands against a background full of cloying shadows. In one hand, he holds a wand. With the other, he channels energy, which emerges as three spheres of brilliant light, illuminating his space.

Meaning: *Development.* Giving expression to thoughts and/or dreams. Learning to harness inner power and express it in the external world. Establishing one's strength and/or skill.

Reversed: There is not enough follow-through the get ideas off the ground. Energy is scattered due to a lack of organization or focus. An idea seems great in theory, but falls short in reality.

Interpretation: The Three of Wands builds directly upon the action of the Two. In the Two, the Watchers learned how to harness their inner fire and make it manifest in the physical world, thus initiating a new age of magick. But the process was raw, uncontrolled, and highly volatile. By the Three of Wands, we see a refinement of technique: an angel, clutching a wand as a focus, evokes vital energy in the form of three glowing balls of force. With will alone, he maintains their shape and structure as they hang in the air before him, illuminating the space in which he works. The tips of his fingers glow with vital light, clearly indicating that the source of the power is not the wand clasped in his other hand but the angel himself. Here, then, the Watchers are on their way to mastering the expression of their celestial fire within the earthly realm. The angel's style of dress echoes that of the Hellenized world. This is a nod to the essentially Hermetic character of the suit of Wands. The Hellenic world, which yielded the *Leyden Papyrus,* the *Testament of Solomon,* the *Corpus Hermeticum,* and a whole slew of other foundational magickal texts is most representative in the Western imagination of an ideal age of early magick. Thus an echo (more accurately, a pre-cursor) to this time is evoked throughout the Wands in our deck.

When this card comes up in a reading, it heralds some amount of success on the part of the querent. A goal which the querent has been striving for has been – or will soon be – achieved. However, there is still room for further refinement and growth in the project. The Three of Wands, as a card of development, indicates only that the essential ground-work has been accomplished. Much potential remains, and there is yet a good deal of work to do in order to fully harness it. Implicit in its aspect of development, the Three of Wands is also a card of care and dedication: the querent must focus their passion and apply their will to the endeavor in order to fully bring it into being. No great work is achieved in a day, and so the querent should keep working, even when the initial process begins to bear fruit. As we see with the angel, even though he has produced balls of light, his focus remains on them as he continues to direct them and exert control. In this, the card can also be a reminder to the querent that any project he or she is thinking about launching is something that will require more than simply the initial thought to get it off the ground. A novel, if it remains as an idea or outline only, will never see publication. An invention in schematics is little more than a dream. The real work of inspiration is to take the initial spark and bring it into the world in its most realized form. The Three of Wands tells us that this can be a long process, requiring patient and dedication, but the rewards are definitely worth it in the end.

Four of Wands: *Achievement*

Image: A human form transfigured through an awakening or release of (psychic) energy. Four chakras have opened and expanded, spilling light. The wand rests upon the solar plexus, representative of magickal Will.

Meaning: *Achievement.* Perfected work. Manifestation of self. Satisfaction with a recent effort or enterprise. Realizing one's potential.

Reversed: Appreciate the little triumphs in life. As projects unfold and progress is made, don't forget to pause and enjoy what has been accomplished. Balance the striving of spirit and/or intellect with physical joys as both are part of human experience.

Interpretation: In the more traditional Rider-Waite-Smith version of this card, four flowering posts are planted in the foreground while in the background, two garlanded figures raised bouquets of flowers in a celebratory gesture. There is a sense of festivity in the urban scene behind them. Waite gives the meaning of the card as prosperity, harmony, and perfected work. As the fourth expression of fire, the Four of Wands represents solidity of purpose: the ultimate direction of the Will has been determined, and there is a stable foundation from which to work toward this goal. In our deck, as the Wands overtly represent magick, this establishment is represented as spiritual Awakening. The main figure of the card has been engaged in meditation and has just achieved a full opening of the upper chakras, from the solar plexus through the crown. This is the path to spirit, reaching up to the oversoul beyond (or Higher Self, depending on the system). The magickal light that explodes forth from these opened energy centers floods the card, momentarily eclipsing the lower portion of the figure, which represents the tie to flesh.

This is a moment of spiritual ecstasy in its original sense of *ekstasis* where the experiencer feels lifted out of and beyond the physical body. It is important to note that the main figure here is that of a mortal, not an angel. In the Two and Three of Wands we have seen the Watchers relearning their ability to harness spiritual fire. Here, in the Four of Wands, we see one of their human charges making the necessary spiritual break-through to enable a being with feet of clay to harness the same power. He (or she, the figure is left intentionally ambiguous) has awakened the Kundalini fire, drawing it up through the crown. The signatory wand of the suit hangs before the figure's solar plexus to indicate the importance of this chakra to both that work and the Wands suit in general: this is the chakra tied to the fiery sun and it represents willpower in a magickal sense. Although our image is very different from the traditional representation, the meaning remains essentially the same. This is a card of achievement: the figure has focused a great deal of effort and energy into developing his or her inner fire, and we witness the very moment of break-through. This is perfected work in the sense of spiritual alchemy.

The Four of Wands is a very positive card. When it comes up in a reading, even reversed, it carries nothing but good news. This card usually means congratulations are in order: the querent has achieved something of substance. A desired goal as been attained, and now there are further opportunities to build upon the accomplishment. The querent who receives the Four of Wands in a reading has a well-developed idea of what he or she wants to achieve. More than that, they have a plan, and have already demonstrated the ability to dedicate their time, energy and willpower to developing the basics. So long as the same amount of effort and focus is applied to the future work, success is virtually guaranteed. Manifested will has opened doors for the querent. The only real question will be how many is the querent willing to walk through?

Five of Wands: *Challenge*

Image: An angel with a wand clasped casually in one hand stands beside a mortal student. The angel demonstrates how to release and give shape to energy. The student scowls with effort, struggling with the lesson.

Meaning: *Challenge.* An effort or activity that narrows one's focus, possibly to the exclusion of all else. Competition. Struggling through a difficult task or situation. Fear of inadequacy fueling a desire to succeed.

Reversed: Activity. Exercise. The challenge implicit in the mortal figure fades from the spotlight and instead the focus is on the angel and all he represents: possibilities; lofty goals, and the opportunity to achieve the same.

Interpretation: Here we see one of the Watchers instructing a mortal student in the arts of magick. With his wand balanced in one hand, the Watcher evokes four glowing spheres of light with an almost casual gesture of his hand. He glances over at his mortal charge who strains to bring forth even one such sphere. If any of you have ever engaged in the psychic exercise of making energy balls, you will recognize the mortal's pose – especially the way he is holding his hands to gather the energy between them. The expression on the angel's face is placid, almost bored. In contrast, the mortal is hunched over with effort, face straining: he's not really having a fun time, and the ease with which his angelic tutor has summoned this spiritual fire is not helping matters any. Here we see the first blush of competitiveness, a sentiment that will wend its way throughout the rest of the suit of Wands. The mortal wants to match the angel, but his skills are not yet up to snuff. The angel is spirit, descended into

191

flesh. Harnessing this power comes naturally to him. The mortal is flesh, striving toward spirit – it is an uphill journey for him every step of the way. Nevertheless, he pushes, willing himself to succeed.

Note here that the mortal figure has closely-cropped hair. In the story of the Wands, all of the action between angels and their mortal students plays out in a mystery school dedicated to the development of magick. In some systems, the newly initiated shave their heads, shedding their hair to represent a new beginning. We wanted an echo of this practice in the mortal students in the suit of Wands. The fellow in the Five of Wands has hair that has just begun to grow back in: he's relatively new to this path.

The Five of Wands is a card of challenges. It tends to come up in readings to represent obstacles that have moved into the querent's life or will soon manifest. These obstacles will put the querent in a position where he or she must fight for what they want. The challenge may be a quarrel with a friend, family member, or other person in the querent's life – typically focused on a situation or subject that the querent is passionate about. The challenge may involve progress in personal development, whether this is in a career, a sport, a field of study, or magickal practices. The querent is put in a position where he or she must defend what they feel is right. Although these challenges can place great demands upon the querent's willpower and mental energy, they are not wholly negative in nature: if properly addressed, they have the potential to make the querent stronger and more capable of facing similar challenges. In this, the Five of Wands embodies the Nietzchian sentiment of, *"That which does not kill you makes you stronger."*

Looking back to our image of the card, the figure that best represents the querent is the mortal student. He strives to overcome his limitations as a mortal to match (or possibly exceed) the skill and finesse demonstrated by his angelic instructor. The comparison may seem impossible: can someone with feet of clay really ascend to the heights of the heavens? The Wands tell us if there is enough willpower involved, the answer can be yes. Thus the Watcher stands in this card to represent the goal that lies beyond the obstacles, that which the querent must strive toward. The implication is this: push past this present barrier, and see how much you can achieve.

Six of Wands: *Victory*

Image: A human figure, awash in light, holds aloft a wand. He commands six spheres of power. All burn brightly in the space.

Meaning: *Victory.* Triumph after struggle. Gaining confidence. Reaching a stable place of power in one's growth and development. Welcome news.

Reversed: Victory is achieved, but by a rival. The competition is lost. The journey is postponed. The accolades are abandoned or unjustly given to another. The querent falters in their progress due to pride or insolence.

Interpretation: The Six of Wands is a direct promise of what one can achieve if they push past the obstacles presented in the Five. Here we see a triumphant mortal figure, holding aloft a wand and surrounded by glowing spheres which he has clearly managed to call forth with his own power. There is no Watcher present overseeing this student's progress and, in fact, the Watchers take a back seat to the mortals in the rest of the numbered cards in the Wands suit. The students of the mystery school, like the fellow depicted in the Six, have progressed to the point of independent study. They have made the necessary break-throughs to begin evoking their sacred fire, and now it is only a matter of mastery and direction. There is a great deal of pride inherent in the stance and expression of the figure on this card, but he has earned it. Through his dedication, hard work, and passion for success, the mortal student has managed not only to call forth the magickal fire, but he holds it in six swirling balls of force neatly arranged around his person. Gone is the pinched expression of effort we see on the face of the student in the Five, replaced with a serenity that almost matches that of the angel from the previous card.

This is a good card to have come up in a reading. It is not only a card of success, but it is also a card of just desserts. Dedication and hard work have paid off. A struggle has been surmounted. Victory has been rightly earned and is that much sweeter due to the effort involved in achieving it. In addition to triumph, the Six of Wands also carries a suggestion of progress and forward motion. This can sometimes refer to literal travel, where the querent is given an opportunity to go somewhere, perhaps to speak or make another sort of appearance where his or her particular achievements are to be lauded or otherwise appreciated by an audience or a group of peers. The forward motion may also refer to victories yet to come: having gained a certain amount of momentum through a judicious application of dedication and willpower, the querent finds that he or she has paved the way for further development and growth in the matter at hand.

If the querent is involved in academics or the sciences, this card can represent a break-through – that thrilling "Eureka!" moment where a flash of inspiration suddenly makes the work of weeks or even years come together in a brilliant and innovative way. In sports, in represents a pinnacle of achievement and is usually tied to winning a competition or achieving an award or other distinction. In magick, it represents a similar flash of inspiration: the querent has broken through the previous plateau in their development and now has a whole new level of awareness unfolding before them. The only caution inherent in this card involves a tendency toward hubris, or of "resting on one's laurels." A concerted application of passion and will are what got the querent to this place, and now is not the time to let those falter simply because victory has been achieved. The querent should use the momentum, continue to press forward, and hold dear the expression, *"Excelsior!"*

Seven of Wands: *Adversity*

Image: Two mortal students struggle together. A wand lies discarded on the ground, its energy spilling forth uncontrollably. This manifests as chaotic swirls that whirl madly around the two figures.

Meaning: *Adversity.* The need for courage in the face of opposition. An unexpected challenge or test of one's skills. A loss of control and the fear that comes with it.

Reversed: Indecision. A lack of direction. The querent too easily backs down from a fight. Bullying becomes an issue. Trouble standing up for oneself.

Interpretation: The undercurrent of competition inherent in the suit comes to a head in the Seven of Wands. Here, two students in the school of magick wrestle together, actively fighting over some aspect of their study. A wand lays abandoned on the floor between the two, clearly dropped in the course of the fight. Power streams forth from the wand, made wild by the fevered emotions rolling off of the grappling figures. At this point in the progress of the fight, it's not clear who started it or who will ultimately emerge the victor.

The action depicted in the Seven of Wands is a direct consequence of the triumph from the Six. In matters of success, two main types of obstacles typically present themselves. These are internal obstacles, which arise from the limitations or perceived limitations of the person in pursuit of the success, and external obstacles posed by rivals who would seek to frustrate, undermine, or even steal the hard work of another. Passion fuels success, and we often get competitive, reactionary, or protective over those things we are passionate about. The figures here are clearly passionate enough

195

about some aspect of their studies that they are willing to come to blows over it. Perhaps the successful student from the Six of Wands bragged a little too freely about his progress; perhaps the simple fact that he was singled out for an acknowledgment of his skill was enough to inspire a fiercely jealous response. Either way, forward motion may be halted as the querent must fight his or her way through the competition that has arisen as a result of prior success.

When this card appears in a reading, it may refer to competition looming before the querent or it may refer to a struggle that has already played out in the past. In either case, the effects of the struggle still have an impact on the querent in his or her drive to succeed. The card can refer to a literal competition where the querent's drive and talents are pitted against those of others with similar interests, whether this is in sports or gaming, art, academics, or entrepreneurial affairs. It may also more generally refer to situational adversity, where problems or setbacks mean struggling toward a goal. Whatever shape it takes, the way to face this adversity is through courage and dedication.

In our card, a hint for success lies with the wand itself. For the moment, the two figures are too engrossed in the actual act of conflict to consider that a very powerful weapon has been abandoned in favor of brute force. This is not the wand itself, but what that wand represents: focus, willpower, and inner strength. If passion is allowed to go unchecked, the struggle remains chaotic and the results may be disastrous for both parties. But if the effort is made to stop and focus that passion, victory is assured. This card may also come up in a reading as a caution against useless jealousy on the part of the querent. In this case, it is the querent who feels competitive and is essentially creating his or her own adversary. Rather than wasting energy in hating another for his or her success, the querent should focus more on his or her own development.

Eight of Wands: *Movement*

Image: A man lies in a meditative trance, his wand on the floor beside him. Spheres of light emerge from his physical body, connecting it with the subtle or astral body projected through his meditation.

Meaning: *Movement.* Forces, plans, or activities head forward at a swift pace. Progression. A transition Pioneering concepts, inventions or perceptions. An expansion of power, understanding, or realization.

Reversed: The push for movement is too bold or the direction too unconventional for success. Expected messages are delayed or do not arrive. Forces move against the querent, fueled by jealousy or violent intent.

Interpretation: As the Wands unfold, they show us that they are all about progression and development: ideas, invention, personal transformation, and that which we are most passionate about. But the progress expressed within the Wands does not occur in a straight line or in one unbroken push uphill. In keeping with the fiery and sometimes unpredictable nature of the suit, the forward momentum that carries us through the Wands often moves in different or unexpected directions. This innovation of movement gains its fullest expression in our Eight of Wands. The movement of this card takes on a wholly unconventional direction: out of body and into the subtle reality or astral plane.

At first glance, there are two figures in this card: one lying supine in the background, sleeping or perhaps meditating. Another stands above him, looking and gesturing behind. However, careful examination of the card reveals that both figures represent the same

197

man. A student of our school of magick, he reclines beside his wand, projecting his astral double into the world. This is a supreme expression of magickal will and internal energy manifested outward. The balls of force which represent the pips of the card move from the figure's physical body to the astral double at his side, connecting the two along a vibrant path of light. The ethereal double glances back at the physical shell, but continues to step forward, intent on exploring the world from this unique perspective.

When this card emerges in a reading, it is a sign of progress. Some project in which the querent is engaged is nearing completion. A goal that the querent has been working toward is now swiftly approached. New ideas manifest and are rapidly put into action. As you can see from these possible interpretations, there is a sense to this card not only of a burst of energy, but also of a definitive direction in which that energy moves. This is not a card that simply says, "and the journey continues," but a card that tells us, "we move on the journey with a destination in sight." Given the way in which this movement manifests in our card, there is also an underlying implication of new or unexpected directions. There is forward motion in a project, but it may take a definitive turn down the road less traveled. In order to fully take advantage of the potential momentum inherent in this card, the querent may have to adapt to rapidly changing circumstances or be prepared to think outside of the box. If a path is blocked and one can no longer go forward or back, try going *up*. In addition to the symbolic movement of ideas, projects, and personal development, the Eight of Wands can also signify literal travel. This may be travel by air, or even the astral travel that is represented directly on the card.

Behind the Cards: The model for the Eight of Wands is Shawn Kurko (aka Sorrowsheart), the Counselor Caste Second in House Kheperu. A seer with gifted vision, Sorrowsheart has a unique approach to astral travel, dreamwork, and moving through multiple layers of reality. We felt this made him the perfect model for a card where movement is expressed as astral travel.

Nine of Wands: *Perseverance*

Image: A mortal student crouches among a collection of scrolls. He reads a spell and directs nine glowing spheres which swirl above his head. His wand lies among the papers, near at hand.

Meaning: *Perseverance.* Dedication that pays off. Persisting in one's efforts until the desired goal is obtained. A mastery of power through consistent effort and hard work. The strength that comes from self-discipline.

Reversed: The querent lacks endurance in mind or body to keep up the fight. Alternately, the querent wastes their dedication in fighting for lost causes. Digging in stubbornly, to the detriment of self or others. A refusal to yield causes one to break, sacrificing mental or physical health.

Interpretation: The student we witnessed astral projecting in the Eight of Wands returns in the Nine of Wands. Here he continues his studies, working toward a mastery of the magickal arts. He kneels on the floor, surrounded by a number of papers covered with magickal characters. His focus is on one in particular while, with an emphatic gesture of his right hand (traditionally, the active hand in magick), he directs the nine vibrant spheres of light around him. He uses his left hand to follow the characters of the scroll, symbolizing a reception of the knowledge therein contained. Thus, he works bodily as a conduit of magickal force: with one hand, he takes in potential, with the other, he expresses this into the world. The unseen portion of the equation is the inner alchemy wherein his Will is married to the potential, allowing it to manifest in a form of his desire. The intensity, beauty, and orchestration expressed in the gleaming spheres implies a level of mastery on the part of this magician. Not only has he progressed to the point where he can manifest his inner fire in the exterior world, he can do so and make it dance.

The Nine of Wands represents strength of purpose. It is a card in which the will to succeed has been honed to a fine edge and now can be wielded either as a deadly weapon or a powerful tool. In either case, it is an object wholly under the main character's guidance and direction. Although it is not as overtly expressed within the action of the card, the Nine of Wands, like the Five and Seven, is also a card of challenges. However, the Nine represents the ultimate development in response to prior challenges, which is preparedness. The figure here has dedicated himself to mastery of his power, and he has marshaled the resources necessary to further develop – and to defend – his empowered position.

When the Nine of Wands comes up in a reading, it generally indicates that the querent has survived several challenges to his or her development in a project, area of study, or field of competition – and that the querent is prepared to face such challenges again with an eye toward success. This is a card of courage and inner strength, combined with the ability to call upon these when faced with adversity. For the querent who receives the Nine of Wands, failure is not an option, and past failures, when encountered, have only served to inspire a greater sense of purpose in the struggle toward the goal. There is an unyielding quality to the character in this card: he knows what he wants, and he will not back down from the challenge until he has achieved it. His is the magickal Will, carefully cultivated and perfectly honed. In this, the Nine of Wands can also be a card of stubbornness and obstinacy. Querents who find themselves in the main action represented by this card may be unwilling or unable to back down from a challenge – and depending on the input from the rest of the spread, this may not be their best quality.

In some cases, the Nine of Wands may be a suggestion to the querent to cultivate the kind of strength of purpose embodied by the card, or it may indicate that only by adopting such an unyielding approach will the querent successfully obtain his or her goals. The card may also be a reminder to a querent who feels overwhelmed that he or she really does have the strength in reserve necessary to conquer the current situation – if only they are willing to put nose to grindstone and press on.

Ten of Wands: *Stagnation*

Image: A mortal student, collapsed with effort, huddles defensively on the floor. Around him, ten spheres of light crowd the space, so bright they wash out the fiery color of the card. The wand hangs ominously over the figure, pinning it to the ground.

Meaning: *Stagnation.* Oppression Profligate power which threatens to oppress even its user. Growth or change that outpace one's ability to adapt. Progress and/or work pursued to the point of exhaustion. Too much too fast.

Reversed: Selfish ambition and lack of foresight. Someone who shifts burdens unfairly onto others. Mismanagement of a project by a superior, usually to the querent's detriment. Being buried under work while someone else reaps the benefits.

Interpretation: Even with the challenges that punctuate the Five, Seven, and Nine of this suit, the Wands overall tell a positive story of inspiration and development – right up until you get to the Ten. At the Ten of Wands, everything falls apart. The figure in this card is hemmed in on all sides by brilliant spheres of energy so bright they've practically gone super-nova. There is so much light that he and the signatory wand are almost washed-out. This is a card of progress that has jetted along unchecked. Faced with so much development and so many possibilities, there is a danger of entropy and stagnation, and the only functional way out is to take things down a notch.

The Ten of Wands is a cautionary tale for people who do too much. Even if you're good at juggling, there is a point where something is going to get dropped. If there is no conscious choice to put something down, fate will usually make the choice for you – and often to your detriment. When we were designing this card, the story I had in my mind was that of the Magician's Apprentice. You've probably seen Disney's version in *Fantasia:* the apprentice tries to summon brooms to clean, only to find himself quickly overrun by self-propelled magickal brooms. He had enough ability to evoke all that power, but not enough focus or follow-through to maintain control. This dovetails nicely with the narrative of the Watcher Angels. The Watchers' revelation of magickal knowledge superficially seems like it could only benefit humanity. But in the *Book of Enoch,* it is precisely this revelation which leads to disaster and the Flood. The implication is that humanity was not ready to responsibly handle this information or the abilities to which it gave access. Outside authorities, in the figures of God and the archangels, step in to clean up the mess.

Of course, in the real world, we rarely have the luxury of being bailed out by some superior force: instead, it's usually up to us to sink or swim in the situations we've created. A querent who gets the Ten of Wands in a reading is feeling the pressure of a heavy load – either mental or physical – and something needs to be done about this. If the Ten of Wands indicates a potential future state, then it appears as a warning to querents, cautioning them to slow down and make a more conservative use of their energies. If the Ten of Wands refers to something in the querent's past, he or she is probably still feeling the effects of this pressure, possibly as burn-out.

The oppressive sensation under which the querent labors may also manifest in the form of choice paralysis: the querent is faced with so many possibilities or directions for growth that he or she cannot begin to choose just one – and as a result of this indecision fails to choose any. This is perhaps the most insidious expression of the Ten of Wands because, at least on the surface, the querent appears to have it all: a world of opportunities, projects, and limitless options for development. But limits and boundaries exist for a reason. They don't have to be constricting. Instead, they can provide a manageable range within which to work. In this, Ten of Wands may be a suggestion for the querent to set his or her own boundaries clearly before being overwhelmed. "I want it all," although ambitious, is not a workable business model in the end.

Page of Wands: *The Free Spirit*

Image: A figure, naked and bald, dances with its back to the viewer. Its gender is uncertain. Filmy veils the color of flames swirl around the figure. Its arms are outstretched, reaching, striving, celebrating.

Meaning: *The Free Spirit.* A person resistant to or unburdened by convention. Someone who speaks and acts freely, often without regard to social expectations or tact. A restless, yearning individual, impatient, always seeking another insight, evolution, or experience.

Reversed: Grandiose and theatrical. Unstable. Irresponsible. Given to wild turns of mood that can do harm to them and/or the people around them. Fleeting in affections and interests. Inconstant and superficial.

Interpretation: The Page of Wands is probably not the most reliable person that you know, but they are almost certainly the most *alive.* Creative, inspired, and unconventional, individuals represented by this card love new experiences for the sake of having them, but like flickering flames, they tend to be restless, never staying the same for long. This changeability encompasses every aspect of life for the Page of Wands: this is someone who changes careers, lifestyles, living situations, social circles, hobbies, and even ideologies frequently and rapidly, at least by everyone else's standards. To the Page of Wands, however, it's all good. Changing is simply a part of experiencing. They throw themselves with an impassioned intensity into their current "thing," and when something else comes along to replace it, they shift that intensity almost seamlessly, rarely looking back to what they have moved away from. In this, they may seem to be slaves to fashions and fads, but Page of Wands people don't necessarily follow the herd. They are just as likely (and perhaps more so) to make up their own trends, following the whimsy of their restless minds and hearts.

When this card comes up in a reading, it can be a reference to a person already in the querent's life, someone soon to be encountered, or it may represent an aspect of the querent him or herself. As a person moving into or already present in the querent's life, the Page of Wands is someone who conveys messages related to their fiery suit. However, in keeping with their restless and unconventional spirit, the Page of Wands doesn't usually just walk up to the querent and tell them what they need to know in a few bland and boring words. The Page of Wands is much more likely to charge up to the querent, grab them by the hand, and excitedly drag them off onto some kind of adventure. This is an adventure of experience, often focused on trying new things, and the adventure itself is the message. Reckless and daring, it may be as simple as sampling exotic cuisine or as hair-raising as going sky-diving. But no matter how strange or terrifying the new experience might seem, the Page of Wands usually manages to make it seem like a good idea at the time.

The downside to the Page of Wands is that he or she doesn't just walk the line between "careless" and "carefree" – this person jumps rope with it, blithely and sometimes blindly. As exciting and inspirational as the Page of Wands can be, this person can also lead the querent to make rash decisions, to leap headlong into the fire, and to behave a little too irresponsibly. As a partner or spouse (or gods help you, a child!), especially for a querent who is timid or conservative, the Page of Wands can be a challenging character to have in one's life. The querent who has to interact closely with this person may find themselves constantly running after the Page, struggling to keep up with the latest turn of whimsy, and occasionally picking up the pieces left behind by yet another frenzy of experience. The Page of Wands lives very much in the *now,* rarely worrying about the future, and often leaving the mistakes of the past to be somebody else's problem. As such, while the *joie de vivre* of the Page of Wands may bring an amazing amount of dynamism into the life of the querent, he or she can also be exhausting.

Knight of Wands: *The Instigator*

Image: A brooding figure holds a glowing wand. His other hand guides or shapes a large sphere of force whose rays resemble the sun. His eyes are intense; his face mostly in shadow. Above his head swirls another orb of power.

Meaning: *The Instigator.* An intense and sometimes impulsive individual, full of pride. He may present himself as an adversary, forcing one to grow through competition and/or struggle. Hot-tempered, he does not easily back down. He can bring about great growth or great harm by pushing limits and defying boundaries.

Reversed: A violent temper and explosive personality. No control. The Knight challenges others, but works from an inflexible or narrow-minded perspective of his (or her) own. Someone who sows discord and inspires conflict simply to watch the resulting chaos.

Interpretation: Of all the people to encounter with a fiery nature, the Knight is likely the most difficult. A challenger by nature, the Knight of Wands is someone never content with letting things rest: not people, not assumptions, not ideas, nor ways of life. A rebel in mind and heart, the Knight of Wands is driven to push boundaries, challenge assumptions, topple traditions, and passionately speak out against anything he or she feels is in need of a change. As such, this is a very Luciferian card in the sense of Lucifer as a Romantic ideal (as in the literary movement, not Harlequin romances): the light-bringer who had the audacity to challenge even the greatest authority simply because he could.

When the Knight of Wands makes an appearance in a reading, if the card represents someone in the querent's life, this person is not necessarily a friend. The Knight of Wands is much more likely to appear as a rival or even an enemy. Even when the Knight of Wands turns out to be a friend or a relative, it's almost a guarantee that there are things about this person the querent doesn't like or at least isn't comfortable with: the Knight of Wands often brings his challenges directly to the querent, pushing him or her to grow, change, dare, and reassess assumptions in his or her life.

The Knight of Wands can be pushy with his agenda, even overbearing. He or she does not like to let things rest. The Knight will poke and prod, agitating the waters until the querent can't help but respond. This may involve direct confrontations with the querent, but in certain circumstances, the Knight of Wands can successfully get under someone's skin simply by being true to his or her nature *around* that person. In this case, the Knight instigates by example, demonstrating some idea, lifestyle, or behavior that the querent finds disturbing or objectionable and, in the end, inspiring the querent to confront the reasons why. This can manifest as a direct conflict with the Knight of Wands – and he (or she) will probably enjoy it on some level – or it may resolve itself internally, with the confrontation taking place within the querent's own mind. Either way, the Knight of Wands will have done his or her job if the querent questions beliefs and assumptions about the issue at hand.

If the Knight of Wands is a reflection of the querent, it represents this almost restless need for rebellion. These querents are driven to challenge assumptions in people, in society, and in themselves. Depending on the querent's level of finesse in addressing these matters, this rebellion may not seem endearing to others. The Knight of Wands may present itself to remind the querent to stay true to his or her nature, even when this nature means being in conflict with others. However, it may also be a reminder that not everyone likes to be challenged constantly. Tempering these tendencies may make the querent a little more approachable or likable to others. While it may be in the Knight of Wands' nature to swiftly spur others into thoughts and/or actions, it may also be a good idea to pick and choose these battles carefully.

Queen of Wands: *The Guide*

Image: A richly dressed woman with hooded eyes stands on a veranda. She holds a wand like a scepter of authority. Mists swirl around her. She raises one hand to the viewer, beckoning.

Meaning: *The Guide.* Passionate and insightful, the Queen possesses an unyielding sense of self which she is able to inspire in others. Slow to engage emotionally, once she has taken an interest in something, she will not readily back down, whether her interest is an object, a person, or a cause. She can seem haughty and cruel, but her courage can serve as an example to others.

Reversed: Strict and domineering, she has a jealous streak and can turn on others in a flash. She (or he) makes friends quickly but just as quickly drops them, often for petty reasons. Stiff-necked and full of pride, she grows tired of people when not given the attention she thinks she deserves.

Interpretation: Our Queen regards us from the veranda of her country manor, which could be a villa in the Tuscan hills or some ethereal corner of the imagination. She regards the viewer with a serene and almost sardonic expression, regal in her robes and seemingly self-assured that any who are worthy of what she has to offer will come forward to answer her call. Fortune favors the bold.

In readings, the Queen of Wands is a guide who encourages those brave enough to follow her not to retread the steps of others but to forge ahead upon their own path. A staunch individualist, she nurtures this individuality in others, helping them to find the strength to believe in themselves. A very commanding figure, in her most ideal state, she uses this command not to subjugate but to inspire. She is the queen bee, in-charge and industrious, and it is her role to guide others in their best realization of these self-same qualities. Her unwavering sense of confidence can be contagious, and those who understand her look up to her. She makes an excellent role-model, even though she may seem a bit emotionally detached. Although she is a queen of the element of fire, she represents fire carefully harnessed and intensely contained – qualities which make her energy both far more effective and far more dangerous if turned toward destructive ends. She is often also a home-maker, but not in the sense of some barefoot and pregnant housewife. Rather, the Queen of Wands is that individual – male, female, or otherwise – who represents the heart and soul of a family: the steel rod at the center holding everything up, providing structure, direction, and identity.

The main qualities the Queen of Wands brings to the querent are her intensity, her drive toward industry, her carefully directed passion, and her sometimes stiff-necked individuality. The Queen of Wands may also be a magickal instructor and initiatrix, someone who both perceives and knows how to cultivate that inner fire expressed throughout her suit. In this, she comes into the querent's life as an evoker, drawing out and guiding them through the development of their inner potential.

As an aspect of the querent, the Queen of Wands can represent a call to guide and inspire others toward a greater expression of their passions, their individuality, their creativity, and their inner fire. The Queen of Wands is also a general affirmation of the value of individuality, both one's own as well as that of others. This may be a suggestion for the querent to respect a person's sovereign right to make their own choices, rather than pushing choices upon them.

King of Wands: *The Visionary*

Image: A leonine man in Greco-Roman attire lounges upon a throne. His hair is mane-like and behind him is a starburst of light in solar colors. His wand sits atop a staff of impressive length.

Meaning: *The Visionary.* Confident and proud, he is in tune with his desires and does not hesitate to pursue them. He possesses great charisma, which can make him a great leader or a dangerous tyrant. He can be hasty and cruel, with a violent streak. His self-confidence and unwavering will make him a force to be reckoned with.

Reversed: Harsh and unyielding, with a tendency to push too hard and to demand too much. He is not only idealistic, he is unrealistic in his goals. He may be fiercely judgmental of any vision other than his own, or prejudiced against those who deviate from his favored ideal.

Interpretation: The figure Ozymandias, from Percy Bysshe Shelley's poem of the same name, neatly embodies the best and the worst qualities of the King of Wands. In an ancient inscription on a shattered statue, the character declares: *"My name is Ozymandias, king of kings. Look on my works, ye Mighty, and despair!"* All around stretch the desert sands, empty and bare. That is the moral of the story, and of this King: he has the fire necessary to ascend to great heights, but when he falters, he falls in flames.

The King of Wands is a visionary leader in the spirit of Alexander the Great. Driven and bold, his desires are always ambitious in scope, if sometimes unrealistic in application. Passionate and idealistic, he sees the world as he wants it to be, and has an enviable talent for making even unrealistic visions a reality –

in part because of his sheer refusal to fail. Although his reach often exceeds his grasp, he nevertheless has a gift for persuading those around him to believe in his goals and to help him achieve these impossible dreams. He can be domineering and even petulant. This King is definitely a "my way or the highway" sort of leader. But no one can argue that he gets results – at least when he's in good form.

When the King of Wands comes up in a reading, the querent should get ready to strap on the seat belt and prepare for a wild ride. This King is a force to be reckoned with, and he (or she) rarely takes "no" for an answer. When this King turns his eye to the querent, it is with the intention of recruiting him or her to a project or cause, and the querent will find the King's fire and charisma very hard to resist. If the card represents a person coming into the querent's life in the near future, this at least allows for some preparation. The querent should consider what he or she really wants and believes, then be ready to stick to these things very firmly when confronted by the King. It can be hard to stand one's ground in the face of this embodiment of mental fire, but it is sometimes necessary. The King of Wands is seductive and persuasive, and it's easy to become so blinded by his shining ideals that realistic concerns are eclipsed. This is almost universally the source of failure when a King of Wands goes down in flames: for want of a nail, the battle is lost. Big things fall apart because someone overlooked the little things. And the King of Wands almost never concerns himself with what he considers the little things. It can be very exciting to work with the person represented by the King of Wands, but also very demanding. Such a person inspires others to strive toward greatness, and his influence may push the querent to discover his or her own ideal self. "Be all that you can be," commands this King, "and then go one better!"

When the King of Wands appears as projection of the querent him or herself, it is an acknowledgment of all of these qualities – either as qualities currently expressed and manifested in the querent's life or as potential qualities to be cultivated in the future. In either case, the card is a suggestion to use these abilities wisely. Don't be afraid to harness the fire, but temper the vision with pragmatism – for one's own sake as well as for the sake of one's followers.

Ace of Swords: *Conquest*

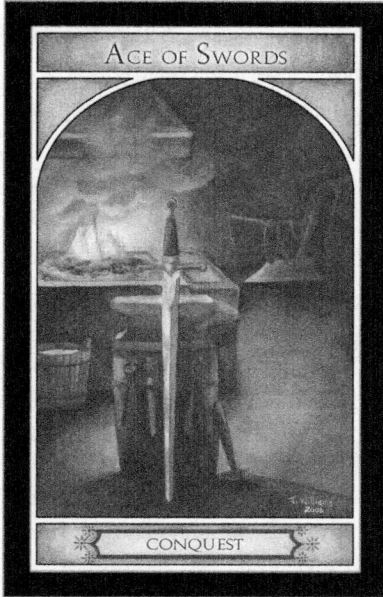

Image: A smoke-filled smithy with a newly forged sword in the foreground. A primitive plow is visible amidst the shadows of the background.

Meaning: *Conquest.* A change or redirection of power. Nascent force used for protection, triumph, or destruction, depending on its application. The beginning of conflict.

Reversed: Destruction. An excessive use of force. Tyranny. Power that is mishandled, cutting its wielder. A warning against starting fights or championing unjust causes.

Interpretation: In the tale of the Watcher Angels, after leaving Heaven to live among mortals (Pentacles), the Watchers indulge in sensual pleasures (Cups), and reveal the forbidden arts of magick to humanity (Wands). As heavenly beings interjecting their powers and desires on the earthly plane without a proper respect for the balance between spirit and flesh, the Watchers bring about discord, and in the *Book of Enoch,* there are repercussions for this. One of the primary judgments passed against the Watchers is for their sons to turn against one another, battling and dying by the sword. This war-torn and bloody stage in the Watchers' mythic history plays out in the Swords suit, and the seed of conflict begins with the Ace of Swords.

This card depicts the forging of the first sword. In the Three of Pentacles, we saw a metal-worker crafting at a forge, but the items produced were decorative in nature. Now we see a plowshare in the background, a conscious nod to the notion of "beating swords into plowshares." But here that action is turned on its head: the sons of the Watchers have taken the metal of their plowshares and beaten it into swords. In this we see the legacy of the Watcher Azazel, who is credited with teaching humanity the forging of swords, armor, and all the tools of war. In the book of Genesis, the children of the Watchers are described as heroes and "mighty men of renown," but it is only toward the end of the Watchers' earthly empire that they succumb fully to their bellicose tendencies and take up arms against one another.

When the Ace of Swords appears in a reading, it is an ominous card. It heralds the beginning of a period of strife and conflict in the life of the querent. This may indicate literal warfare, but as Swords are tied to the element of air and thus to the intellect, it may also represent a war of thoughts and/or ideals. An alternate meaning to this card is the emergence of a champion or war-leader. This may refer to the birth of a child destined for such a calling (or a young protégé coming into the querent's life through other means), or it may suggest that the querent will soon find him or herself called down the warrior's path. This may not mean that the querent will find themselves literally leading troops on the field of battle, although soldiering and a call to the military is not beyond the scope of this card. But – especially in this modern age – battles are waged on many fronts, and the card may be a sign that the querent will be called to lead the charge in a more figurative battle: championing causes, engaging in verbal skirmishes, or defending family and loved ones from prejudice, bullying, or other domestic threats. Interwoven with the looming threat of conflict represented by this card is also a potential for courage and valor. This is a call to arms, and the querent may ultimately triumph. Within the scope of the Ace, however, that triumph is only one possibility among many – a whisper of a promise that may not become a reality. One thing is certain: there is work ahead for the querent who receives this card, and it will not be easy work, nor will it be accomplished without some loss and pain.

Two of Swords: *Stalemate*

Image: Two young men, possibly brothers, stand back to back in preparation for a duel. They are almost identically outfitted and each bears a sword of similar appearance. Behind them is a bleak winter landscape.

Meaning: *Stalemate.* A struggle where no one is the winner. Divided viewpoints. Opposing forces that are locked in balance, for the moment.

Reversed: Built-up tension suddenly released. An unexpected resolution between two opposed forces. The dam breaks, but the subsequent flood is unpleasant.

Interpretation: Once a weapon has been forged in the Ace of Swords, it doesn't take long for people to take up arms against one another. In the case of the Two of Swords, we see a duel that pits brother against brother. There is little difference between them: dressed in similar garb, their hair is only shades apart and they bear identical weapons. Behind them is a barren landscape of denuded trees, the black branches stark against a gray winter sky. There is a bleak aspect to this scene, and as the keyword of the card implies, it does not look like either side in this conflict will emerge a winner. One brother grimly regards the viewer, testing the edge of his blade. The other turns his face toward the trees, staring into the distance.

The Two of Swords is a card of conflict, but it represents a struggle that is so equally matched as to be futile. The two sides are in balance – even if they themselves do not see this. When this card appears in a reading, it represents a war of forces, ideas, or people in the querent's life that is split down the middle. The two sides strive with one another, equally matched yet equally stubborn. No one

213

wants to strike the first blow, but no one is willing to back down, either. As a result, there is indecision and lingering tension where neither side gives any ground.

The querent stands somewhere in the middle of this: in our card, there is a third party present for this scene, essentially off-camera. He is the observer. He bears witness to the duel between the brothers, unwilling to help either overcome the other yet unable to dissuade them from their course of action (this observer doesn't step visibly into the action himself until the Three of Swords). His position and that of the querent are the same: he is caught in the balance, with sympathy for both sides. For the querent, this often indicates a hesitancy toward action in the midst of opposition. This may involve a situation in the querent's past, something ongoing, or a situation moving into the querent's future. Rather than make a decision between one side or the other, the querent opts to make no decision at all – which is itself a decision. The lack of action on the part of the querent does not help matters in this card and, in fact, may actually make things worse. As much as the querent may feel pulled in both directions at once and is reluctant to pick sides, this card often manifests as a warning against inaction. In some cases, the card can also indicate a sudden calm in the midst of a storm or a momentary truce in the conflict. But this is little more than a caesura. Although there is balance, the swords remain unsheathed and held at the ready.

Three of Swords: *Sorrow*

Image: A sorrowful figure bends to retrieve two discarded swords. In his hands he holds a third. The red of his cloak is reminiscent of spilled blood. The surrounding birches are bleak and bare.

Meaning: *Sorrow.* The sense of loss that comes in the wake of difficult choices. A schism among family and/or friends. Being torn between loyalties or ideologies. Mourning words, thoughts, or actions that cannot be undone.

Reversed: A tense situation devolves into chaos. An error in judgment brings a potentially devastating conflict to a head. There is confusion and heartache, with an implication that the querent may be at fault.

Interpretation: The Two of Swords pitted brother against brother in a duel of equal forces. Off-camera, a third party observed the conflict, unable and unwilling to intervene. This figure steps forward in the Three once the fight is done and over – and from the two swords lying next to one another in the snow, we are given the impression that both of the brothers lost the fight. Heartbroken and mourning his friends, the figure bends to retrieve the swords of the fallen brothers. The scene is washed-out and pale, from the white of the birches to the marked pallor of the figure's face. His woolen cloak is a harsh splash of color against all the white and gray, pooling around him in a conscious echo of blood.

The Three of Swords is a harsh card to emerge in any reading. It is a card of heartache and sorrow and is traditionally represented by a heart pierced with swords. Within the narrative of our deck, that heartfelt emotion manifests in the figure crouched against a bleak winter landscape, mourning the loss of close friends – if not literally his brothers, then surely his brothers-in-arms. This card represents the logical conclusion to events sparked by the Ace and hanging in balance in the Two. When conflicts arise between enemies or friends, it is only a matter of time before they reach a head and someone walks away a loser. Of course, in many conflicts, both sides take losses, and that is reflected in the two fallen swords in this card. Fighting hurts, and for the querent who receives this card in a reading, it is an expression of this heartache. It may signify a pain that lingers from a conflict past or it may herald pain in the future. The only good news this card can offer a querent is that matters at least have the potential to be resolved – once the dust settles. The conflict that inspires the sorrow expressed within this card can involve friends or family; it may be a physical conflict or a battle that plays out between hearts, ideals, or words. Though it is not the case with our two fallen brothers, for the querent, there may be a definitive winner and a loser: but everyone comes away bloody. The best advice for a querent who gets this card is to work through the pain and attempt to learn from the conflict – even if the lesson is simply, "Let's not do that again."

There is a promise hidden in the birch trees that stand in the background of this card. Birch trees are very adaptable, often surviving in harsh conditions. They are also very flexible trees, bending before the force of a storm. They eagerly repopulate areas of forest devastated by fire, and in this are symbols of renewal. They suggest to the querent that, no matter how bad things look right now, it is possible to survive.

Behind the Cards: This one's a little weird. We used a lot of friends as models and inspiration for our cards, and the Three of Swords is no different. The fellow depicted in this card, whose personality and regional ties had an influence on the whole setting and feel of the Swords, is someone both Jackie and myself consider a good friend. Except that he happens to be dead and has likely been dead a long while. We identify him as a Celtic warrior, and he is something of a family guardian. So, there you have: one of our models is a ghost.

Four of Swords: *Recuperation*

Image: Four cairns surmounted by four swords. In the foreground, a young woman sits, hugging her knees and staring into the distance. The background is full of evergreen trees. The woman's red cloak pools like blood.

Meaning: *Recuperation.* A moment of rest in the midst of struggle. A period of recovery and/or seclusion, possibly forced. Recovery from loss and/or illness. Retreat. The need to marshal one's strength.

Reversed: Disquiet. Unrest. Inner tumult that demands circum-spection. The period of rest only increases problems and/or tensions. May indicate a strike or a rebellious and/or dysfunctional refusal to engage in the world.

Interpretation: The conflict sparked by the Ace has claimed lives by the Three of Swords, but within the mythos of the Watcher Angels, the fight extends well beyond the pair of brothers depicted in our Two. All of the children of the Watchers are pitted against one another in this final conflict. Fighting develops and continues throughout the Swords, and by the Four of Swords, we see that there have been further losses. After a battle, there must be time to bury the dead. In ages past, when wars were waged with a certain sense of etiquette and propriety, a momentary truce sometimes arose between the two armies facing one another so that each side could bury its dead. The peace didn't last, but it offered a brief respite in which to mourn and to catch one's breath. Here in the Four of Swords we see that moment of rest and reflection. A young woman pauses by the cairns of the dead. The sword of each fallen soldier marks his grave, thrust point-down into the pile of stones. The young woman stares

217

into the distance, perhaps thinking of those she has lost and those she stands to lose as the conflict wears on. The evergreens behind her are the only sign of hope in this otherwise bleak card. As trees that do not loose their leaves during the chill months of winter, they are sometimes seen as symbols of eternal life. Nevertheless, the figure's back is turned upon this promise and instead she gazes uncertainly into the future. The promise may be there, but she is not prepared to see it at this time.

When this card comes up in a reading, it does not represent death, but the stillness that comes after. This still and quiet time is generally more symbolic than not. Rarely does the Four of Swords come up to indicate an actual period of mourning in the wake of a death. However, the card may be concerned with the aftermath of symbolic deaths: it may represent a period of semi-forced rest following a protracted illness, or it may suggest a time of withdrawal and recuperation in the wake of significant and upsetting life changes. The overall sense of this card is not focused on the pain of loss or the act of losing something but rather on the time of retreat that is generally sought afterward. This is a delicate time for the querent. He or she feels overwhelmed or even numbed by recent experiences. There is a need for time to sort one's thoughts and marshal one's strength. This can be a time of healing, but it is also a melancholy time. The querent's thoughts can't help but stray to the incident or situation that inspired the retreat in the first place. Although there is peace enough for reflection, it can turn to brooding if the querent isn't careful. An alternate meaning of the card is "exile," and in this, it suggests that the period away from the action is forced or imposed upon the querent. This can tie into the concept of recovery from illness addressed above, where the querent must take time away from favored activities while he or she rests and heals. However, the querent may grow restless with this enforced removal from preferred activities and grows restless, feeling trapped and/or isolated.

Behind the Cards: The model for this card is our friend Andrea, the head of House Kheperu's Counselor Caste. She also modeled for The Star, a card well-suited to her personality and magickal affiliations

Five of Swords: *Defeat*

Image: A pale woman sprawls upon the ground, holding a shattered sword. In the background, four more swords stand point-down in a tightly-packed bundle. They loom over the fallen figure.

Meaning: *Defeat.* Dishonor. Submission. A feeling of being overwhelmed. Yielding to a superior force, be this another person, a circumstance, or simply fate.

Reversed: An empty victory, or one achieved through under-handed means. Low blows. Someone stoops reprehensible actions in order to lay low another. Debasement. Groveling.

Interpretation: In the Four of Swords, we see a moment of rest and withdrawal from battle. But elsewhere, the battle rages. As a result, in the Five of Swords we see a poignant moment of defeat. A woman lies collapsed upon the ground, her shattered sword still clutched in one limp hand. Her white dress is tattered in places and has been pushed half-way up her thighs. Four swords are thrust into the ground beyond her. The rest of the card is empty and bleak. From the woman's pallor, it is difficult to say whether or not she is alive.

This is not a happy card. It represents not only defeat and surrender, but dishonor and degradation as well. This is definitely the card of adding insult to injury. Additionally, there is the suggestion that something of value has been taken away from the figure on the card – and rather forcefully. In our deck, since the main figure of the card is female, the implications of this forceful theft and subsequent degradation take a particularly unpleasant turn. She has been overwhelmed by a superior power and forced into a position of surrender. Her posture of despair and submission should eloquently speak for all that she has lost. The broken sword implies that she did not go down without a fight, but even so, she was overcome.

When this card appears in a reading, much as with cards depicting death, do not feel that you must interpret it literally. Our image for the card does carry an intimation of rape or sexual abuse: this is often the fate of women who find themselves in the midst of war. However, this ***does not*** have to hold literal meaning for the querent. Rather, the card is suggestive of surrender, defeat, and the sense of being hopelessly overwhelmed by a force both vicious and violent. This defeat can result from a mental, emotional, or otherwise figurative battle – but notably, whoever came out the victor felt the need to rub it in. The challenge in reading this card is that the querent may equally be the victim or the victor represented by the image. Thus, the way in which this card is read relies heavily upon the other cards appearing around it. It is not merely a card of surrender and defeat, but also represents the act of demanding and/or forcing such a surrender. In this, it is essentially both edges of the blade. The despair and desolation embodied by the woman on the card may be something the querent is experiencing or a state which the querent, through his or her actions, has inspired in another. As already noted, read this in relation to the other cards carefully before concluding which way it is meant to go. The actual action that has lead to the state of submission and surrender may be in the past or it may be a situation in the immediate future. In this, the card may come up as a comment upon the querent's current mental state, or it may be a warning to prepare for – or attempt to avoid – bringing out this state in the future. For querents who have found themselves at the wrong end of abuse – be it emotional, physical, or otherwise – the card can reflect echoes of that abuse impacting the querent's current state or may serve as a reminder for the abused not to fall into the common trap of eventually becoming an abuser themselves.

Six of Swords: *Passage*

Image: A lone traveler marches along a riverbank. Four swords stand in the high grass beside him, another is strapped in a scabbard at his hip. A sixth sword, ethereal, hangs in the distance, a visionary marker of his destination.

Meaning: *Passage.* A journey. Movement, which may involve struggle, from one place, idea, or state of being to the next. Travel.

Reversed: Entrapment. No way out. Delays or setbacks in physical journeys. The querent cannot seem to make the mental transition necessary to change or improve ideas or attitudes.

Interpretation: In the Six of Swords, a ranger walks through a trackless field of high grass alongside the bank of a river. His back is turned toward the viewer and he fixes his gazes ahead. The four swords thrust into the ground beside him are a reminder that, although the scene around him is calm, there is still a war going on somewhere. Notably, our figure is moving away from these, his attention focused on the countryside ahead, suggesting that perhaps he has chosen to leave the battle behind. Maybe there was a conflict in ideologies, maybe he found that his heart was no longer committed to the cause. Either way, he is walking away – not out of cowardice but with determination. He clearly has a destination in mind, and this is represented by the ethereal sword hanging in the distance. It points like an omen to the green hills on the other side of the river: a safe haven, perhaps, or possibly his home. Whatever his destination, we see him in transit, moving from one thing to another. He is still girded for battle with a dagger at his back and a sword at his side, but the sword rests in its scabbard, safely sheathed. For the moment, the scene is placid. He is leaving behind the concrete threat of the unsheathed blades to his right, and although his destination is also marked with a sword, it is a symbolic one – suggesting that his future battles may be of a more intellectual or even spiritual nature.

This is a card of movement, as the image suggests. Notably, it often appears in a reading to indicate that the querent is moving out of or away from current troubles and conflicts. The card may appear to represent a change in residence, where the querent moves away from a place in which he or she felt physically or mentally embattled. It may signify the move from a job where incessant conflicts created an atmosphere poisonous to the querent. The card may also represent removing oneself bodily from a threatening situation or person. Depending on the circumstances, the card may indicate that the querent is in the midst of this move, or it may show up as a suggestion for the querent to consider such a move. Although the scene of the card is rather serene, our figure is nevertheless trudging through high grass in a trackless expanse: for the querent, this is a reminder that the move is not necessarily going to be easy or without risks. But a transition is looming – or has become necessary.

Another aspect of the card lies in the ethereal quality of the visionary sword. This represents a movement from physical concerns to issues in the realm of the mind. In this, the card may indicate that the best answer for the querent's present situation is to try to seek refuge within. A movement in thoughts or in attitude may be the solution to the current conflict. Finally, the Six of Swords often carries the traditional meaning of a passage by sea: it can emerge to represent travel that crosses water, much as our main figure's journey seemed destined to take him to the other side of the river. The card may come up to indicate a literal journey on the part of the querent, one that takes the querent to the other side of a river, an ocean, or other body of water. It may also remain symbolic, telling us that the querent is moving mentally from a troublesome situation to a far and distant shore.

Behind the Cards: The image for this card came to Jackie in a dream. It's one of the inspired cards that emerged almost effortlessly.

Seven of Swords: *Betrayal*

Image: A man crouches in the shadows of a tent. Stealthily, he takes swords from a rack of armaments. With a guilty look, he scans the night to see if anyone is witness to his theft.

Meaning: *Betrayal.* Theft. Shady dealings. A need for caution. Anxiety over exposure. A situation requires cunning, and even then success is uncertain.

Reversed: Over-thinking or over-strategizing. The querent is making a situation far more complex than it needs to be. A thief has second thoughts and returns what was stolen.

Interpretation: In the Seven of Swords, this bellicose suit takes a turn toward the under-handed. A lone figure has stolen into an enemy encampment under the cover of darkness, but rather than confront any of the soldiers directly, he merely makes off with their weapons. If you examine the figure closely, you should recognize the fellow from the Three of Swords. He has changed up his cloak – adopting the enemies' colors to better infiltrate their camp – but he knows his ruse can only last so long. So he moves quickly, looking furtively around to be certain that his act of subterfuge is carried out without raising an alarm.

The Seven of Swords is the card of sneaks and thieves – which is great if you're the thief, but not so great if you're the target of the theft. This can mean literal theft of objects or ideas, but the card also represents the attitudes and strategies necessarily adopted when one's goal is winning at all costs. When it represents a person or situation that is happening or will happen to the querent, it means that the querent is likely to get played. But the card can just as easily represent the querent, indicating a need to adopt careful and even underhanded techniques in order to come out the winner in a difficult situation. There is conflict in the Seven of Swords, but it is indirect. Rather than face opposition head-on, the warrior in this card has brought his full mental faculties to bear on the situation, applying stealth, subterfuge, and rather novel tactics. Faced with a superior force in strength of arms, his solution is not to overpower but to disarm them, literally.

Querents finding themselves faced with such cunning are in for a difficult time. The person, force, or group represented by the Seven of Swords does not fight fair, and the querent will feel stabbed in the back, out-maneuvered, and betrayed. Whether or not these actions are right or proper, they are nevertheless necessary for success in the present endeavor – which means, if the querent is at the receiving end of this action, he or she must also work smarter and not harder to avoid being taken advantage of. If the card shows up as a suggestion for the querent to adopt these techniques, all these things should be kept in mind. Tactics like these generally inspire a great deal of bad feeling. A wily approach to opposition where one plays the friend only to get close and learn the secret weaknesses may lead those on the sidelines who witnessed this conflict to approach the manipulator suspiciously in any future dealings. While these tactics may be effective, they are not strictly honorable.

Behind the Cards: Jackie tells me that anyone who has ever gone to the Society for Creative Anachronism's annual summer event, Pennsic War, is likely to recognize this scene with the tent. Though if some fellow came skulking about to steal anyone's swords at Pennsic, he'd likely to get a taste of rattan come morning.

Eight of Swords: *Imprisonment*

Image: An angel, stripped to the waist, rests on her knees, hemmed in by eight swords. She covers her nakedness self-consciously. The swords do not allow her space to stretch her wings.

Meaning: *Imprisonment.* A sense of being surrounded on all sides by restrictive and/or threatening forces. Overwhelmed by too many people, ideas, or choices. Mental paralysis. Indecision.

Reversed: Release. Liberation. An end to restriction. The stifling situation resolves itself. Doors open to offer new directions of growth and development.

Interpretation: Within the unfolding narrative of the war-torn Swords, the Eight depicts someone who has been taken as a prisoner in the conflict. Her captivity may be a consequence of the theft and betrayal depicted in the Seven of Swords, but it is just as likely that she is yet another victim of the strife unfolding within the suit. She is stripped to the waist but covers herself modestly. The swords thrust into the ground do not wound or pierce her, but they pen her in on all sides. She looks cold and dejected, without even room enough to stretch her wings. The ground beneath her is rough and the background is dark and brooding, matching her despondent mood.

When this card appears in a reading, it represents a situation in which the querent feels trapped. This can sometimes signify a literal imprisonment, but more often, the card represents a sense of captivity that is situational. The details of the situation can vary; the real import of the card involves the querent's interior experience of and response to this sense of imprisonment. The card represents sensations of frustration, constriction, and the inability to take satisfactory action. These sensations may result from a very real restriction upon the querent's freedoms, or they may merely be perceptions on the querent's part. The querent may feel trapped at home or work, embattled by confrontational, domineering, or even abusive individuals. The querent may be faced with several difficult choices, and rather than err on the side of one or the other, he or she remains stagnating in between, trapped in inactivity.

The imprisonment represented by the card may also be self-imposed: the querent is caught in a situation where he or she feels unhappily trapped, and yet it is within the querent's power to escape. In this case, a resolution lies in finding the strength to take positive action, rather than allowing the sense of imprisonment perpetuate despondency and inaction. As Swords are the suit of the mind, the underlying message of this card is best expressed in poet Richard Lovelace's ageless lines, *"Stone walls do not a prison make, nor iron bars a cage."* Although outside forces, people, and circumstances certainly have an influence upon what and how much we can do in any given situation, true liberation begins in the mind.

Nine of Swords: *Nightmares*

Image: A young man sleeps on a rough pallet, wrapped in his traveling cloak. His sword lies unsheathed beside him, as if he expects trouble. Above him, chilling specters loom, each bearing swords of their own.

Meaning: *Nightmares.* A period of great anxiety, restlessness, and/or fear. Struggling with inner or outer demons, whether real or imagined. Doubts about actions, beliefs, or people.

Reversed: Faith in ones own strength or in a higher power can help overcome the nightmares and fears. Patience is key to enduring current hardships. However dark the night, dawn is sure to come.

Interpretation: The recurring figure who is essentially the main character of the Swords suit has returned. We see him at some point after his escapades in the enemy camp (the cunning theft depicted in the Seven of Swords). Here in the Nine of Swords, the warrior lies sleeping, covered with his familiar red cloak. Wherever he has chosen to lay his head, he does not feel safe, for his sword lays ready beside him, unsheathed and within easy reach. We can only imagine that he sleeps fitfully, for above him swarm specters – real or imagined. They loom ominously in the darkness, each bearing a sword like an omen of doom. The shadowy wraiths dominate the spaces of this dark card, practically dwarfing the slumbering figure. One lies stretched on top of him, in a conscious echo of hag attacks or night terrors.

The Nine of Swords is traditionally the card of nightmares. Fears, anxieties, and the mental exhaustion that comes from protracted conflict all are made manifest within this card. We've all experienced the scene presented in this Nine: the worries of the day loom large in the dark and lonely hours, crowding our minds once we've dropped our defenses to sleep. In the next moment, the young man resting in his card will wake with a start, heart pounding and stomach clenched, unable to focus at first upon anything except the anxieties flooding his mind. Every little worry from the day before – every argument, every deadline, and each improperly spoken word – seems suddenly too massive a burden ever to be overcome. All of this stomach-churning anxiety may fade away in the light of morning, but in the instant captured upon this card, fear is the only thing that matters.

When this card appears in a reading, it means that the querent is really feeling the mental and emotional burden of a difficult situation. The querent may literally be losing sleep over the issue, mental distress manifesting as nightmares. Doubts and suspicions wear away at the querent's mental fortitude. All of these worries may exist only within the querent's mind, but the main message of this card is that this is enough to cause distress. The looming specters may be nothing more than a projection of the querent's agitated mental state – but this does not make the fear any less real, and whatever issue or situation has lead to such agitation on the querent's part must be addressed before he or she can once again rest easily.

Behind the Cards: Although the Tolkienesque resemblance was not wholly intentional, among our friends the Nine of Swords has become affectionately known as "The Ringwraith Card."

Ten of Swords: *Tragedy*

Image: A lone figure in a red cloak stands on the edge of a wind-swept lake. A funeral barque burns upon the waters. In the foreground, ten swords are thrust among the high grass lining the shore. In the distance, the light of dusk or dawn kisses the horizon.

Meaning: *Tragedy.* The darkest hour before the dawn. All options have been exhausted, leaving no choice but to accept and let go. Being isolated in one's thoughts, beliefs, and/or ideologies. A loss of everything one has valued coupled with a need to move on.

Reversed: Survival against all odds. The courage to get back up, even after being sorely defeated. Suffering and/or loss engenders mental fortitude. Surviving the crucible. Ordeal path work. Shamanic death and rebirth.

Interpretation: The warrior whose experiences thread throughout the suit of Swords returns for a final curtain call. Here in the Ten, he appears as a lone figure standing on the shore of a lake in the last hours of the night. A funeral barque launches into the waters, its pyre already burning. Ten swords, representing the fallen, are thrust into the high grass of the foreground. The figure is dwarfed by the scene – lake and trees and the sky beyond – giving us a sense of how small and ineffectual he feels in the enormity of his grief. Head down, he huddles against the wind, his crimson cloak blowing about him. He has stood witness to each step of this conflict, from the first duel between brothers to this moment at the end of war, when all other combatants have fallen. There is a sense of the desperate courage in this gloomy scene: *"I alone have lived to tell the tale."* Yet, as dark and despondent as this moment is, there is nevertheless a promise of hope. First of all, there *is* a survivor to the conflict, and implicit within his survival is the notion that at least one soul has seen the cost of war and learned the lessons necessary so that future tragedies may be avoided. The harsh winter that has served as the setting for most of the Swords suit has broken: the feathery leaves that adorn the trees denote early spring. And finally, far over the waters of the lake, the first pale light of dawn is breaking. As one thing ends, something new is beginning. The Ten of Swords is a conclusion, and a definitive one, to the cycle of experience represented by the suit. It is a suit of harsh lessons, but once one has endured them, there is a chance to move in a different direction. Within the myth of the Watcher Angels, this chance for renewal is significant: the sons of the Watchers are turned against one another, but once the chaos of battle concludes, a new age for fledgling humanity begins.

The Ten of Swords is a challenging card when it comes into a reading. It is one of the darker cards within the cycle of the Tarot, and its overall message is one of endings. Generally, the card emerges to denote a difficult time in the querent's life, but the good news is that the card represents the conclusion to those difficulties. It can't get any worse. In fact, once the issues represented by this card have been endured, things can only get better.

There is a great sense of loss inherent in this card. It may represent a death among family or friends – but *always* use caution when bringing up death in any reading. More often than not, the death is figurative rather than literal, and with the Swords, it is likely to have more to do with the death of a way of thinking, the death of previous attitudes, or the death of an idea of oneself rather than the physical death of a person connected to the querent. The Swords are a very cerebral suit, and the conflicts, betrayals, and endings thus represented more often play out in the theater of the mind – although for some people, this makes them harder to bear. Enduring the circumstances of this card with an eye toward survival is the best possible approach: endings are harsh, but they are also necessary. If nothing else, the querent should try to learn from the experience so that the same mistakes are not repeated again.

Page of Swords: *The Mediator*

Image: A young woman wearing a light breastplate crouches near a standard. She is watchful, but at rest for the moment. Her unsheathed sword lies on the ground before her. A river traverses the distance.

Meaning: *The Mediator.* Someone who serves as a messenger, diplomat, or spy. A person with a logical and detail-oriented mind who may also be calculating. An individual who seeks to speak to both sides of an issue or debate with an eye toward resolution or triumph.

Reversed: Someone who is a gossip, with changeable loyalties. A cunning individual, mentally evasive. A sharp mind, but one that distorts or twists messages, often with an ulterior motive.

Interpretation: Our Page of Swords is dressed for battle, but her armor is light, implying someone who needs to be swift and maneuverable: she is a scout. She pauses by a standard, looking intently to one side. Her sword rests on the ground before her, but it is clear from her posture that she is ready at any moment to grab it and dart off. In the way that she gazes to one side of the card, she seems to be observing something that we cannot yet see. This quality of observation, as well as her readiness and maneuverability are hallmarks of this card.

The page of Swords is someone who possesses a quick mind and keen observational skills. This Page often notices things that others do not, and he or she is inclined to communicate those observations, usually with an eye toward enriching others with the information. Often involved in carrying messages and disseminating ideas, the Page of Swords also has some control over how the message is presented – and he or she understands the value of this control. When cast in a good light, this is a useful skill for the querent. It means that the Page of Swords is someone who respects that most wars are not won through strength of arms alone, but also through ideas and through words. This is a person who manages the message as much as he or she passes it along. Some might call this spin-doctoring, and sometimes it is. The Page of Swords always has an idea in mind that influences what information – and how much of that information – he or she shares with each individual person or group. When the Page of Swords appears in a negative light, this isn't a beneficial quality for everyone involved. Rather, the Page of Swords (especially when this card comes up reversed) can adopt the role not only of an informant but also of a gossip. In this case, the observations of this quick-minded Page are made for his or her benefit (or amusement!) alone, and information is passed along either indiscreetly or with an intentional goal of sowing confusion, discord, and/or misunderstandings. Cunning and manipulation become a part of the information game.

Given the nature of the Swords as a suit, the information itself almost always is something that could lead to conflicts if shared indiscreetly: intellectual property; personal details; trade secrets, and similar ideas of value. Not everyone around the Page of Swords may realize the full import of the information being shared, but it has certainly caught the Page's attention. The Page of Swords has an uncanny knack for catching details that might sail past the observation of others, giving this person an edge in any situation where knowledge is power. If the Page of Swords emerges as an aspect of the querent him or herself, the card may be a reminder to guard information a little more carefully, or to think a situation all the way through before opting to share a juicy tidbit with another.

Behind the Cards: The model for this card is our friend Rez, another member of House Kheperu. She has a passion for working on race cars and must be nimble in both mind and body when repairing them with her pit crew on the track.

Knight of Swords: *The Philosopher*

Image: A man with intense and focused features stands with a massive book open in one hand. His other hand rests on the pommel of his sword, which is sheathed.

Meaning: *The Philosopher.* A warrior whose battleground is the mind and/or the realm of words. Courageous and clever, with the potential to be overbearing. A fierce intellect that may be divorced from emotion or the practical application of ideals.

Reversed: Secretive and plotting, he (or she) rarely engages with others except to start a fight. Confrontational and argumentative. A violent streak, often cruel.

Interpretation: A conceptual revolutionary and an intellectual provocateur, the Knight of Swords is someone who challenges others to change the way they think. He (or she) is an intense individual with a sharp and probing mind, who is always seeking and sharing new ideas. Where the Page of Swords merely communicates information (sometimes putting a personal spin on it), the Knight of Swords innovates on information, sometimes pushing the boundaries beyond what others might accept – or find comfortable. He is a deep thinker and possibly a radical, intellectually, politically, or otherwise. In our card, he carries his sword sheathed and his real focus is his book, signifying how much of this knight's action takes place on the battlefield of the mind. He pauses to look up from the massive tome, clearly ruminating on the contents. This Knight is not content to take information at face value or to let ideas simply stagnate. He pushes for everyone around him to think as deeply about things as he himself does. The ideas he presents and the questions he raises may

233

not always be welcome among those around him, but they always have the effect of making others consider their meaning.

When the Knight of Swords comes up in a reading, the querent should brace for a change. This figure enters the querent's life swiftly and with the intensity of a hurricane. He wields his fierce intellect like a weapon, analyzing concepts that others are content to ignore, challenging assumptions, and introducing explosive new ideas into other peoples' lives. His work can sometimes be disruptive and it's not always appreciated – but that doesn't mean it lacks value. The Knight of Swords pushes the boundaries of the mind, expanding the vision of others and pointing out intellectual blindspots to which they've grown complacent. Throughout this process, he is constantly learning himself, which means that he is also constantly revising and elaborating upon his own points of view – and is happy to share the details of this process with anyone willing to listen.

Although the Knight of Swords may manifest as a teacher, he is much more likely to be a student, co-worker, or new friend. He is that radical coffee-house philosopher we've all encountered, someone who is always eager to strike up a conversation and who spends the next three hours expounding upon the state of the world and why everything could be improved – and he's got a theory as to how this can best be done. When he's coming from the querent's past, the Knight of Swords represents an influential thinker who changed the querent's ideas, attitudes, or understanding of a key topic pertinent to the reading. As someone coming into the querent's life now or in the near future, the person represented by the Knight of Swords is going to challenge what the querent thinks – and he or she will not likely be content until something has been added, innovated, or changed.

Queen of Swords: *The Strategist*

Image: A proud and fierce woman stands with her hands resting upon her unsheathed sword. The background of the card is empty, save for a play of light and shadow.

Meaning: *The Strategist.* Someone who relies on patience, cunning, and superior intellect. Professional, organized, driven. Keenly perceptive, she swiftly interprets and communicates ideas, enacting plans with confidence. She sometimes makes choices without consideration or value for their emotional impact.

Reversed: Cold, severe, and calculating, she has a harsh streak and is often cruel. Emotionally detached, she uses words to both manipulate and deceive.

Interpretation: Our Queen of Swords stands, stately and severe. Her gaze is distant, turned within. She appears in an empty expanse colored predominantly in shades of gray. In this, she echoes gray-eyed Athena, conceived as thought and living within the expanse of her father's own mind. She is a lady of ideas before she is a lady of action, and as a Queen, her role is to encourage intellectual capacities in others, guiding them to a greater realization of their own mental faculties.

I have always thought of Lady Macbeth when working with the Queen of Swords. She is the ultimate strategist, conceiving the plot to kill the king and place her husband on the throne. She not only develops the details, but she is there every step of the way with Macbeth, urging him to take the thought into action. Of course, in Shakespeare's play, she is undone by her thoughts as well, a hazard for any who live so completely in their minds.

Our Queen of Swords may not plan out the murder of a king, but she is nevertheless a cold and calculating individual. Sharp-witted and keenly insightful, there is rarely a detail that escapes her notice. Even when she seems to be withdrawn or removed from a situation, she is paying attention, gathering information as a warleader might gather munitions for a coming battle. The Queen of Swords is a person (male or female) who likes to be prepared, and who likes to plan things out well ahead of time. She approaches life like a game of chess and is always planning five or six moves ahead.

To others, she may be seen as a plotter or a schemer – and this is certainly true. Her primary capacity is the development of goals and the plans for achieving them. As an ally to the querent, The Queen of Swords can be a helpful and inspiring force. Typically in some position superior to the querent, her wise council and valuable insights provide strategies for success. When she takes action, she likes to move swiftly and decisively, but she is never rash. Every choice is carefully considered, and even if her behavior may surprise those around her, she herself has been planning it out quietly and patiently for quite some time.

When she appears in a negative cast, the Queen of Swords is sly and vengeful, with a bit of a sadistic streak. She never forgets a slight and only rarely forgives them. When crossed, she does not act in the heat of the moment but instead sets her passion aside, bringing the full force of cold intellect to bear on any complaint she has against another person. This makes her effective and deadly, and if she is turned against the querent, she is a vicious enemy. The only way to succeed against the type of person represented by the Queen of Swords is to both out-think them and out-wait them – neither of which is very easy. If this card comes up in reference to the querent him or herself, it may indicate that the querent will have to draw on all of these many traits in order to succeed in the matter at hand. Depending on the reading, it may also manifest as a warning not to be overcome by the harsher qualities of this card, and to temper cold logic with a bit of heart now and then.

King of Swords: *The Judge*

Image: An aging king sits on a stone bench, clasping a sword in one hand. He wears a simple crown and a crimson cloak. One foot rests upon a sealed chest. Mountains brood in the distance above a placid lake.

Meaning: *The Judge.* A cunning observer who measures the worth of actions, ideals, and/or people and who does not hesitate to remove anything perceived as flawed or wanting. Someone who imposes his thoughts or values upon others. Can be harsh, plotting, or over-cautious.

Reversed: Stubborn and un-yielding, his judgments are unfair and motivated by a personal agenda. He is malicious and unnecessarily harsh. Biased and narrow-minded, he projects his prejudicial points of view onto others.

Interpretation: The King of Swords sits on a monolithic stone bench, his weapon unsheathed and at the ready, although for the moment, it is not actively pointed at anyone or anything. He regards the viewer with a stern look of cold command, his gaze harsh and appraising. His cloak spills about him, partially covering a large chest at his feet. He has the chest trapped under one boot, guarding it protectively. The chest represents the truth – or at least the king's view of it – and he keeps this treasure close, measuring all he comes into contact with against it.

The King of Swords is a judge, sometimes literally in the sense of his professional career. He is someone whose nature and purpose is the analysis, measurement, and estimation of people, ideas, and actions. Discerning and insightful, he sees the true worth of things and is not afraid to express these perceptions. A well-established person, often in a position of authority, his appraisals of people, situations, and ideas carry the weight of pronouncements, and he can be very influential to the querent in both good ways and bad.

The King of Swords uses his blade to separate the gold from the dross, the worthy from the unworthy, and he brings all his piercing intellect to bear upon this judgment. The results of this for the querent can depend on the circumstances as well as on the king himself. If his judgment is flawed, or he is an unjust person by nature, the King of Swords can be a very destructive individual. Harsh and narrow-minded, he imposes his point of view on others, measuring them up and finding them wanting. In this, he may be someone who is exceptionally conservative, unwilling or unable to entertain a new perspective. He may also be prejudiced against those who do not measure up to his ideal, and this can manifest literally as prejudice against people of a certain race, religion, or identity group. He may also be so sure of his own perspective that he feels no need to further investigate the details of a situation, and once he arrives at his judgment, he is unwilling to change it.

But the King of Swords doesn't have to be all bad. He may represent an unyielding authority against which the querent find him or herself opposed, but he can also be someone who directs the querent to a better assessment of his or her own ideas, actions, and/or abilities. A more flexible and expansive King of Swords is willing to at least consider the views of others. In this case, his judgments can be beneficial and productive. He helps to point out flaws and shortcomings not to damn people for their failures but in an effort to correct problems. This is the ideal role of the King of Swords, and it is the ideal use of the judgmental qualities embodied by the card: to perceive, point out, and help redact in order to improve.

Behind the Cards: The model for this card is Jason, House Kheperu's Warrior Caste Second. He also appears on Trump XX, Judgment, and in this sense is both the "big" judge and the "little" judge in the deck.

Tarot Part VII b:

Extended Interpretations

The Major Arcana

"It matters not how strait the gate,
How charged with punishments the scroll:
I am the master of my fate.
I am the captain of my soul."

--"Invictus," William Ernest Henley

0. The Fool: *Shemyaza*

I Enoch 6:3 *"And Shemyaza, who was their leader…"*

Image: An angel, naked, hugs himself – either in regret or in pain – after sacrificing his wings. A lone, white feather drifts down, a poignant reminder of this choice. The background is replete with verdant shadows – green for newness or the realm of flesh.

Meaning: The start of the journey; taking the leap. The loss or sacrifice of innocence for a deeper experience of the world. Blind faith. Child-like wonder combined with child-like trust. The one who dares take action regardless of the consequences. May indicate a lack of foresight. Warns that an impending action or decision will change everything.

Reversed: The disregard for consequence is dangerous to self and others. The choice is frivolous, made for shallow reasons. Indiscretion. Also can suggest a failure to jump at opportunities, often due to fear. Holding oneself back unnecessarily.

The Fool as Shemyaza: Identified as the chief of the Watchers, Shemyaza is the one who instigates their descent to Mount Hermon. Here, he urges that they all swear to commit themselves to their proposed endeavor of joining themselves to the daughters of men. Shemyaza is many things – a lover, a leader, and a powerful magician – but where he distinguishes himself most is in his willingness to take the leap.

Interpretation: The Fool is a card of action. As the first card in the cycle of the Major Arcana, The Fool lights the spark that sets off the entire chain of events that takes us through the challenges, revelations, and transformations expressed by the twenty-two Tarot Trumps. Some renderings of The Fool show us the moment *just prior* to the action. These versions of The Fool can feel like a moment of suspended animation: the traveler poised just on the edge of revelation, one foot on solid ground, the other foot caught in mid-step. This is the moment that begins every journey, every quest that leads from here, to there, and back again: it is literally the first step. Seeing The Fool frozen in their process, just before the plunge over the edge of the cliff can allow us to consider all the implications of taking that first step, of making the decision to act, to take the leap.

The Fool in the Watcher Angel Tarot shifts the focus somewhat. Our Fool is not caught in the moment immediately preceding the decision to jump. Instead, we see him in the moment immediately after the fall. We still get to see this process frozen in time: the decision to act, to become something else, to leap from the sanctuary of heaven to the uncertainties of a life on earth. The primary difference between our Fool and more traditional renderings of the first of the Tarot Trumps is the implication of sacrifice. The most popular images of The Fool show him stepping off a cliff, blithely unaware of the danger he's in, with a little dog seeking to give warning. We can imagine this version of The Fool picking himself up from the bottom of the cliff a few moments later with a shame-faced "oops." But I think this implication that his initial leap is an accident undermines a great deal of power in The Fool. Revisioning the card even in traditional representations, can we definitively say that The Fool is ignorant of the cliff yawning before him – or does he simply not care? Maybe The Fool is not looking where he is leaping – or maybe he has decided that, if his steps *must* take him off a cliff, he'd rather not look too hard at that first drop. Otherwise, he'd lose his nerve and, in losing his nerve, he also loses everything he might learn from this new experience.

And that is the message of Shemyaza, The Fool in the Watcher Angel Tarot. We don't see Shemyaza in the moments before he makes his fatal decision. We see him in the moment immediately afterward, no longer perched on the edge of the cliff, but having fallen, at least figuratively speaking. As a Watcher Angel, that "fall"

– the decision to leave the safety of heaven for a taste of the mortal world – is represented by a sacrifice of wings. Bloody wounds gape on Shemyaza's back as a testament to the change. A lone, white feather drifts to the ground (and it is no coincidence that this feather is reminiscent of an ostrich plume, the feather of the Egyptian goddess Ma'at, weighed on the sacred scales against a mortal's heart to learn the true measure of his or her actions).

The single feather reminds us what those wounds imply, and what has been given up in order to pursue their new part of his experience. And, while we see no obvious implement for severing the wings, every implication is that it was Shemyaza himself who accomplished the deed. His back is to the viewer in the card, and he hugs himself in a mixture of regret and pain. This is no blithely ignorant Fool. Rather, this Fool is all about the loss of innocence. We know this has cost him. And yet, here he his, embarking on an earthly journey. He has chosen to act regardless of the cost or other consequences. Maybe such a bold decision is impetuous, even foolhardy. But the fact remains that without this action, we have no beginning to our story. To strike out on one's own, to learn, to change, to experience the world, one must become The Fool. The Fool swallows fear and hesitation and what might otherwise be good sense to cut himself loose, and dare to leap away into the unknown, the unforeseen, and the uncertain. And everything else follows that first audacious jump.

I. The Magician: Armaros

I Enoch 8:3: *"Armaros taught the resolving of enchantments..."*

Image: An angel sits in a posture of meditation. A pentacle levitates above his upturned palm. Around him are other symbols of the suits: a cup, a sword, and a wand. His gaze seems a challenge to the viewer. A symbol of eternity hangs just above his head.

Meaning: A master of appearances and a manipulator of reality. Someone who has the tools but not necessarily wisdom to use them. Magick as the act of bringing the unrealized into being – and the inevitable imperfections and illusions that must inevitably occur when the infinite is made finite. Sophomoric comprehension. A shaper. A dreamer. Someone who can open the door to something amazing but may not have the capacity to follow all the way through.

Reversed: A lack of skill or foresight scuttles plans. Power is used selfishly or irresponsibly, with dangerous results. Fumbling. Fakery. A con-artist who manipulates and misleads.

The Magician as Armaros: In the Charles translation of the *Book of Enoch,* Armaros (called *Pharmarus* in Syncellus) is named immediately after Shemyaza in Chapter 8:3. His powers are presented in counterpoint to the leader of the Watchers. Where Shemyaza teaches enchantments, Armaros teaches the resolving or "loosening" of enchantments. The terminology is important, because it implies that Armaros had the ability to undo binding spells, a significant form of magick used in throughout ancient world. In the

Nickelsburg translation of *I Enoch*, the wording is expanded, giving us a much greater sense of Armaros' significance: *"Shemyaza taught spells ... [Armaros] taught sorcery for the loosing of spells and magic and skill."* His name appears here as *Hermani,* closely echoing Hermes. This cinched his association with The Magician in our deck.

Interpretation: In the 18th century Marseille Tarot, the Magician appears as *Le Bateleur.* This translates to "the Juggler," implying that there is a good deal of sleight of hand involved in his art. Implicit in his identity of Juggler is the threat of chicanery – magickal fakery perpetrated for effect rather than true magick worked with an enlightened cause. As the interpretation of Tarot imagery has evolved over the years, particularly through the influence of nineteenth century occultists like members of the Golden Dawn, this implication of fakery has faded somewhat from the Magician. Instead of a charlatan seeking to mislead our eyes with his tools and tricks, we see someone in the process of learning real magick – and like many beginners, he is in effect tricking himself into believing that his tools *are* his art, rather than objects of focus harnessed to direct his own Will. True magick comes from within and is reliant upon no items. In the real world, only a fledgling magician would ever need a wand to channel his power.

With all this in mind, the Magician can be seen as the "fake it till you make it" card. Where the Fool has taken the leap, the Magician has gone through the door encountered in the darkness below and now stands just inside the threshold. He is in the process of the journey, and he is beginning to learn that there is more to the world – and to himself – than previously understood. Like many people who find themselves in the midst of such an Awakening, the Magician makes the mistake of getting lost in the magick. Suddenly, *everything* is about magick, its influence on people and its manifestations in the world. In keeping with his sophomoric view of his new, magickal Universe, the Magician also makes the mistake of assuming that he is in complete control. Or, when he is not, he is too proud to admit it or ever let it show.

That pride is a key to understanding the essence of the trickster that is also present in the Magician card. There is simultaneously magick *and* trickery in the Magician's work. He uses his tools and flashy appearances (in our deck, he's adopted the posture of a Hindu Yogin, perhaps disingenuously, given his blonde hair and pale skin) to convince not only his audience but also himself of his power. As any practitioner of magick knows, there is a certain amount of mental prestidigitation involved in working magick: visualizations, neural linguistic programming, auto-suggestion, and so forth – and all of these are used to essentially trick the mind out of its own disbelief. Symbols, items, personal mantras: each can be used to better tap into and harness one's magickal Will. The danger for the Magician (as well as for his audience) is to lose perspective about the real nature of these tools and to begin mistaking the gestures, objects, and general flash and dazzle for the magick itself. In readings, this card indicates a beginning with great potential for power and mastery – but for whatever or whomever The Magician represents, there is a lot of room to grow.

II. The High Priestess: Kasbiel

I Enoch 69:13: *"And this is the task of Kasbiel, the chief of the oath which he showed to the holy ones…"*

Image: A priestess stands at the curtain leading into the inner sanctum. Both she and an altar are partially visible beyond the curtain. Seductively, she beckons the viewer to approach the guarded, interior space.

Meaning: The anima. Keeper of mysteries and hidden truths. Gnosis. Occult knowledge revealed. Inspiration and intuition of a spiritual or psychic variety. An initiatory experience. Esoteric and interior revelation. A mystical encounter with the ineffable.

Reversed: The initiation leads to irrational thoughts and behavior. The mind is clouded. Someone promises to reveal mysteries, but the knowledge is superficial. Sense, reason, and/or inner vision become occluded. Someone who reveals only to obtain/retain power or to gain control.

The High Priestess as Kasbiel: Kasbiel appears in a later restatement of the Watchers and their magickal functions that appears in chapter 69 of the *Book of Enoch.* This is a curious passage, almost certainly composed after the more familiar I Enoch 6-9 then later integrated into the larger text. It is garbled in places and the translation is uncertain, but in the Charles edition, Kasbiel is described as "the chief of the oath which he showed to the holy ones when he dwelt high above in glory…" (*I Enoch* 69:13, Charles; Nickelsburg offers a very different reading of this entire section). In verse 14, we learn that this "oath" is actually the secret or hidden name, almost certainly the Ineffable Name of God, codified in later magick as the Tetragrammaton. In a passage that echoes the Jewish legend of the Star Maiden, Kasbiel convinces the archangel Michael to reveal this name "The he might enunciate it in the oath so that those might quake before that name and oath who revealed all that was in secret to the children of men." This is, of course, a reference to the Watchers. We have taken the liberty of changing Kasbiel's gender for the High Priestess. *I Enoch* assigns all of the Watchers masculine pronouns, a Jewish default for angels in general, regardless of whether or not they are perceived as having a true physical gender. As a keeper of secrets among the Watchers, particularly the secret name of God, Kasbiel is a perfect choice for the High Priestess.

Interpretation: In the early examples of Tarot cards, such as the Tarot of Marseille, the card we know as the High Priestess appears instead as *La Papess,* a female pope. This may be a reference to the legend of Pope Joan, a woman who was thought to have ascended to the Throne of Peter in the Middle Ages. Though there is no historical evidence for an actual Pope Joan (if she ever really existed, do you think the Vatican would keep records of something like that lying around?), she was nevertheless a controversial figure. Rather than deal with such controversy, some decks switched out the Papess, replacing her with a variety of figures, from the goddess Juno to the character of the Spanish Captain from the *Commedia dell'arte.* French occultist Court de Gébelin established the tradition of renaming this card the High Priestess, a change in character that altered the meaning of the card significantly. As *La Papess,* the card held implications of female power subverting traditional roles of male authority. As the High Priestess, instead of a rebel, she becomes the initiatrix, gaining associations with the Gnostic Sophia and the Jewish Miriam. Waite strongly evokes this sense of the Miriam, depicting her as the keeper of the Torah.

As our associations with the Tarot have continued to evolve, the High Priestess has regained a little of her subversive character. Standing in counterpoint to the High Priest (once the Pope card and thus representative of worldly religious authority), the High Priestess has come to represent the interior path to mystical knowledge gained through direct experience and inspiration. This stands in opposition to the dogmatic revelation of religious practice as dictated by an authority figure. Thus, the High Priestess and the High Priest represent two different paths to the same revelation: spirituality versus religion, direct personal gnosis versus mediated (and thus controlled) religious experience. Neither one is strictly superior to the other: they are point and counterpoint, embodying approaches that are effective for some and destructive for others.

The appeal – and the danger – of the High Priestess is that her approach involves total immersion in the mysteries, often unstructured and unmediated. Within the story of the Watchers, she represents the invitation to learn forbidden knowledge – which may possibly expose us to forces or ideas for which we are unprepared. Such revelation can be electrifying, but it can also be overwhelming. In our card, she beckons for us to enter the inner sanctum and view the holy of holies with our own eyes. Parting the curtain, she allows some of the light of this revelation to spill forth enticingly. There is almost a sense of seduction in her posture, but it is a seduction inviting us to experience spiritual rather than physical ecstasy.

Such an intense mystical experience is not for everyone: it can eclipse our connection to the physical world, overwhelming the senses. It is the path of the non-rational, and it requires a great deal of courage and focus to successfully navigate. As Initiatrix, the High Priestess serves to open the door, but when it comes to the mysteries that lie beyond, she is but a guide. The querent presented with this card should keep in mind the amount of focus, dedication, and hard work that must be applied to properly interpret and contextualize the resulting experience in order to bring it back out of the inner sanctum and make it functional as part of one's life within the practical, everyday world.

III. The Empress: Hananel

I Enoch 7:7: "And these are the names of their chiefs ... Hananel, thirteenth to [Shemyaza]..."

Image: A matronly angel sits presenting a rose to the child beside her. One hand is curled about the child's waist in a gesture both protective and possessive. The colors of the card are warm and rich with red and rust tones.

Meaning: The mother as creatrix and guardian. The fertile force which gives life and can either nurture it or stunt its growth. The incubation of forms, ideas, or causes. Fecundity in people, animals, or the earth. Love manifested as protectiveness or, negatively, as possessiveness.

Reversed: The mother in her shadow-aspect as devourer. The nurturing necessary to flourish is lacking or withheld intentionally. The creative power is closed off or somehow inhibited. Love turns to control and/or manipulation.

The Empress as Hananel: Hananel, also spelled Ananel, is one of those Watchers whose name is also associated with a heavenly angel. In Davidson's *Dictionary of Angels,* the name of this angel is presented as meaning "graciously given of God." Selecting a Watcher for the Empress card presented a challenge because technically all of the Watchers are male. Yet the Empress is all about feminine energy – especially in her capacity as creatrix and mother. It was discovering the further meaning of "grace" or "gifts of grace" implicit in the name that ultimately swayed my choice. Accordingly, our Empress is passing the gifts of her power along to an inarguably female child in the form of the budding rose.

Interpretation: Where the High Priestess and the High Priest represent diametrical approaches to religious and/or spiritual experience, the Empress and the Emperor cards represent two diametric expressions of worldly and/or secular authority. In their most basic sense, the Empress and the Emperor are iconic representations of Mother and Father. The two cards embody all the worldly authority and approaches to love (as well as discipline) which these archetypes represent.

In her identity as Mother, the Empress is much more than simply a parent. She is, in many ways, an embodiment of Mother Earth herself. She is the source of riches, fertility, and a stable worldly foundation upon which to grow. In our deck, she is midwife to the Watchers, helping to bring the gift of children into the world and then serving to nurture those children as they grow. She holds the secret to successfully pairing spirit with flesh, and bringing this productively into the world. As the card shows us, she passes the gift of a rose to her daughter (the models for the card are real-life mother and child), symbolizing the earthly riches and experiences which she promises as a legacy. However, the rose depicted is merely a bud – in this, the Empress is passing along the *potential* for material splendor, with the implication that there is still some participation required in helping it to bloom.

With its implications of harvest, fertility, and the riches of earth, the Empress card is often portrayed in fields of green or gold. Our Empress card, however, is rich in rusty hues – reds, ochres, and burgundies. Sanguine colors, they echo not the rolling green of fertile fields but the warm and nurturing interior spaces of the flesh. Our Empress is enthroned in a space evocative of the womb and the colors were consciously chosen to represent the sense of being surrounded on all sides by a mother's love. She is at the very heart of the Watchers' aspiration to join with the earthly realm, and the knowledge she keeps is how to successfully live in the world.

Behind the Cards: The figures depicted in this card are real-life mother and daughter. The Empress is embodied by Jane Pierce, a member of House Kheperu's Priest Caste and long-time magickal worker.

IV. The Emperor: Azazel

I Enoch 8:1: *"And Azazel taught men to make swords ..."*

Image: A stern-faced warrior or general gazes out of the card, his hands folded across his chest and his feet positioned in a solid stance. He is dressed in armor and a cloak reminiscent of imperial Rome. The background of the card moves from dark to light, and the ethereal wings of the figure seem to be the source of light revealing structure, sense, and form in the darkness.

Meaning: The father as autocrat and disciplinarian. Government. Secular authority. Conquest, expansion, action, and ambition. The potentially domineering force that provides structure and stability in society. A person, institution, or ideology that seeks to quell chaos, sometimes at the cost of freedom.

Reversed: Misuse of authority. Tyranny. Discipline and structure that sacrifice liberty and individuality. Oppressive and/or dictatorial regimes. A vision of order that fails to allow for personal expression, diversity, or growth.

The Emperor as Azazel: Azazel was one of the easiest Watchers to place within the Trumps of the Major Arcana. Although later Jewish legends depict Azazel as a corruptor and a reprobate (in what Reeves identifies as the Adamic template, in contrast to the Enochic template), within the *Book of Enoch*, he is a civilizing, if bellicose, authority. It is through his teachings that mortals learn the arts of metallurgy and smithing, for he "taught men to make swords, and knives, and shields, and breastplates, and made known to them the metals of the earth and the art of working them…" (*I Enoch* 8:1). Interestingly, Azazel does not merely reveal the craft (and presumably the use) of all the tools of war. He is also concerned with the decorative applications of precious gems and metals, teaching how to fashion "bracelets, and ornaments, and the use of antimony, and the beautifying of the eyelids, and all kinds of costly stones and all coloring tinctures." Simultaneously, he shows how to conquer the earth and how to enjoy its spoils. Azazel as a civilizing force among humanity, guiding mortals toward empire-building and worldly luxury makes him the de facto choice for the Emperor.

Interpretation: In the myth of the Watchers, Shemyaza and Azazel both emerge as leaders. Shemyaza, the Fool, is the head of the Watcher Angels, and it is at his instigation that they choose as a unit to "jump" into the experience of the mortal world. Once in this world, Azazel also emerges as a leader. Where Shemyaza is the visionary, Azazel commits himself to more practical concerns, working to make the Watchers' existence in the mortal realm both productive and functional. In the *Book of Enoch,* Shemyaza is criticized for binding spiritual beings to the world of flesh. Azazel, on the other hand, is criticized for propagating dangerous knowledge. He is a civilizing force in the Watchers' world, raising and leading armies, expanding territories, building empires, and succeeding in his earthly endeavors by any means necessary. As such, he represents the concepts of leadership, worldly authority, dominance, imperial expansion, and practical or pragmatic stability. Shemyaza may have the vision, but it is Azazel that applies that vision to reality, building and even bending the material world to meet the idealized form.

The Emperor, as the active embodiment of Father as Autocrat, is a scion of structure, stability, and authority. Connected astrologically to Mars, this martial current is expressed in the armor so reminiscent of the Roman Empire. In the Western world, few civilizations better embody the notion of order, militaristic expansion, and imperialism – and all of these come together in the figure of the Emperor. The character of the Emperor is not the nicest or most subtle force that one can encounter, but he is a force that gets things done. Through strength of will or strength of arms, he imposes order upon chaos, structure onto that which is weak and undisciplined. And he rarely takes "no" for an answer. When the force represented by the Emperor is working for the querent, he is a powerful ally and the querent has a great deal of energy and power that can be harnessed – so long as he or she is willing to follow the rules. When the Emperor is a force opposed to the querent, he is a devastating enemy, imposing his version of order, structure, and worldly rule onto everything, often without regard to freedom or individual expression, facts which can lead his stability to stifle, his structure to potentially crumble beneath its own weight.

Behind the Cards: Posing for The Emperor is Jason Crutchfield, the Warrior Caste Elder of House Kheperu. In both his magickal and his mundane identities, he is a living archetype of this card.

V. The High Priest: Ramiel

I *Enoch* 6:7: *"...Ramiel, sixth to Shemyaza..."*

Image: A religious leader, crowned with golden laurels and bearing a staff of authority reclines upon a throne. The scroll of a decree is unrolled almost carelessly upon the figure's lap, but its pages are empty. A supplicant kneels worshipfully at the figure's feet, head bowed. A starburst of light in the space above the figure represents the divine authority of which the priest is the earthly representative.

Meaning: A mediator between the earthly and the divine. The interpretation and transmission of religious and/or spiritual revelation. The structuring of mystical truths into words and doctrines, removing or denying the need for direct personal experience. Religious authorities and institutions and the power they wield over the masses.

Reversed: Unorthodox or heretical beliefs. Someone who claims the title of an established belief system, but freely (and often erroneously) reinterprets this. Cherry-picking the teachings of an established religion to forward personal agendas or beliefs. A delusional, fanatical, or otherwise damaging use of religion.

The High Priest as Ramiel: The *Book of Enoch* doesn't give us much on Ramiel. He appears in the list of the "chiefs of tens" (and in many nineteenth century translations, he is accidentally combined with Urakiba/Arakiba into one run-on name). What may be a variation of his name (spelled *Rûmjâl*) appears in the reiteration of the "chiefs of tens" passage in Chapter 69, but he is absent from either of the "teachings" passages. From these slight entries, we know nothing of his powers or areas of expertise. However, Ramiel appears in another piece of Apocalyptic literature. This is the *Apocalypse of Baruch,* or more precisely 2 *Baruch*, a Syriac Jewish text written around the first century of the Common Era.* In 2 *Baruch* 55:3, we meet "the angel Ramiel who presides over true visions." (Ramiel is presented here as a heavenly angel working in the familiar capacity as a messenger of the divine, but many of the Watchers appear to shift allegiances in this manner: Sariel, the Watcher who taught the courses of the Moon, is also named as an archangel, working alongside Michael, in the Nickelsburg translation of *1 Enoch.*) Ramiel as an *interpreter* of visions is the key for his association with our High Priest. Baruch has a vision, which he believes is inspired by God. Ramiel appears as a mediator between the earthly and the divine, dictating to Baruch what the dream-vision is really supposed to mean. The angel doesn't carry a message directly from the divine and pass it along unaltered to Baurch; he offers his take on it, thereby imposing at least a little of his own will and meaning upon the vision. This notion of filtering the divine *and then* passing the revelation along rests at the heart of our High Priest.

Interpretation: The first thing that will stand out about our High Priest is the fact that the religious leader depicted in the card is not a man, but a woman. Traditionally, the first four cards after The Fool represent masculine and feminine dyads: Empress and Emperor, High Priestess and High Priest. In revisioning the cards, one thing we felt driven to question were stereotypical gender roles. The Empress and Emperor, with their connections to the archetypes of Mother and Father, have distinct feminine and masculine characters, and so these were retained. But the High Priestess and High Priest represent issues less concerned with gender and more concerned with approaches to religious (or spiritual) revelation. And this, we felt, had no reason to be tied to male or female bodies. It doesn't matter if the High Priest is male, female, or otherwise: that person is merely filling a role, and the real message is found in the role itself.

* p. 512 *The Apocrypha and Pseudepigrapha in English,* vol. 2, edited by R. H. Charles, Clarendon Press, 1913

In many ancient cultures, the High Priest of a religion was the mouthpiece of the god. The relation between the High Priest and the deity was so close, in fact, that it was not uncommon for the High Priest to be viewed not only as the god's representative in the earthly realm, but also as the god's incarnation on earth. Essentially, the High Priest *was* the god, speaking for the god and dictating the god's will and desire to the people. Beliefs like this underscored the authority of Egypt's god-kings the Pharaohs and ultimately led to the Medieval notion of Divine Right: a king ruled because God had chosen him to do so. As the vessel of divine will, only the High Priest was in a position to properly interpret the meaning of religious inspiration, and this is the real key to the High Priest as a Tarot card. The High Priest represents not only the position of an earthly mediator between the worldly and the divine but also the need, function, and inevitable results of such mediation. This card represents organized religion and everything it brings into the world, both good and bad. The meaning and tenor of the card will be determined not only by the other cards around it, but also by the querent's own experiences and attitudes regarding religious structure.

Behind the Cards: Jackie originally painted the High Priest as female because she assumed from the robes of images of the Hierophant that the figure was a woman. I was unaware of this at the time and thought her reinterpretation of the figure was a brilliant stroke of genius. Because I wanted to present the High Priest as a function independent of gender, we decided to keep Jackie's image.

VI. The Lovers: Na'amah

Legends of the Jews p. 150: *"Na'amah, the lovely sister of Tubal-Cain, lead the angels astray with her beauty..."*

Image: A voluptuous and dusky-skinned mortal woman tosses her hair back and stretches her naked body invitingly, openly seducing the angel who stands above her.

Meaning: Decisions. Temptation. Dualities and polarities. The simultaneous tension and attraction of opposites. The path of pleasure versus the path of wisdom. The forces released when two disparate things come together or fall apart.

Reversed: Outside forces interfere with or disrupt the balance. Being pulled off balance, particularly by emotion or desire. A schism between two people where one seeks to harm or subjugate the other. Love turns to hate, passion to obsession.

The Lovers as Na'amah: In the *Book of Enoch* itself, the lovers and wives of the Watchers remain unnamed. They are merely mentioned in reference to the Watchers' admiration and desire, and the overall implication is that the Watchers themselves took the first steps toward seducing and ultimately mating with these beautiful "daughters of men." However, in later Jewish legend, the women of the earth are not merely passive players in the unfolding drama of the Watchers. We have already touched upon the story of the pious star-maiden, Istahar, but her tale is often presented as a counterpoint to the story of Na'amah. Sister of Tubal-cain and thus the daughter of Cain himself, we learn in Ginzberg's *Legends of the Jews* that, "Naamah, 'the lovely,' earned her name from the sweet sounds which she drew from her cymbals when she called the worshippers to pay homage to idols" (Ginzberg, p. 118). As a daughter of Cain, she is a devoted Cainite, the branch of humanity described in the same work as being "shameless" and prone to "bestial indulgences" such as "walking abroad naked" and having sex with angels (Ginzberg, p. 151). The implication here is that the women, and Na'amah in particular, actively seduced the Watchers from what might have otherwise been a righteous path. But this is merely another tired iteration of "woman as temptress" that fails to recognize the fact that seduction is a two-way street. Na'amah may have been lovely, but her angelic lover (in *Legends of the Jews,* his name is Shamdon, likely yet another variant of Shemyaza) is hardly a non-consenting party in this arrangement. And that is the heart of The Lovers card: neither of them coerces the other. Their pairing is a partnership, consensual on both sides. As they say, it takes two to tango.

Interpretation: The Lovers, like so many Tarot cards, is not intended to be strictly literal. Just as the Death card doesn't really herald someone's physical demise, The Lovers card rarely comes up in reference to an actual romance. While the pleasures and pitfalls of a relationship may be implied, The Lovers is concerned with *any* type of relationship between two things. Broadly speaking, The Lovers addresses the issue of relating itself: how things come together, why they come together, and how they manage to balance qualities that may, in essence, oppose one another.

There is a sense of dynamic tension underscoring the character of this card. In the Rider-Waite-Smith deck, the Lovers appear to be Adam and Eve, overseen by the angel Raphael. In this, the card depicts not only the polarities (and thus the tension) of male and female, but also of heaven and earth – but the Biblical imagery lends the card a balanced and strangely beatific character. Going back to an earlier representation of The Lovers, we find that the card once had a very different image. In the Tarot of Marseille and in Oswald Wirth's Tarot based upon this (produced in 1889, a full twenty years before the publication of the RWS), the Lovers shows the central figure of a man flanked by *two* women. The angel in the sky above is rather obviously Cupid, blind-folded and with an arrow nocked. This earlier version gives us a better sense of the tension inherent in the card. The women appear to be fighting over the man in the Wirth and Marseille decks, each competing for his affections and offering a different set of charms.

The Lovers are not only about polarities, but about decisions and the amelioration of opposites. Na'amah, throwing her hair back and displaying her body before the angel Shamdon, represents one choice along the path to self-awareness. Hers is the path of pleasure, coming to know spirit through an experience of the flesh. The angel himself represents the path of wisdom, or at least its potential: knowledge and discovery through a connection to and an exploration of spirit. Na'amah reclines on the ground, connected to earth. Shamdon bends to her from above, wings spread to show his allegiance to heaven. He is pale. Her flesh is as richly colored as the earth itself. At some point, a decision must be made: come together or remain apart. Each choice has different repercussions, different challenges, and different rewards. The querent who receives this card is similarly faced with choices and the need to balance between people, forces, ideas, or institutions that seem in opposition to one another. The key may lie not in choosing one thing over the other, but in combining, reconciling, or striking a balance between the two. Na'amah may teach Shamdon all the pleasures of the flesh, but the angel also teaches her the secrets and mysteries of heaven. Whenever two people or forces come together in union, each adds something to the other. The real decision, then, is how exactly to achieve the most harmonious balance allowing each side to best express itself. This is the ideal path of The Lovers.

VII. The Chariot: Enoch

I Enoch 14:8: *"...And the winds in the vision caused me to fly and lifted me upward and bore me into heaven."*

Image: An angel with wings outspread bears a mortal figure into the heavens. In the background, soft golden light spills from between parting clouds. The earth is nowhere to be seen.

Meaning: Triumph, victory, and forward motion – specifically that achieved through the amelioration of powerful and potentially conflicting forces. Sublimation in a psychological sense. A unification after struggle that allows for increased strength, power, and/or effectiveness.

Reversed: There is a need to move forward but no strength or motivation to do so. Passions and/or ambitions get out of control. A delicate and necessary balance is upset. Defeat or failure through a mismanagement of drive. Slacking and squandering great potential due to fear, inaction, or sloth.

The Chariot as Enoch: The *Book of Enoch* begins, not with the story of the Watchers, but with a declaration about Enoch himself who saw "the vision of the Holy Ones in the heavens" (*I Enoch*, 1:2). The adventures of the Watcher Angels are compelling enough that Enoch – the real focus of the *Book of Enoch* – can become eclipsed. But Enoch's journey into the heavens and his revelation of the wonders there comprises the real meat of the book, placing *I Enoch* definitively in the genre of Apocalyptic literature. As far as marrying the Enochic mythos to the Tarot, Enoch's portion of the story completes the cycle of the Major Arcana. Where the Watchers represent heavenly forces that are only fully realized once they become involved in the world of flesh, Enoch represents the earthly spirit that strives for its fullest expression through an apotheosis of spirit. Thus, Enoch and the Watchers each represent the two primary paths to experience. Enoch makes his first direct appearance in The Chariot, caught up by an angelic guide and borne bodily into the heavens – presumably for his initial tour of the celestial hierarchies.

Interpretation: The Chariot is a card of motion, but more than that, it is a card of victory through struggle. Initial images of this card depict a triumphal chariot with a decorated hero at the reigns, displaying his success for all to see. The charioteer thus represents not only the triumphant spirit, but also the drive and the will to succeed. Later depictions of The Chariot shift the focus from the charioteer to the animals pulling the vehicle. In the Rider-Waite-Smith deck, these are not horses but sphinxes. These mythic composite animals remind the viewer that the work and triumph encoded in the card are not only physical but also mystical: the charioteer triumphs on all planes. One sphinx is black, the other white, representing the balance and control required to manage these two diametrically opposed forces while still keeping the chariot in motion. This message of success and/or progress resulting from the careful management of powerful and potentially conflicting forces finds an altogether different visual expression within our deck.

In the Watcher Angel Tarot, we see Enoch in the moment of rapture – that is, being "caught up" or "carried off" – the original meaning of the word. Clasped in the arms of an angel, Enoch is carried up to the heavens – but he's not there yet. There is a sense of the splendor and triumph inherent in The Chariot in the beatific moment of this flight: the clouds open up around them revealing a glowing light. But the angel and Enoch have not completed their journey. They are still in transit, and a delicate transit it is. Enoch, a son of earth, is not equipped to fly up to the heavens. He is not even fully dressed, clasping a coverlet around him. In keeping with most of the descriptions of his visions as they unfold within the *Book of Enoch*, the Patriarch seems to have been caught up from his bed. The majority of Enoch's visionary experiences are described as dream-visions, and dream incubation was a common method of communicating with both gods and their messengers in the ancient world from Sumeria onward. Given his unwieldy burden of one startled Patriarch, the angel has his work cut out for him trying to insure that they both safely make their passage from one world to the next (let's not even discuss the physics of flight involved for one humanoid with wings!)

In order to get Enoch from earth to the heavens, that winged humanoid has to somehow also manage the weight of a second person and hold on without dropping him. And in this, we have our expression of the two horses or sphinxes drawing the chariot. Forces of heaven and earth, Enoch and the angel must work together in order to make this flight a success rather than an unfortunate disaster. If Enoch struggles too much in his terror at the experience, if the angel falters the least in his grip, there will be no tour through heaven – Enoch will be little more than a smear on the unseen ground below. The charioteer as an external, guiding force for these two forces is removed entirely and the card focuses on the experience of motion and control itself: the forces involved in striving toward the querent's goal must be harnessed responsibly and in tandem in order to achieve success. In this, The Chariot is also the card of work in general, but also spiritual work in its broadest sense. *Yoga*, for example, means "yoke," as in the yoke connecting two oxen. The oxen are the horses are the sphinxes are the emissaries of spirit and flesh: both must work in unison for the real work to be complete.

VIII. Strength: Turiel

I Enoch 6:7: *"And these are the names of their chiefs ... Turiel, eighteenth to [Shemyaza]..."*

Image: An angel, powerfully muscled, sits submissively at the feet of an elegantly dressed woman. The angel wears cuffs on his wrists connected to a delicate silver chain held loosely in the woman's hand. She rests her other hand lightly upon his shoulder. From the angel's build, it is clear that if he stood up, he would dwarf her and should be able to easily overpower her, yet he chooses not to.

Meaning: Inner strength. Mental, spiritual, and/or emotional fortitude. Beauty conquers the beast. Love and/or lust as a power that can lay low even the fiercest warriors. True power as the ability to yield. A surrender of Self and/or ego. Negatively: manipulation.

Reversed: A fear of being dominated by one's passions, or the danger of the same. Spiritual matters eclipsed by material concerns. A failure to find one's inner strength. Mental or emotional weakness. Servitude to superficial or inconsequential matters.

Strength as Turiel: Named as one of the "chiefs of tens," Turiel's name appears in most variations of this passage. Unfortunately, like so many of the Watchers named in the *Book of Enoch*, little else is mentioned of Turiel, beyond his rank in relation to Shemyaza. No special art or science is attributed to him, or if it once was, this detail has been lost to time. However, the character of this angel is clearly expressed within his name. Turiel is from the root for "rock," implying not only stability but also strength. Rock or stone as a crafting or building material in the ancient world was one of the most lasting. Heavy and powerful, it was (and still is) excellent for foundations and could produce some of the strongest fortifications and defenses. When we say that someone is "rock-solid," we are drawing upon many of these associations. Strong, enduring, unyielding – these are all qualities tied to a being whose name means "Rock of God."

Interpretation: In his Thoth deck, Crowley changes the title of this card to "Lust." While I agree with many of the concepts behind this change, I would personally be more inclined to rename the card "Beauty" – if I felt the card absolutely had to be renamed. But Strength works just as well, so long as we keep in mind that the strength implied by the card is not the obvious physical strength possessed by the submissive angel. The real power here is the woman. She is Beauty to his Beast, and she is definitely the one in charge.

Traditional representations of this card depict a maiden conquering a lion through a gentle application of her hands to its powerful jaws. If we want to be blissfully (and perhaps naively) romantic about it, she is able to overcome this creature by the power of her purity and grace, in much the same way that a maiden was once thought able to attract a wild unicorn and get the proud creature to lay its head meekly in her lap (a Medieval fancy gorgeously illustrated in the Unicorn Tapestries). Without getting too deeply into the Freudian imagery of a beast with one long horn bending that prominent member toward a maiden's lap, let us simply say that Crowley was onto something when he reframed the card as "Lust." This is the card of "Yes, dear," and "Whatever you say, dear." It represents the impulse harbored by many of us to surrender our power (and sometimes our dignity) to something that we love. This is not necessarily a bad thing: it also contains the lesson that true power lies not in strength of arms. Removing lust from the equation entirely, how many otherwise fierce and intimidating individuals may be utterly disarmed by the antics of a cute puppy or kitten? Sometimes being vulnerable is the key to holding all the cards.

The Strength card, with all these layered meanings, is particularly relevant to the tale of the Watchers. The *Book of Enoch* doesn't say much about the "daughters of men" for whom angels fell – beyond the fact that they were fair and the Watchers lusted after them. But there is a whole side to the story hidden there in the hearts of the women. Here are Watcher Angels – sons of Heaven, so strong and powerful that any children they sire are destined to become giants and leaders among men. What strength of purpose and sense of self must their wives possess in order to stand up to these beings and ask them to take the garbage out? On the part of the Watchers, this must be a willing submission – Turiel could easily stand and snap the chains binding him (and in this, there is an echo of The Devil, which takes the implications of Strength to the extreme). Yet he sits meekly, disarmed not by the woman's physical prowess, but by her softness, by her sweet and gentle touch.

When this card comes up in a reading, the querent may relate more to the angel or more to the woman – the true message of the card will depend upon the other cards around it. As the angel, this card represents the power of learning when to bend and when to yield, although it can also caution against surrendering control too eagerly. As the woman, it shows the querent another face of the same strength: confidence can replace physical prowess, a superior position can be achieved through non-physical strengths. There are implications of dominance and submission, but the power exchange here is a positive one, supported by consent and choice.

Behind the Cards: This card is Jackie's homage to the work of Czech illustrator Alphonse Mucha, one of the artists whose work influenced her approach to the cards. The lines, costume, and lush Art Nouveau aspect of the woman depicted here are a conscious echo of Mucha's art.

IX. The Hermit: Penemuê

I Enoch 69:8: *"Penemuê [who] taught them the secrets of their wisdom and instructed mankind in writing ..."*

Image: An angel crouches in a darkened wood. With one hand, he gathers power. With his other hand, he holds a staff, its glowing tip the only reliable source of light in this remote location. Fireflies or some manner of faerie light dot the landscape, lending a mystic feel to the scene.

Meaning: The Wise Old Man who leads you back to yourself. The need to withdraw and seek within. A guide or mentor who manifests to help one navigate a dark or confusing time. Wisdom, offered or sought. Sometimes: a need for silence and/or secrecy.

Reversed: A rejection of wisdom. A refusal to learn from one's experiences. A resistance to maturity – either one's own or that of others. Fumbling blindly through a difficult path and ignoring help when it is offered – either through pride or obstinance. The guiding light is clear, but one refuses to see.

The Hermit as Penemuê: Perhaps appropriately, Penemuê was one of the inspirations for this Tarot. In my research on the Watchers, the knowledge and qualities attributed to Penemuê struck me as being a perfect representation of The Hermit. As the angel who teaches writing and "all the secrets of their wisdom," Penemuê is the first scribe (and is thus also connected to Enoch), guiding humanity not only to learn but to record their knowledge. He also teaches "the bitter and the sweet," a phrase that Andrew Collins (author of *From the Ashes of Angels,* a fascinating take on the Watchers' myth) conjectures may refer to herbalism and, specifically, poisons. However, I feel the phrase is better reflected simply as the act of differentiation. Penemuê teaches discernment, in the Biblical sense of the word – the ability to recognize signs and visions. He is the quintessential guide, not only lighting the path, but offering the tools necessary to best equip those who choose to follow.

Interpretation: The journey represented by the Trumps of the Major Arcana is a difficult one. As an exploration of our own interior landscape, the way is not always clear, and there are many obstacles along the path. When we have lost ourselves in the dark, The Hermit appears to light the way. We may not always recognize him or even trust him at first, but he is patient. He can wait. He has learned that all things come in their proper time.

The Hermit card represents wisdom – not necessarily the wisdom of the seeker, but the wisdom offered by someone who has taken the road before and learned its twists and turns the hard way. There is a lesson in humility captured in The Hermit. Anyone who is lost can keep plodding along, stumbling and flailing and making random turns until – perhaps by accident – the desired destination is achieved. But in the midst of all that confusion, it takes a certain kind of person to stop and ask for directions – because, of course, in asking for directions, you are admitting that you don't actually know the way. The Magician would stubbornly push forward, pretending to anyone who observed him that he totally knew where he was going. But we've come a long way from The Magician. At this point in the journey, we should know better. It should be obvious that superficial appearances are not as valuable as inner truths, and stopping for directions may save everyone valuable time. The Hermit understands this, and he (or she) stands by patiently, waiting for a traveler to demonstrate wisdom by seeking it from another.

There is more than a little of Diogenes and his lamp captured in the figure of The Hermit. This Greek philosopher was said to go about in broad daylight with a lighted lamp. When asked about this curious behavior, he said simply that he was searching for "an honest man." The Hermit holds his lamp (or glowing staff) up in the darkness in a similar search: he is seeking people honest enough with themselves to admit that they need this to help light their way.

X. The Wheel: Uriel and Raphael

I Enoch 72:1: *"The book of the courses of the luminaries of the heaven, the relations of each ... their dominion and their seasons ..."*

Image: Two angels, otherworldly in aspect, stand beside portions of a great machine. Although they do not interact with the gears directly, their hands are raised in guiding gestures. The machine stretches all around them, dominating the background of the card. A coppery sphere in the upper right-hand corner appears enmeshed in or overlaid by the interaction of the gears.

Meaning: The machinery of fate. Forces beyond one's control have influence over the outcome. Destiny. Fortune. Inevitability. Inexorable cycles. Macrocosm and microcosm – and the interconnected nature of the Universe. God *is* the machine.

Reversed: Fate is working against the outcome. Factors beyond one's control impede the chosen direction. Fighting against destiny. Toiling against the current rather than going with the flow. Feeling oppressed by circumstances or forced in an unwanted direction.

The Wheel as Uriel and Raphael: What we know as the *Book of Enoch* is actually a compilation of several books, including the *Book of the Watchers*. Beyond the story of the Watcher Angels, one of the most intriguing books in *I Enoch* is known as the *Book of the Course of the Heavenly Luminaries*. This treatise, presented as information revealed by angels to Enoch during his tour through the heavens, seeks to describe the courses of the sun, moon, and stars through the heavens. The book is concerned with measurements of time and how

269

the passage of the days and seasons reflect the work of the heavens. Two guides who reveal and explain the celestial mysteries to Enoch are the angels Uriel and Raphael. They are not his only angelic escorts through the machinery of the heavens, but they are the two most frequently named. As such, they make an appearance on our version of The Wheel, continuing to work in their capacity as guides and guardians of the heavenly machine.

Interpretation: This is the card of *deus ex machina* – "a god from the machine." This Latin phrase originated as a critical reference to a conceptual device in Greek theater (most frequently used by Euripides) where difficulties in plot were resolved by the introduction of a god who solved everything. All the trials and efforts of the mortal players amounted to nothing, because an outside force had influence over the outcome, funneling the plot to its desired conclusion. While applying a "god in a box" to solve problems in one's narrative is a cheap option in storytelling, it nevertheless reflects a situation that can arise in the real world: sometimes things are out of our hands. There are forces greater than us at work in the Universe, and they don't have to be gods or Fate or anything more than other people to sometimes muck up our plans.

The Wheel card, in its broadest sense, represents these forces: something that the querent cannot control has an influence in the outcome. It's no coincidence that The Wheel is also the tenth card in the cycle of the Major Arcana: it sits in the middle of the progression, representing the very force of progress itself. It is the gears of fate or – if you believe in an intelligent Universe, then The Wheel represents the intelligent design, the unfolding pattern of the fractal. Within the Watcher Angel mythos, The Wheel is essentially God's plan, which is inscrutable, but merrily ticks along regardless of whether we have the capacity to understand or even to perceive it. That there is a shape to things, even in apparent randomness, is something we learn from chaos theory, and this notion is embodied by The Wheel. Even though we are sometimes steered by forces bigger than ourselves, this is not always a bad thing. It generally seems worse when we resist, fighting against the grinding of the gears.

Consider that the myth of the Watcher Angels arises from a religious system wherein the Creator is perceived as both omniscient (all-knowing) and omnipotent (all-powerful). Angels are little more than an expression of God's will, an extension of the colossal mind whose very existence seems dedicated to manifesting (or communicating) that will to the material world. With this in mind, even the Watchers, who *appear to* rebel in their choice to abandon Heaven, are nevertheless expressions of that will: they are as much a part of the machine, its ultimate purpose and expression, as Uriel and Raphael, who more overtly serve its function. The Wheel tells us that we have no choice to be other than what we are, and all of our choices – a much as they may seem to be an expression of free will – are nevertheless part of something bigger, which is constantly unfolding. And when it seems that fate has dealt us a rotten hand, the best thing – at least when we are caught up on The Wheel – is to relax, enjoy the ride, and see where it's going to take us.

XI. Justice: Satariel

Waite: *"The Concealment of God ... [who] hides the face of mercy."*

Image: A veiled angel stands with its hands outstretched in equal positions. The left hand balances a dagger, point-down, while the right balances a feather. The entire figure is covered with white drapery, obscuring its face and its gender. The colors of the card are white and gray – everything is neutral, echoing the balanced position of the angel's hands.

Meaning: Weighing the balance. Being measured and/or held accountable. Assessment. Probity. Equilibrium. Legal proceedings. A time to consider the justification of one's actions. Secular or divine justice. Karma.

Reversed: Inequality and injustice. The scales are tipped unfairly. Bias, especially in judgment. A corrupt legal system. Measurements and assessments are skewed. False testimony.

Justice as Satariel: For several of the Tarot Trumps, I did not know which Watcher was going to be assigned to the card until that card was finished. This was not at all the case with Justice. In the case of Justice, the finished card was inspired by the name. I had an idea for Justice but was having trouble conveying this to Jackie. Growing frustrated with my subjective attempts at description, she asked me which of the Watchers fit the card best. As the *Book of Enoch* only has heavenly angels in judgment of others, I wasn't certain, so once

---

* *The Doctrine and Literature of the Kabalah,* A.E. Waite p. 80 Theosophical Publishing Society, London 1902

again I started sorting through the list of the "chiefs of tens," trying to track down the meaning of these names. Satariel, named in the Charles translation, intrigued me, so I started flipping through Davidson's invaluable *Dictionary of Angels*. It was here that I came across the phrase "who conceals the face of mercy" (p. 262) I reported this back to Jackie as "the veil which conceals the face of mercy." Her eyes lit up in that way artists have when gripped with inspiration. The image of this card poured out over the next day or two, catalyzed by that phrase. The concept of Satariel as a concealing veil is drawn from Waite's own work on the Holy Kabalah. Under the spelling Sathariel, he gives the name as the averse correspondence to *Binah* in the Tree of Life (the dark mirror of the Tree, sometimes also called the Qlippoth).

Interpretation: The name of this card is Justice, implying not the act of judging but the qualities required for judgment. Notably, Judgment appears as an entirely different card almost at the end of the cycle of the Major Arcana. There, Judgment is much more active. In Trump eleven, there is no motion: all things hang in a balance. And it is that very balance that is the key to this card. In modern court rooms, there is often a representation of Justice, personified as a woman with scales of measurement. She is invariably blindfolded, indicated that justice is – or at least should be – blind.

Appearances, superficialities, misleading façades – all of these should be of no consequence to the proper carriage of justice. In our card, the blindfold is replaced with a veil. This not only obscures the figure's vision of whatever or whoever is being weighed in the scales, it also obscures the face of the figure itself. This has a depersonalizing effect that shifts focus from identity to function. Our angel of Justice does not merely hold the scales. This figure *is* the scales. She – or he, for gender is irrelevant for this card – holds hands outstretched in perfect balance. The dagger on the left represents punishment. Were the scales to tip to the dagger, the judged is found wanting. The feather in the right hand is the ostrich plume of the Egyptian goddess Ma'at. She is frequently identified as the goddess of justice, but her role was more complex than that. She represented the balance of the scales themselves, and through this, she was truth, order and balance incarnate: the right way of things. In ancient Egyptian beliefs, a soul was judged in the underworld by weighing his or her heart against the feather of Ma'at. If the heart was heavier than the feather, the soul was deemed unworthy and subsequently devoured by Ammut (whose name means simply "The Devourer"). The figure of Satariel in this card is a conscious echo of the scales of Thoth, with the dagger replacing the possibility of a heart heavily laden down with violent and/or harmful deeds.

When this card appears in a reading, it can indicate a literal lawsuit. Right-side up, the card generally indicates that justice will be favorable to the querent. Reversed, justice is turned against the querent. But far more than literal legal proceedings, this card represents the quality of justice in a broad sense. One does not have to enter a court room to be judged by others. People judge one another every day, both fairly and unfairly. The querent who receives this card has some connection with being weighed in the scales. This may indicate a tendency on the querent's part to judge and the card may be a reminder to abandon prejudices and seek impartiality. The card may also reflect a situation or state of mind in which the querent is the focus of the judgment. As with all of the Major Arcana, Justice represents broad, sweeping forces at work in the querent's life: ideas, concepts, and themes. As such, it can sometimes be hard to pin down the little details connected with the card, should there be any. The other cards in the spread should help to shed light on the particulars.

XII. The Hanged Man: Baraquiel

I Enoch 8:3: *"Baraquiel taught the signs of the lightning flashes."*

Image: And angel, tangled in chains, is suspended upside-down in the air. One wing is caught in the bonds while the other hangs uselessly. He twists against the fetters, though his resistance seems to entangle him more. The background of the card evokes a sense of smoke and flames.

Meaning: Insight acquired through self-sacrifice and discipline. The mind suspended in itself. An interruption. Psychological constriction. Penance. Transition. Renunciation. A period of withdrawal and reflection – possibly forced. Self-initiation.

Reversed: A refusal to look within. An inability to find inner quietude. Self-focused to the point of narcissism. A preoccupation with inconsequential matters. Allowing oneself to be distracted from the path of interior revelation. A stubborn clinging to ideas or a sense of self one knows is wrong.

The Hanged Man as Baraquiel: In the *Midrash of Shemhazai and Azael* that appears in the *Chronicles of Jerahmeel,* we are told that, after the cataclysmic destruction of the empire of the Watchers, "Shemhazai repented and suspended himself between heaven and earth, head downwards…" In several versions of the Watchers' myth, this penance of suspension was meted out to all of the Watcher Angels. As immortal spirits, they cannot be destroyed, but by their deeds they belong properly neither to heaven nor to earth. Thus they hang between the two, heads down so they can better contemplate

275

the issues that got them into their predicament in the first place. As noted earlier, although Shemyaza is most frequently named in connection with this penance, he already occupies the Trump of the Fool. And so I sought out another Watcher whose qualities also tied him to this notion of suspension. Araquiel, identified in the Charles translation as the teacher of the signs of the earth, was my first choice, however I ran into some trouble with this. As I further researched the names of the Watchers, it became clear that the name Araquiel doesn't really exist. Although identified in the Charles translation as the angel who taught the signs of the earth, Araquiel is merely a variant of Baraquiel. Baraquiel (whose name may share a root with *baraka,* meaning "blessing," but also can refer to a kind of spiritual power possessed by certain things), is named as one of the "chiefs of tens." Furthermore, he is associated with lightning, that lance of power that appears suspended between heaven and earth (the Charles translation connects him with the teaching of "astrology," but Nickelsburg demonstrates how this is a misrepresentation of a term meaning "portents in the sky" and is connected with lightning flashes). These connections made him my ideal choice for The Hanged Man.

Interpretation: The Hanged Man represents contemplation and surrender. Although the card may have originally depicted a thief strung up by one leg from a gallows as punishment for his crimes, the card has come to share associations with Christ on the Cross and Odin on the World Tree. It is seen as a descent into one's interior realms for the purpose of achieving insight and understanding, and as such, it represents an ordeal path. The Hanged Man is the belly of the whale in Campbell's sense of the Monomyth, that moment where we are alone with ourselves, whether we like it or not, and in order to come out of it, we must face – and possibly wrestle with – what we encounter there. Odin's *Rune Song,* a section of the *Hávamál,* eloquently captures the state of the Hanged Man, who at once resists and desires the moment of suspension and the insight which it brings: "I knew that I hung on a wind racked tree nine whole nights with a spear wounded, and to Odin offered, myself to Myself…"*

*p. 133 Anne Evans, "Norse Mythology," *The Theosophical Quarterly*, Vol. 12; Theosophical Society Publishing, NY, NY 1914.

Within the mythos of the Watchers, the Hanged Man depicts that moment after everything has fallen apart. Removed from the material world, at least for a time, the Watchers contemplate what went wrong. It's important to note that in some versions of the myth, the Watchers go down to the earthly realm with God's blessings. They have high hopes for what they can accomplish in the physical world and they feel that they can do a better job than what they're seeing mortals do. In these versions of the tale, God is essentially setting them up for a fall because spirit cannot commingle with flesh without some level of complication – but the experience itself is important. The Watchers have to learn the lesson directly. The suspension between heaven and earth that comes after is indicative of their plight from the very beginning: their desire leads them down one path, yet their essential nature pulls them toward the other. In their penance of suspension, they are removed from direct experience and all the distractions that it entails, and thus can gain perspective. They are literally looking down from a distance at what caused them to err, and from this position, they can see that the problem was perspective all along. Spirit and flesh exist in tension with one another, and unless an active effort is made to achieve balance, one eclipses the other – always.

Although the pay-off in personal revelation is ultimately worth the pain, the ordeal of the Hanged Man is not an easy one. Most traditional depictions of this card show the figure in a serene pose of surrender, but ours struggles against his bonds. We chose to capture the Hanged Man in process: we don't surrender our old views easily, and even when we go seeking revelation, we resist it at the same time. The key to our Hanged Man lies in the nature of his bonds. The chains are not locked in place at any point; they are merely wrapped around the figure, tangling him. His own struggles against the bonds are what work them ever tighter. If he simply relaxed and surrendered to the experience, the bonds would slip away and he could fly free. And that is how one survives the Hanged Man and all it represents: stop struggling and just accept the experience. No lesson worth learning ever comes easily.

XIII. Death: Kasdeya

I Enoch 69:12: *"Who taught the blows of the infant in the womb, so it may pass away..."*

Image: A cowled figure stands against a dark background, clutching a gnarled staff. The robes of the angel are black, as are the angel's wings. The face is obscured by the cowl, but what little can be seen is somber in expression and deathly pale. Rather than a scythe, a cocoon dangles from the end of the staff.

Meaning: Change. Necessity and inevitability. A transition from one state to the next. Loss that makes room for something new. Sacrifice that leads to transformation. A period of destruction where one is stripped of illusions. Learning to let go.

Reversed: Stagnation. Resistance to change. Fighting change to the point where it can only come with destruction and pain. A disastrous upheaval.

Death as Kasdeya: There were several candidates for the angel of death. In *I Enoch* 69, we encounter Gadriel, who "taught all the blows of death," and while this seemed like the most ideal fit imaginable, further reading on Gadriel's areas of expertise reveals that he is really another version of Azazel – though why he is renamed Gadriel in this corrupt later passage is anyone's guess (according to Davidson, the name is from Aramaic and actually means "God is my Helper"). In related literature (Ginzberg's *Legends of the Jews,* Rappoport's *Myth and Legend of Ancient Israel*), there is an entertaining story that casts Sammael as the angel of death sent to take the soul of Moses (Moses is such a powerful mortal that he pretty much kicks Sammael's ass). But even though Sammael is often counted among the fallen (and has ties to that same *Sem/Shem* root that seems to lie at the heart of several of the Watchers' names), I felt this may be going a little too far afield. So I turned back to the *Book of Enoch* and reread the entry for Kasdeya – sometimes also spelled Kasdeja. This is a Watcher who teaches "smitings," and while the precise implication of these smitings isn't clear in every phrase, once there is a reference to infants in the womb, it becomes obvious: Kasdeya teaches people how to kill things, possibly with poison and possibly with magick. Considering that Kasdeya doesn't seem to discriminate on what he teaches people to kill – spirits, demons, serpents, and embryos are all mentioned in the passages describing the knowledge he shared – he makes an ideal Death. Death, in both the real world and in the Tarot, doesn't care who or what you are when it comes time to raise the sickle. Death simply cuts things down when it is time.

Interpretation: The death embodied by this card is not literal but conceptual. Death in the Tarot is *change* – and it is only painful when we resist it. We encounter this message again and again in the Major Arcana, "Don't fight. It's so much easier when you don't fight." This is not to say that we are to be passive players in our own lives, but that our natural impulse is to resist change, even when it is good for us. We grow attached to familiar things, no matter how destructive they may be in the long wrong. Letting go of old habits, places of residence or employment, relationships, attitudes, identities, and self-images is a frightening prospect mainly because we can never be certain of what will come next. The familiar, even if we aren't really satisfied with it, is at least a known quantity. It's predictable and therefore bearable. And yet, card number thirteen in the cycle of the Major Arcana tells us that we *must* let go at some point. Stagnation is the real death, and as terrifying as it may be to move on to something different or new, that movement is also necessary if we have any hope of progressing in our lives and our development.

There is an echo of form between the Death card and Justice in our deck. One prepares us for the other. Justice raises questions about what is worthwhile in our lives. It demands an assessment –

whether anything is found wanting depends on the person and the circumstance. The Hanged Man is, in many ways, a reaction to this assessment: we've been told to let go of something or to change it, and we really don't like this. We struggle with ourselves, refuses to see the truth that's staring back at us even as we gaze into the mirror. So along comes Death to make the change for us. We can fight it – but we already know from the Hanged Man how that turns out. Fighting the inevitable forces simply makes our progress through their lessons that much more difficult. The ideal reaction when faced with Death is to accept the change and move on.

Death is not an end by any stretch. Death is a transition from one state to the next, whether that is a literal state with regards to a move or a figurative state of mind. When one thing ends, something else begins in a constant cycle. In this, Death is also a promise for renewal. This promise is represented on our card in the detail of the cocoon. Although the figure of Death is foreboding, one must surrender to death if one seeks to be reborn.

Behind the Cards: The cocoon depicted on the Death card belongs to a particular species of moth (actually one of three related species in the genus *Acherontia*). This is known as the Death's Head moth, so named for a peculiar marking on its thorax that resembles a human skull. Because of this mark, these moths have long been associated with death and supernatural portents.

XIV. Temperance: Zaquiel

I Enoch, 6:7: *"Zaquiel, eighth to Shemyaza..."*

Image: An angel stands wreathed by a current of force or heavenly flame. It courses about him in the symbol for infinity. Wings and arms outstretched, his head is uplifted. The fingers of his left hand are cupped in a receptive gesture turned toward heaven. Two fingers of his right hand are extended in a directing gesture and point to earth. Only the lower portion of the image has color; the upper portion fades to monochrome grays.

Meaning: Moderation. Balance. Compromise. Mixing two things to create something new. A delicate blending of disparate states: flesh and spirit, intellect and emotion. A process of refinement, purification, or homogenization. Inner alchemy.

Reversed: Imbalance. Forces or drives that are badly managed. Competing forces; being pulled in different directions. Poor judgment, especially when it comes to an attempt at harmonizing people, ideas, or forces. Things are out of tune.

Temperance as Zaquiel: Zaquiel's name appears in the list of the "chiefs of tens." Little else is said of this Watcher. The Nickelsburg *I Enoch* renders this name *Ziqel* and has him teaching "the signs of the shooting stars." An angel by the name of Zakkiel, possibly related, appears in Ginzberg's *Legends of the Jews.* He is identified as an angel of storms and is one of the angels who bears witness to Enoch's transformation into the Metatron. Between clouds, storms, and shooting stars Zaquiel's true nature seems difficult to pin down.

To be honest, the ultimate choice for assigning Zaquiel to Temperance has little to do with textual references. In the end, it simply felt right.

Interpretation: Temperance is about combination and moderation. The word comes from Latin, *temperare,* "to control." The idea of temperance is most often expressed in connection with alcohol and implies responsible imbibing and sobriety. Traditional images of this card depict an angel mixing fluid between two vessels. This is a visual reference to the act of mixing water with wine in order to dull its effects. By extension, Temperance refers to the harmonious reconciliation of two things, generally with the idea of comingling them into order to produce something new and more balanced.

Within the narrative of the Watcher Angels, this is expressed through the commingling of spirit and flesh in the character of the Watchers themselves. In Ginzberg's *Legends of the Jews,* we read that the angels "...were invested with sublunary bodies, so that a union with the daughters of men became possible" (p. 151). Sublunary means "below the sphere of the moon," which is to say, within the sphere of the earth – the physical, the mundane. In this view, prior to their descent upon Mount Hermon, the Watchers were beings of pure spirit (a common belief about angels). In order to achieve descent, they took up bodies as garments because that is what must be done to interact with the physical world. Our Temperance captures that moment of descent at the very crux of its process: we see the commingling of spirit and flesh.

The placement of the current of energy flowing around the angel is significant: half above, half below, with the two halves converging over the figure's midsection, near the vicinity of the solar plexus. Thus our figure is split into his two conceptual halves: head and heart, feet and loins – that which is above and that which is below. The card expresses the process of spiritual alchemy, the amelioration of these two apparently disparate halves. It is a balance that the Watchers must achieve in order to clothe spirit in flesh and to retain their essentially immortal natures while still taking up the appearance and function of mortals. For Temperance, it represents the supreme balancing act: living in the world while also retaining one's connection to spirit.

XV. The Devil: Setnael

Book of Mysteries: "Then Setnael, the most mighty of God's angelic creation, rose up and made war upon him..."

Image: An angel stands against a bright white background. The man and woman at his feet are naked save for tethered cords at their necks. The angel beckons all who observe to come and join him. Only the upper portion of the angel seems wholly solid. His legs and the bottoms of his wings seem to fade into the light.

Meaning: Spirit's descent into flesh – and subsequent distraction by it. Sensuality. Excess. Addiction. Obsession. A challenge of limits or boundaries. Things, people, or states that are dangerous, yet seductive. Bondage, mental or spiritual, with the implication of a willful surrender.

Reversed: An unhealthy relationship with physical desire. Repression. Perversion. A total lack of control. Indulging in physical pleasures specifically to drown out or avoid emotional, cerebral and/or spiritual concerns. Escapism.

The Devil as Setnael: The Devil is really another face of Shemyaza. By rights, the card should bear his name, but I felt this would be confusing, even if I simply used *Shemhazai* or a similar variation. Fortunately, Shemyaza has many names, and the archetype he represents can be found in a number of different texts. For a little while, I considered *Lucifer,* but as much as the Son of Morning has developed into a recognizable figure, the name's connection with the Devil is really a construct arising from a misinterpretation of Isaiah

14:12. Besides, Lucifer is a little too obvious, and I didn't want to weigh the card down with the baggage that names like Lucifer or Satan represent. It's bad enough that it's called the Devil – a lot of people see that and miss its real meaning.

In the Slavonic *2 Enoch* 18:3, the name of the leader of the Watchers is given as *Satanail*. Obviously, this is the familiar name *Satan* (which is from a word meaning "adversary" -- a job description rather than a proper name) retrofitted with an angelic ending. This was a possibility, but I was still concerned that people would see "Satan" and freak out. So I cast around for other literature related to the Ethiopic *I Enoch* and found *The Book of the Mysteries of the Heavens and the Earth*. This is another Ethiopic manuscript believed in the 17th century to be a version of the *Book of Enoch*. To make a long story short, it's not, much to the disappointment of Nicholas Claude Fabri, the Seigneur of Peiresc who probably paid quite a bit for the book. However, this text does contain variations on the story of the Watchers in what has obviously developed as a unique blend of Christian, Jewish, and wholly Ethiopian folklore. And, perhaps because the Coptic Ethiopian culture retained some remnants of Egyptian influence, the main leader of the Watchers is named, not Shemyaza, not Satanail, but *Setnael*.

This is something I couldn't pass up. There has long been conjecture that the Egyptian god Set, demonized even within his own culture, served as one of the archetypes for Satan – but textual evidence showing the progression is scarce, if it exists at all. In this text, Set seems to have been rendered into an angel and linked directly with the Luciferian archetype. Why does this fit our Devil card so well? Because long before he became identified as a god of chaos, Set was the god of the desert as well as a god of foreigners (storms and earthquakes, too). He represented extremes as well as that which lay beyond the bounds. This dovetails conceptually with the origin of our English word for "evil" – originally *yfel* – derived from a root meaning "over-reaching the bounds." Evil originally was what lay beyond the bounds of what was considered normative, and for me, our misunderstanding of "evil" in its original context echoes our misunderstanding of the Devil as he is presented in this Tarot Trump. The behaviors represented by this card are only evil in the traditional sense once they have gone beyond an acceptable limit. Hence, though the path to the decision may seem rather discursive to anyone but me, Setnael was the ideal choice for our Devil. As an interesting aside, the Nickelsburg translation of *I Enoch* has a name very close to this appearing in the "chiefs of tens" list. Here, the name appears as *Setawel.* In Syncellus, it is *Sathiel* or *Sethiel.*

Interpretation: When Temperance fails, the Devil is what results. In Temperance, we witness a descent of spirit into flesh, but Temperance depicts their ideal state. The two exist in balance. There is an echo of that process in our Devil card: the lower portion of the Devil seems somewhat insubstantial, as if he were not as solid as the upper portion of his body seems to imply. This is a reminder that he is a being of spirit merely experiencing flesh. This insubstantiality is visibly counterbalanced by the man and woman crouching on either side of the angel. Beings of flesh, the leashes worn around their necks serve to tether the angel to the earthly realm even more than they tie the mortal lovers to the angel. With the Watcher Angels, the bondage goes both ways: experiences of the flesh are what attracted most of the Watchers in the first place. Thus, these experiences serve to hold the angel to the physical world. The two lovers sitting naked at the angel's feet are essentially his anchors to a physical body and all that it represents. Our Devil is also a pusher of boundaries. He is the one who lead the descent of spirit into flesh. In this, he challenged the limits placed upon the Sons of Heaven. He is an instigator and a rebel in the truest sense of the Luciferian ideal promoted by the Romantics – but to break boundaries and to shatter pre-conceptions, the person who gets there first almost always has to go to an extreme. This extreme nature is as much a part of the Devil as his need to push the limits of what others accept as "right" or "normal."

Traditional depictions of the Devil are fairly grotesque. Ours retains the ethereal beauty befitting a Son of Heaven. There is a reason for this: flesh can be beautiful and enticing. It is not always bad. This is an important message that many other depictions of the Devil seem to miss. The attitude that matter is necessarily base while spirit is necessarily pure is a remnant of Zoroastrian dualism that has wormed its way into the Western imagination, obscuring the idea of balance seen in the Temperance card. Spirit and flesh are each different ways of approaching and experiencing the Universe. Problems arise only when one eclipses the other. The danger of the

Devil, then, is getting lost in experiences of the flesh, to the exclusion of all else (note also that the woman kneeling before the High Priest reappears here in the Devil: fanaticism is another form of excess that can lead to this Trump).

One key to the Devil card is choice. The bonds worn around the necks of the human lovers are tokens only. They imply consent. The man and the woman sit naked and submissive at the feet of the angel because they choose to be there. By taking up the tethers, the angel, also, makes a choice to engage in physical experience. All of the figures on this card are engaged in this sensual play because it is something that they *want* to do, not something that they are compelled to do. And this is the underlying meaning of the Devil, above and beyond the simple lure of the flesh: if we over-indulge and lose sight of ourselves, it is because, at some point in the process, we made a choice. Whether the indulgence is food or drink, sex or something stranger, we are always the only ones responsible for our choices. If we get in over our heads, only we can save ourselves by finding the strength to say, "Enough!" When this card comes up for a querent it's a warning, not a guarantee. There is a tendency to over-indulge or the querent must face some temptation. Whether the querent conquers this or succumbs to it depends entirely on how well he or she has learned the lesson of the Trump before: *Temperance.*

Behind the Cards: You knew that one of the cards in this deck was going to be me, but I bet you didn't expect it to be The Devil. Here I am anyway, cast in the role of Setnael aka Satanail aka Shemyaza aka Lucifer. If you know me, you know why. *Fiat lux!*

XVI. The Tower: Mount Hermon

I Enoch 6:6: *"And they were in all two hundred who descended in the days of Jared on the slopes of Mount Hermon…"*

Image: Craggy mountains rise against a stormy, brooding sky. An otherworldly white city sits atop the highest crest. A cruder city of clustered mud-colored buildings rests in the valley far below. Lightning reaches for the highest towers of the white city and two lights streak like comets, descending to the land below.

Meaning: Destruction. Ruin. The price of hubris. Ambition laid low. Disaster brought upon oneself. Decisions that are ultimately self-destructive. Calamity and disgrace. Sudden and devastating insight. Pride that leads to one's downfall.

Reversed: A refusal to learn from one's mistakes. Ignoring signs, requests, or portents that a particular course of action is foredoomed. Dragging others down with bad choices. Willful self-destruction and/or self-sabotage. Pursuing failure from a fear of success.

The Tower as Mount Hermon: Originally, the Tower was going to be named after Azza and Uzza, variants of Shemyaza and Azazel who appear in some Enochic texts. However, the concept of the card was always the pact sworn upon Mount Hermon, and in the end, it seemed most logical to simply express it as that fateful locale. What we see here is a white city built by the Watchers in an effort to recreate the city of heaven. Its placement on the peak of a mountain is significant: in the ancient world, mountain-tops, or "high places" were seen as half in the mortal world and half in the heavens, and thus these were the locations where angels and gods were likely to come down. Had the Watchers remained in this space merely as observers, perhaps none of the tragic events of their history would have ensued. However, the temptation of the mortal world proves too much: the two lights represent Azza and Uzza, Shemyaza and Azazel, in their moment of descent. The lightning that arcs toward the highest towers of the white city portends the disastrous results.

Interpretation: If you falter with the Devil, you get the Tower: *ruin.* As the tower of ruin, it is not just some sweeping cosmic force that happens to you. The Tower represents destruction that you have brought upon yourself. The Trumps, from the Lovers onward, have carried messages of balance. Several also suggest that, when faced with sweeping cosmic forces, the best approach is to yield to them rather than fight their effects. The Tower represents the hubris of pushing things too far and it comes with an additional message: *"You really should have known better."* When the Fool jumps into the abyss, a certain amount of naïveté protects him from the harshest repercussions. It's almost as if he's too blind to see the danger he's thrown himself into, and his very ignorance protects him. By the time we get to the Tower, however, a certain amount of perspective is implied. This is not our first time at the rodeo, so to speak, and we should know what we're getting ourselves into when we continue to push the limits. The higher the climb, the harsher the fall.

Of course, the thing about the Tower is it's not the last card in the cycle. This is only card sixteen in a twenty-two card progression. There's still further to go. So the real message of the Tower is not to *never* fall. Rather, it is an acknowledgment that *everyone* falls. There is always that one choice, that one goal where our reach exceeds our grasp, and yet we keep pushing. Pride prevents us from backing down, even when we know failure is near at hand. So the Tower, at least when it's right-side up, is a card of harsh lessons – but the most important lesson it harbors is not about falling. It's about how – or if – you pick yourself up after the fall. If you just dust yourself off and start climbing the mountain the exact same way again without learning the benefit of, say, some protective gear, then you've missed the message of the Tower. The Tower is about learning the hard way. You've only failed if you've learned nothing at all.

XVII. The Star: Kokabiel

I Enoch 8:3: "...Kokabiel [taught] the constellations..."

Image: A female figures appears in the sky, robed in sheer bands of rose-colored cloth. The figure's wings stream like a burst of light behind her. She gazes down at the viewer, one hand extended in a gesture either of assistance or annunciation. A single star glows in the sky behind her on the right.

Meaning: Hope. A guiding principle. Renewal in the wake of destruction. A glimmer of light in the darkness. The promise of better things to come. Surcease to sorrow. Cosmic forces offer healing for mind, body, or soul.

Reversed: Doubt. Fumbling in the dark. Faltering along the path. Being overcome by hopelessness. Feeling crushed under the weight of life's burdens. Illness resulting from exhaustion, either mental or physical.

The Star as Kokabiel: The Watcher for this card was set from the very inception of our deck. In the "teachings" passages of *I Enoch* 8: 1-4, Kokabiel is associated with the stars. In the Charles translation, we read "...Kokabiel [taught] the constellations..." while Nickelsburg specifically says this Watcher "taught the signs of the stars." However you parse the passage, Kokabiel is tied to the stars and, subsequently, becomes tied to the Star in the Tarot Trumps.

Interpretation: In the aftermath of the Tower, amidst the ruin and desolation of what for many is a dark night of the soul, there emerges a glimmer of light. This glimmer, though it may seem faint and distant at first, is the Star. It is the promise of renewal in the wake of destruction, and it is represented as a literal light guiding us in the darkness. Only a few centuries ago, sailors steered their vessels by the stars. Navigating at night by the light of certain constellations – particularly the fixed stars – is as old as navigation itself. In addition to navigation, the stars have guided humanity in understanding and marking the passage of the seasons as well as much longer counts of time. For those cultures that developed the technology, the stars have helped map cycles of time far beyond the span of human lives, extending all the way to the long count of the Great Year based upon the precession of the equinoxes (sometimes called the Platonic Year, the "hours" of that clock tick along in terms of millennia).

One thing to note about the Star is that it is the first in a progression of cards tied to heavenly bodies that appear within the Tarot Trumps: the Star, the Moon, and finally the Sun. It is no coincidence that these heavenly bodies appear in order, from the dimmest to the strongest. Following in the wake of the Tower, hope does not present itself with the clarity of the Sun – at least not at first. Instead, it shows up first as the Star, like a still, small voice in the darkness that we might miss if we aren't careful. Seeing the light of the Sun is easy, but seeing the light of a star can take work. Navigating by that star is even more challenging: one must understand that the stars move in cycles, dancing across the sky through both the course of the night and over the course of the year (and if we include the concept of precession, further still, over the course of millennia). The cyclical nature of stars is both a secret and a promise inherent in the Star: all things turn round in time and what you have lost sight of in this moment will eventually return. That return may also involve a change, but Orion is always recognizable no matter where he appears along the horizon. And even in those moments when the sky is obscured by clouds and the darkness is deep and cloying, there is hope in the knowledge that the stars still shine on the other side of the barrier. Therefore, once the storm has passed, one can begin moving forward again.

Behind the Cards: The Star features Andrea, the Counselor Caste Elder of House Kheperu. She also modeled for the Four of Swords.

XVIII. The Moon: Sariel

I Enoch 8:3: *"And Sariel taught the courses of the moon…"*

Image: An angel kneels before a scrying pool, craggy rocks on either side. Filmy veils in a cold, lunar blue whirl around the figure, agitated by the same wind that whips the angel's hair. Mist rises from a small chest beside the figure's left knee and something peers out from the interior. Behind this scene, the moon dominates the sky, pale, full, and huge.

Meaning: A light in a dark time that can either reveal or mislead. Deception. Illusion. Lunacy. Dreams and visions. Things are not what they seem. Forces released from the unconscious, primal and uncontrolled. Intuition. Emotion. Instinct. The subversion of rational sense.

Reversed: Mania. Hysteria. Mental illness. Shifting, surging emotions usurp the rational mind. Reason is eclipsed entirely, drowning in delusion or hallucination. The veils are torn away, exposing deception. The querent is being willfully misled; someone or something is feeding their delusions.

The Moon as Sariel: Like the Star, the angel for the Moon card was one of the first to be assigned long before there were images completed for the cards. The *Book of Enoch* is rather clear on the nature of Sariel. One of the "chiefs of tens," he teaches the courses, or phases, of the moon. The only thing that may be confusing about Sariel is that his name occasionally appears among lists of archangels. Nickelsburg renders the spelling of this Watcher *Sahriel* to distinguish it from the archangel Sariel, who takes the place of

291

Uriel in his translation. I, however, rest with the Charles spelling in this instance.

Interpretation: The Moon card has a negative reputation among many Tarot readers, although the card can have positive aspects as well. This is, of course, thoroughly in keeping with the shifting nature of the moon. Following the collapse of the Tower, three instances of light present themselves to the seeker. The first is the weakest, and this is the Star. It is the initial glimmer of hope in the darkness. But then there comes the Moon. This light can be much brighter than that of the Star, depending on the phase. It illuminates more of the path leading away from the experience of the Tower. But the thing about moonlight is that it is shifting and false: it often obscures as much as it reveals. Think of the way that moonlight silvers everything it touches, giving everything an unearthly feel. Touched with moonlight, things can looks fey and strange, and much of this shifting quality manifests in the meaning of the Moon as a Tarot Trump.

The moon itself is inconstant, waxing and waning over the course of the month. Although it has a set pattern, it is not the same from one night to the next (it is at least predictable in its unpredictability). The moon also behaves in ways that may seem irrational to us: we associate the moon with night, but there are times when it can be seen in the sky during the day, as if seeking to compete with the sun. All of these natural observations of the moon's behavior contribute to our mythic understanding of the Moon. Thus this card is about shifting landscapes and the ebb and flow of tides, but the landscape in question is the mind and imagination and the ocean is our unconscious mind.

There is an old superstition that holds if one sleeps with the light of the moon falling upon them, they will awaken moon-struck – insane. The words *lunatic* and *lunacy* arise from beliefs in the moon's mind-warping powers. There is more than a little lunacy to Sariel's gaze as he meets the eyes of the viewer, but his non-rational intensity is almost required to plumb the depths of the Well of the Imagination that lies before him. The agitated wind whipping through his veils is indicative of a shifting and unsettled emotional atmosphere. The veils themselves represent forces which simultaneously reveal and obscure.

The box beside Sariel is a nod to the myth of Pandora: if we seek to plumb the depths of the unconscious, delving deep into the realm of the Moon, we need to be careful about what we release. The forces here are wild and unpredictable, and though they hold great power, they are resistant to control and can easily slip our grasp. In this, the Moon is often a warning of the dangers of uncontrolled visions and imagination. The Moon is also a psychic card, and it reflects the subjective aspect of those talents that can twist perception into delusion if a rational approach to experience is lost. On the upside, the Moon also holds the key for its own control: it moves the tides of our inner oceans, but there is a predictable ebb and flow. Learning the patterns and knowing when and how to prepare for the shifting of these tides helps to manage to Moon. The tides cannot be stopped, any more than one can control the phases of the moon, but one can work within or around their shifting natures. In this way, one can ultimately use the ebb and flow to great advantage once one has acclimated to the ceaseless cycle of change.

XIX. The Sun: Shamsiel

I Enoch 8:3: *"...Shamsiel [taught] the signs of the sun..."*

Image: A figure stands in light so powerful, it can only be seen in silhouette. Wings stretch from its shoulders, but they seem to be made of light. The figure holds a sphere of solar energy, protecting it or offering it to the viewer.

Meaning: Splendor. Radiance. Illumination. That which is made manifest. Supreme consciousness. Secrets exposed and understood. The naked truth. Joy. Happiness. Triumph. Renewal. Witnessing or reclaiming an exalted state.

Reversed: Hope is eclipsed. Promises are broken. Happiness proves fleeting. Potential withers on the vine. Like Icarus, one strives toward the sun only to fall in flames to the earth. The searing force is too much, consuming rather than renewing. The light burns brightly only to burn out.

The Sun as Shamsiel: When discussing the Sun card, there was no question as to its assignation from the ranks of the Watchers. Shamsiel is the sun. He doesn't always appear in the list of the "chiefs of tens." He is absent from this list in the Charles edition, but his name appears in the Nickelsburg translation. He may appear in Syncellus under the spelling *Samial,* though whether this is more accurately related to the name Sammael is difficult to determine. All texts that speak of Shamsiel identify him as the angel who taught the signs of the sun. Interesting lines have been drawn between the name of this angel and Shamash, the Babylonian god of the sun. Notably, the Akkadian word *Šamaš* means "sun" and the two names may share a common origin.

Interpretation: The sun is illumination and revelation, interior as well as exterior. In the sequence of manifest lights which follow the fall of the Tower, the Sun is the brightest and represents the quintessential sense of enlightenment. This is the surest guide out of the darkness, where all the shadows are dispelled save for those which we cast ourselves. And even those shadows not dispelled by the light but defined by it offer revelation by clearly delineating our forms. This is the "aha!" moment, that incandescent sense of epiphany through which all things become clear.

Notably, our depiction of the Sun card features a background so drenched in light that the main figure is cast in shadow. This is a conscious nod to the Jung quote: *"Enlightenment is not imagining figures of light but making the darkness conscious."* Shamsiel, then, is the shadow at noon, the figure standing in the brightest light who must, perforce, cast the darkest shadow. The implication is that the light of the Sun does not completely eradicate the darkness, it simply helps us to understand it and – ultimately – to integrate it. The Sun does not give us the power to go back an undo the action that led to the Tower. Instead, the way in which the Sun lights our paths allows us to gain perspective and understanding. In this clear, pure light of reality, all of our illusions are dispelled and we can contextualize whatever remains.

This is a card not merely of hope, but of achievement. The querent who receives this card has come through their trials better for the experience. They have learned the lesson and now, for a little while at least, they can bask in the radiance of that knowledge. When the issue of the reading involves spiritual, magickal or mystical experiences, this card indicates a moment of gnosis – a brilliant flash of understanding that unveils at least some portion of the nature of the Universe. Notably, we see that the figure silhouetted against the brilliant source of light holds his or her own light as well, having invoked it from within. This is a mini-sun, a microcosmic reflection of the archetypal sun which our figure seems not to stand in front of, but *within*. This implies mystical union. Standing in the light, the figure has connected with the prime force of the universe, and this connection in turn has revealed that he or she has carried a spark of that force inside themselves all along.

XX. Judgment: Michael

I Enoch 10:11: *"And the Lord said to Michael: 'Go, bind Shemyaza and his associates...'"*

Image: The angel of judgment stands astride mountains. He levels his sword at the viewer, left hand raised in an arcane gesture. The sky behind him is dark and streaked with rain, but nothing is darker than his outstretched wings. Below him, waters surge, drowning the land in a flood.

Meaning: A final decision. A sentence passed and implemented. Resolution. An end to deliberation. A literal judgment, which forces a choice. A change of states – which may be positive or negative. Forcing one's hand. No more room for negotiation or appeal.

Reversed: Vengeance. A decision made with finality, but made in error. Burning bridges. Being forced unfairly to a point of no return. Judgments made rashly or which are unnecessarily harsh. Barriers. There is no going back again.

Judgment as Michael: When I first developed the concept for this deck, it was my intention to feature only the Watchers on the Major Arcana. However, as we have toured through the Tarot Trumps, you can see that the deck itself had other ideas. Several other figures – and one location – from the Watcher Angel mythos have found their way onto these cards, and Judgment was perhaps the loudest in clamoring for a place. That judge is Michael, one of the archangels named in *I Enoch* as meting out the punishment handed down to the Watchers for allowing their earthly experiment to get so out of control. Notably, Michael is one of the most consistently named angels throughout Jewish and Christian literature. He appears in the Essene writings we know as the Dead Sea Scrolls at the head of the army of the Sons of Light, pitted against his enemy Belial in the *"Dream-Vision of Amram"* – and this is perhaps the most recognizable aspect of Michael to modern readers: Michael the Warrior, General of Heaven, vanquisher of the rebel angels who once waged war in the celestial sphere. In our deck, he appears in all his fearsome glory as the executor of Judgment in Trump Twenty.

Interpretation: Traditional images for this card, such as that found on the Rider-Waite-Smith deck, depict the angel Gabriel blowing his trump. With this clarion call, he wakes the dead, heralding their final judgment. As such, the card carries a sense of hope, because we don't see the moment of judgment itself. In our deck, in order to continue with the narrative of the Watchers, Trump twenty takes on a much darker tone. We don't get to see that moment *prior* to judgment when there is still some hope that things may go in one's favor. No, we can forget Gabriel and his trumpet. Here, we get Michael and his sword. Judgment has been passed, and in the case of the Watcher Angels, the accused have been found wanting.

The error of judgment on the part of the Watchers lay in a misunderstanding of the fundamental nature of heaven and earth, spirit and flesh. When called from one to the other, rather than attempt to seek a balance between the two, the Watchers sought to simply turn earth into their new heaven. They try to force the flesh to conform to the spirit, and in the process, they lose sight of the value of both. In the Pentacles, they establish themselves, working to bend the very earth to their will; in the Cups, they pursue all manner of emotional and sensual pleasure; in the Wands, they push the limits of the material world in order to evoke the fire and the power they remembered wielding in heaven. And here is where things really start to go wrong, for they drag their mortal charges along a path to spiritual revelation, pushing too hard and too fast. The fire of revelation quickly becomes an all-consuming blaze, burning destructively rather than illuminating productively. This begets the Swords with all their bloody conflict, which is something of a pre-show to the final judgment where flood waters are released to wash everything away so things can start over again. And Michael, fierce and unyielding, oversees this moment to make certain that the judgment is fulfilled.

That is Judgment for the Watchers. For querents who receive this card, it represents judgment as well, but the actual measure of the querent is determined by the other cards in the spread. Judgment is not always harsh, but it is always final. This card represents an end to the cycle, a firm reminder that you cannot go home again. Taken in terms of Campbell's reading of the Monomyth, this card represents the consequence of the "refusal to return." Having achieved that incandescent moment of revelation depicted by the Sun, there is an impulse to remain enveloped in that light. But the purpose of the journey and all of its experiences is to acquire wisdom – and then to return it to the world so that it can be shared. In this respect, Michael points his sword at the viewer to say, "You're done with this. It's time to move on." Refusal is not an option. The waters of the flood may drown the world, but they also cleanse it, clearing away the detritus of past mistakes and preparing the way for a new cycle and a new set of experiences.

Behind the Cards: This card, in all its stern glory, was modeled by Jason, the Warrior Caste Second of House Kheperu. He also appears in the King of Swords.

XXI. The World: Metatron

2 Enoch 55:2 "In the morning I shall go to the highest heavens to my eternal habitation."

Image: An angel, naked and shorn, walks away from the ruins of a city. His path leads toward a heavenly light whose rays spill out above another city, transfigured and new. The angel does not look directly at his destination but instead glances down, thoughtful. There is blood on his wings and blood trailing behind him.

Meaning: Apotheosis. Transfiguration. The Great Work complete. The end of one cycle and the beginning of the next. Refinement of Self. Perfection. Synthesis. Mystical experience. Eternal return. The Fool revisited, only now one is fully conscious of the cost of that final leap.

Reversed: Fixating on what one has lost instead of what has been won. Failing to learn the lesson and thereby repeating the same cycle over again. Clinging to the past in a manner that prevents growth and progress. Losing sight of the goal in the struggle and/or details.

The World as Metatron: In certain streams of Jewish mysticism, such as the Merkaba tradition, Enoch plays a significant role as the Metatron. Having the distinction as the only mortal transfigured into an angel, Enoch completes our cycle in the Tarot of the divine becoming human and the human becoming divine. Originally, I had no intention of placing Enoch – in any of his guises – within the Major Arcana. But the deck had other ideas, and in the end it became clear that I could not tell one story without telling that of the other.

299

The Watchers and Enoch are inextricably linked: each represents a difference side of the cycle of experience. And so we bookend the deck with Shemyaza who leaps into an experience of flesh from the perspective of spirit and Enoch, who finds himself called to leave behind the material world in order to take up an existence beyond the flesh – with the implication that it all comes 'round again in time. There will be a point where Enoch seeks to return to a new physical existence just as Shemyaza and his Watchers will eventually learn all that they need from the world of flesh, choosing to return to a different experience in the realm of spirit.

Interpretation: The World is the end of the cycle – which leads, of course, to the beginning of the next. As our cycle of the Major Arcana began with the descent of spirit into flesh through the figure of Shemyaza, so it ends with flesh being transfigured into spirit through the figure of Enoch/Metatron. The Watchers take center stage throughout this mythic cycle, but Enoch's story is both integral and revealing within the greater narrative. Enoch starts out as one of the wisest of mortals – the King Solomon of his age. Born to the seventh generation from Adam, the number is significant because in the cultural context of this story, seven is a number of completion. There are seven days in a week, and seven spheres to the heavens. Seven is not only the end, but the pinnacle, and in his position of seventh from Adam, Enoch represents a pinnacle of humanity.

Enoch is born in interesting times. He gets to witness the descent of the Watcher Angels as well as their successes and failures in the physical realm. As the story goes, once judgment has been passed upon the Watchers, these angelic Sons of Heaven actually seek Enoch out as ask him to intercede with the Almighty on their behalf. Even God raises an eyebrow over the fact that Sons of Heaven ask a child of clay to petition for them, telling the Patriarch in *I Enoch* 15:2, "Go, say to the Watchers … 'You should intercede for men, and not men for you.'" But the Watchers seem to know more about Enoch and his relation with heaven than Enoch himself – at least at this point. When Enoch journeys into heaven to speak for the Watchers, he is taken directly to the throne of the presence – traditionally, an experience of the divine that even many of the angels cannot bear. This direct communication with God sets the stage for Enoch's later assumption into heaven and his ultimate transformation into the angel Metatron.

Our World card depicts Enoch's departure from the realm of the flesh. Behind him, the destruction of the civilization of the Watchers litters the ground. One broken angelic idol lets us know to whom the shattered pillars of this city once belonged. The blood on the figure's wings is suggestive not only of the cost of previous trials endured but also the pangs of birth: these wings have recently sprung from his back as a part of his transformation, and this has not come about without pain. Before the figure lies a clear path, but it seems to lead simultaneously to two different locales. One is heavenly, and is represented merely with a burst of light. The other is an idealized city – essentially a perfected version of the previous city, reborn. One path leads to an experience that we can assume takes place wholly in the realm of spirit. The other continues in the world of flesh, but represents a fresh start with new possibilities. As far as the story is concerned, Enoch's destination is the brilliant flash of light. But in his angelic aspect, he also echoes every one of the Watchers and his journey in this card parallels the completion of their own cycle. Enoch is destined for heaven. The Watchers have a choice once they have attained the World: continue in the world of flesh in a different cycle having learned from the mistakes of the past or leave the world of flesh entirely to return from whence they came – and there, to pursue whatever new cycle of experience awaits.

For the querent who receives this card, the World is indicative of completion of a cycle of learning. The lessons have been learned, not without cost and not without pain, but it is now time to move on and carry forward that hard-earned wisdom. He querent can choose to revisit some of the issues, situations, and images of self represented by the first cycle – only this time, older and wiser, he or she will try things differently, moving closer to perfection with each turn of the wheel. Or, the querent may choose to move on to a different cycle of expression entirely. In this, the World card may come up to indicate a radical life change. This is not something the querent is forced into nor is it something for which they are unprepared. Nevertheless, it is something that inspires a moment of reflection. Our figure glances back, contemplating everything that has led him to this point – such a retrospective is common for people experiencing the World card, and if there is a caution inherent at all in this Trump, it is this: know the past and do not be ignorant about it, but do not fixate on it so completely that you forget to move forward to apply what you have learned.

The End and the Beginning

We have journeyed through Pentacles and Establishment, Art and Beauty in the Cups, the fire of Magick and Inspiration in the Wands, and Ideology with the Conflicts it begets in the Swords. In the Major Arcana, we have explored sweeping cosmic forces – the faces of the Macrocosm as they manifest in our life during our progress through cycles of learning and experience. And now it feels like we have come to the end of a long and intense journey together. In the process of this journey, we have learned (I hope) a great deal about ourselves and about the nature of the Universe in which we live. There is much more than can be said, but I have to trust that the deep language of the Tarot with its many layers of image and meaning will continue to unfold as you work with it, telling you new tales as you go and enlarging upon the stories you thought that you already understood.

00. Conclusion: Evolution of the Tarot

My personal journey with the Tarot has been a fascinating one. In all my studies, what I have appreciated learning the most is the Tarot's evolutionary capacity: the Tarot is something that began as a simple game yet developed into a profoundly nuanced tool of reflection. The cards have not remained static throughout this development – neither in their appearance nor in their meaning. In fact, it seems that every artist who creates a deck and every scholar who interprets it leaves his or her own stamp upon it. As such, we have inherited a dynamic system that is always shifting, changing, and growing. The Hanged Man started life as The Traitor and depicted a traditional punishment meted out to enemies of the state. The Lovers originally depicted a man between two women, and connoted the path between vice and virtue. The Hermit once held an hourglass rather than a lamp and represented Father Time. And the Magician, far from being a magus, may very well have been a merchant hawking his wares at a table (if any of this comes as a surprise to you, I highly recommend *A Wicked Pack of Cards*). It is through the lens of time and culture (and at least a few printer's errors) that we have arrived at the cards we know today.

When I was first trying to design the Watcher Angel Tarot, I worried constantly about tradition versus innovation. While I definitely wanted to put my own stamp on the Tarot, I did not want to deviate too far from what people expected to find in the cards. I've encountered some hard-core traditionalists over the years (I think of them as Tarot fundamentalists) who tended to react with severe criticism to any deck that dared even the slightest deviation from what they considered to be the "definitive" Tarot. Of course, I have since learned that there really is no such thing. Like so many things related to belief, the Tarot is a consensual construct built from a few fundamental kernels which themselves were essentially woven from whole cloth by innovative thinkers: someone, somewhere, made up a story, and it became canon in its multiple retellings.

In my eyes, this doesn't invalidate the use of the Tarot, nor the meaning which it has come to hold. Rather, it makes the fundamental truths we can perceive within the Tarot that much more reflective of humanity in general. It is a mirror of our own construction, and

303

therefore it is a very accurate mirror because every creation contains at least a spark of its creator. Knowing this, I stopped hesitating with my deck and simply allowed it to be – an unfolding of meaning and imagery between myself and the artist. In this, I have made my own contribution to the Tarot's evolution, and hopefully it will be a viable mutation, rather than an evolutionary dead-end.

I know that learning about some of the true origins of the Tarot may be a bit of a let-down for some people. It's enticing to think of the secret *Book of Thoth* with all its revelations about how to tap into our divine character hidden in esoteric images and handed down throughout the ages as a humble pack of cards. But from our perspective here in the Digital Age, where we have the luxury of immediate access to primary materials from the libraries of the world and we can check and double-check the sources of our sources – well, I think it's fair to say that we would serve ourselves poorly if we took these wild claims at face value.

But consider that the *Book of Thoth* does still exist, after a fashion. It is not carried in a pack of cards, nor is it written upon leaves of gold and stored in some hidden chamber deep beneath the cyclopean monuments of a forgotten civilization. If a book exists that contains the answers to who and what we are – our connection to the infinite nature of the Universe and how best we can go about developing this – that book is not written upon paper or stone or even steel. It is a book that we carry writ upon our souls, and its language is found within our dreams. And in this, the Tarot does hold keys to opening the book and unfolding all that it has to reveal, but we ourselves are the vessels of transmission. The cards are merely a way to project what we already know outside of ourselves, where we can at last recognize it and, recognizing it, bring it fully into being.

Appendix I: Names of the Watchers

In order to arrive at my presentation of the Watchers' names in the deck, I compared a number of different versions of the *Book of Enoch,* focusing on the passage (*I Enoch* 6:7) that lists their "chiefs of tens." For those who are curious, I've included a portion of the chart created in this process on the pages below. The headers indicate the source and, when it is known, its date of publication.

4Q201	G Akhmim	Syncellus* 8th cent.	Laurence 1821
Shemihazah	Semaza	Semiazas	Samyaza
Arataqoph	Arathak	Atarcuph	Urakabarameel
Ramtael	Kimbra	Araciel	Akibeel
Kokabel	Chocharial	Chobabiel	Tamiel
xxxx-el	Tamiael	Horammame	Ramuel
Ramael	Ramiael	Ramiel	Danel
Daniel	Daneial	Sampsich	Azkeel
Ziqiel	Ezekiael	Zaciel	Sarakuyal
Baraqel	Barakiael	Balciel	Asael
Asael	Azaael	Azalzel	Armers
Hermoni	(h)Arearos	Pharmarus	Batraal
Matarel	Batriael	Amariel	Anane
Ananel	Semiael	Anagemas	Zarebe
Stawel	(h)Ananthna	Thausael	Samsaveel
Shamsiel	Rakeiael	Samiel	Ertael
Shahriel	Sammanae	Sarinas	Turel
Tummiel	Sathiael	Eumiel	Yomyael
Turiel	Thoniael	Tyriel	Arazyal
Yomiel	Touriael	Jumiel	
Yehaddiel	Iomeiael	Sariel	
	(h)Atriael		

*From the *Anecdota Oxoniensa: Semitic Series* parts 10-11 I obtained access to the Greek of both Syncellus and the G Akhmim, a fragment now in the Gizeh museum. Jackie helped transliterate the names preserved in these Greek fragments.

Baty 1839	Dillmann 1853	Charles 1893	Nickelsburg 2004
Samiaza	Semjaza	Semiazaz	Shemihazah
Arstikapha	Urakibarameel	Arakiba	Arteqoph
Armen	Akibeel	Rameel	Remashel
Akibeel	Tamiel	Kokabiel	Kokabel
Tamiel	Ramuel	Tamiel	Armumahel
Ramiel	Danel	Ramiel	Ramel
Danyal	Ezeqeel	Danel	Daniel
Zakiel	Saraqujal	Ezeqeel	Ziqel
Barakel	Asael	Baraqijal	Baraqel
Azaziel	Armers	Asael	Azsael
Armers	Batraal	Armaros	Hermani
Bataryel	Anani	Batarel	Matarel
Ananel	Zaqebe	Ananel	Ananel
Thausael	Samsaveel	Zaqiel	Setawel
Samiel	Sartael	Samsapeel	Samshiel
Ertael	Turel	Satarel	Sahriel
Tumael	Jomjael	Turel	Tummiel
Tarel	Arazjal	Jomjael	Turiel
Yomyael			Yamiel
Sariel			Yehadiel

As you can see just from this collection, there is a bewildering variety to these names. Glancing across the comparisons, it is possible to see where certain names repeat or, perhaps, became distorted. Without access to and knowledge of the language of the originals, however, it is impossible to accurately conjecture about the derivations or development. As a side note, 4Q201 is the official designation of the main portion of the Watchers' story that appears in the collection of Qumran manuscripts known to the world as the *Dead Seas Scrolls*.

Appendix II: Tarot Correspondences

Tarot traditionalists will notice that I have left out all mention of the kabalistic and astrological associations with the cards. Originally, it was my intention to include these on each card. If you look carefully at the border designed for the cards, you will see the two spaces arching around the top of the image where we set aside room for the inclusion of a Hebrew letter on one side and an astrological symbol on the other. However, I didn't want to merely copy the attributions of someone else. I wanted to be certain that I had the correct ones. I knew that there was some dispute between Crowley's interpretations and those of the Rider-Waite-Smith/Golden Dawn systems. Crowley himself went back and forth on the Hebrew letter associated with The Emperor and The Star. So I wanted to go to *their* sources. My quest for accuracy led me to research Gébelin and Etteilla more thoroughly, on the theory that, if I went to the very roots of the Tarot as it is known in the occult world, then I would certainly find the "right" attributions.

As we've seen in the Tarot History section, the idea that there is one "right" or "true" set of attributions was terribly naïve. Instead, what I discovered was even more conflict – to the point where early writers could not even agree on the proper order of the cards! As I personally approach the Tarot through a primarily Jungian perspective, I don't feel the same resonance with the kabalistic or astrological attributions as many others do. Therefore, it didn't distress me as much to learn that these attributions were essentially an artificial construct projected onto the cards. But I know many who read Tarot place a great deal of meaning on these correspondences. Accordingly, I have collected in the following charts the Hebrew letters, astrological associations, and card order applied to the Major Arcana by several key innovators of the occult Tarot: Etteilla, Papus, and Lévi. The charts use as their basis of comparison what has become the standard at this time, which is the Golden Dawn system of attribution. Waite sourced Lévi directly for his production of the Tarot, and the similarity in images between the RWS and Wirth decks implies that he also consulted Papus.

Hebrew Correspondences of the Tarot

Tarot Trump & Number	Golden Dawn	Etteilla's Order	Lévi's Order	Papus' Order
0. The Fool	Aleph	Tau	Shin	Shin
I. The Magician	Beth	Samekh	Aleph	Aleph
II. The Priestess	Gimel	Cheth	Beth	Beth
III. The Empress	Daleth	Vau	Gimel	Gimel
IV. The Emperor	Heh	Zain	Daleth	Daleth
V. High Priest	Vau	Aleph	Heh	Heh
VI. The Lovers	Zain	Mem	Vau	Vau
VII. The Chariot	Cheth	Shin	Zain	Zain
VIII. Strength	Tet	Koph	Cheth	Cheth
IX. The Hermit	Yod	Tzaddi	Teth	Teth
X. The Wheel	Koph	Resh	Yod	Yod
XI. Justice	Lamed	Tet	Koph	Koph
XII. Hanged Man	Mem	Lamed	Lamed	Lamed
XIII. Death	Nun	Peh	Mem	Mem
XIV. Temperance	Samekh	Yod	Nun	Nun
XV. The Devil	Ayin	Nun	Samekh	Samekh
XVI. The Tower	Peh	Qof	Ayin	Ayin
XVII. The Star	Tzaddi	Daleth	Peh	Peh
XVIII. The Moon	Qof	Gimel	Tzaddi	Tzaddi
XIX. The Sun	Resh	Beth	Qof	Qof
XX. Judgment	Shin	Ayin	Resh	Resh
XXI. The World	Tau	Heh	Tau	Tau

As you can see, Etteilla, writing in the second half of the 18th century, proposes an entirely different order to the cards, creating his own narrative with the Trumps. Lévi, writing in the middle of the 19th century, begins with the Magician, placing the Fool just before The World. Strength and Justice are also reversed from the order we accept as standard now. Published in the same year as the founding of the Golden Dawn, Papus repeats Lévi's attributions.

The astrological associations of the cards are no less thorny. In the chart below, I have provided what has become the standard next to Etteilla and Papus to give an idea of how some of these associations vary depending on the person writing about them:

Astrological Correspondences of the Tarot

Tarot Trump & Number	Etteilla's List	Papus' List	Golden Dawn
0. The Fool	Sun	--	Air
I. The Magician	--	--	Mercury
II. The Priestess	Moon	Moon	Moon
III. The Empress	Venus	Venus	Venus
IV. The Emperor	Jupiter	Jupiter	Aries
V. High Priest	Aries	Aries	Taurus
VI. The Lovers	Taurus	Taurus	Gemini
VII. The Chariot	Gemini	Gemini	Cancer
VIII. Strength	Mars	Cancer	Leo
IX. The Hermit	Leo	Leo	Virgo
X. The Wheel	Virgo	Virgo	Jupiter
XI. Justice	Cancer	Mars	Libra
XII. Hanged Man	Libra	Libra	Water
XIII. Death	--	--	Scorpio
XIV. Temperance	Scorpio	Scorpio	Sagittarius
XV. The Devil	Sagittarius	Sagittarius	Capricorn
XVI. The Tower	Capricorn	Capricorn	Mars
XVII. The Star	Mercury	Mercury	Aquarius
XVIII. The Moon	Aquarius	Aquarius	Pisces
XIX. The Sun	Pisces	Gemini*	Sun
XX. Judgment	Saturn	Saturn	Fire
XXI. The World	--	--	Saturn

The Golden Dawn's system of attribution is most widely accepted at this time, although sometimes the modern planets of Uranus, Neptune, and Pluto are used to replace the elements which essentially seem to have been used by the Golden Dawn to "fill in the blanks" as it were, since there are only twelve Zodiac signs and seven "traditional" planets, providing only nineteen total astrological signs to distribute among twenty-two cards. As you can probably see, Papus uses Gemini twice. He is also clearly working from Etteilla's example, save for this difference – which may be an intentional deviation or an error.

Bibliography

Anecdota Oxoniensia: Texts, Documents, and Extracts chiefly from the Bodleian Library Semitic series. Volumes 10-11. Clarendon Press, Oxford: 1898.

Budge, E.A. Wallis. *The Book of the Mysteries of the Heavens and the Earth.* Ibis Press, Berwick, ME: 2004.

Campbell, Joseph. *The Hero with a Thousand Faces.* Bollingen Series XVII. Third printing. Princeton University Press, NJ: 1973
--*The Power of Myth.* With Bill Moyers. Betty Sue Flowers, editor. Doubleday, NY: 1988

Charles, R.H. *The Book of Enoch the Prophet.* Weiser Books, Boston, MA: 2003.
-- *The Book of the Secrets of Enoch.* Clarendon Press, Oxford: 1896.
-- *The Book of Jubilees, or the Little Genesis.* Adam and Charles Black, London: 1902.
-- *Apocalypse of Baruch.* Society for Promoting Christian Knowledge, London: 1918.
-- *The Apocrypha and Pseudepigrapha in English*, vol. 2, Clarendon Press, Oxford: 1913

Christian, Paul. *The History and Practice of Magic.* Ross Nichols, ed. Citadel Press, New York: 1969.

Davidson, Gustav. *The Dictionary of Angels.* Free Press, NY: 1967

De Gébelin, Court. *Monde primitif, analysé et comparé avec le monde moderne.* Vol. 8. Valleyre, Saugrain, Sorin, Paris: 1781.

Decker, Ronald; Thierry DePaulis & Michael Dummett. *A Wicked Pack of Cards.* St. Martin's Press, New York: 1996.

Dillmann, August. *Das Buch Henoch.* Leipzig: 1853

Gaster, Moses. *The Chronicles of Jerahmeel.* Royal Asiatic Society, London: 1899.

Ginzberg, Louis *The Legends of the Jews: From the Creation to Jacob.* Henrietta Szold, trans. Jewish Publication Society of America, Philadelphia: 1912.

Gray, Eden. *Mastering the Tarot.* Signet Publishing Group, New York: 1973.

Greer, Mary K. *21 Ways to Read a Tarot Card.* Llewellyn Publications, MN: 2007.

Hoffmann, Andreas Gottlieb. *Das Buch Henoch.* Croeker, Jena:1833

Jung, Carl. *Man and his Symbols.* Anchor Books, NY: 1964.

Laurence, Richard. *The Book of Enoch.* Collingwood Press, Oxford University: 1821

Lévi, Eliphas. *Transcendental Magic: Its Doctrine and Ritual.* Bracken Books, London: 1995.

Nichols, Sallie. *Jung and the Tarot.* Samuel Weiser, Inc., York Beach, ME: 1984.

Nickelsburg, George W. E. & James C. VanderKam. *I Enoch: A New Translation.* Fortress Press, MN: 2004.

Orlov, Andrei. "The Origin of the Name 'Metatron' and the Text of 2 (Slavonic Apocalypse of) Enoch." *Journal for the Study of the Pseudepigrapha* 21 (2000) pp. 19-26. Accessed via Marquette.edu: http://www.marquette.edu/maqom/metatron.html
　　-- *The Enoch-Metatron Tradition.* TSAJ, 107; Tuebingen: Mohr-Siebeck, 2005, pp. xii+383. Except accessed via Marquette.edu: http://www.marquette.edu/maqom/metatronshiurqomah.html
　　-- *The Watchers of Satanail: The Fallen Angels Traditions in 2 (Slavonic) Enoch.* Marquette.edu: http://www.marquette.edu/maqom/satanail.pdf

Papus. *The Tarot of the Bohemians.* A. P. Morton, trans. Senate Books, London: 1994.

Place, Robert M. *The Tarot: History, Symbolism, and Divination.* Tarcher, NY: 2005

Rappoport, Angelo. *The Myth and Legend of Ancient Israel.* Vol. 2. Kessinger Publications, 2005.

Reed, Annette Yoshiko *Fallen Angels and the History of Judaism and Christianity.* Cambridge University Press, NY: 2005

Reeves, John C. "Sefer 'Uzza Wa-'Aza(z)el: Exploring Early Jewish Mythologies of Evil." Excerpt, Scribd.com

Riley, Jana. *The Tarot Book.* Sam Weiser, Inc., York Beach, ME: 1992.

Schodde, George H. *The Book of Enoch.* Warren F. Draper, Andover, OH: 1882

Sharman-Burke, Juliet. *Understanding the Tarot.* St. Martin's Griffin, New York: 1998
　　-- *The Mythic Journey.* With Liz Greene. Simon & Schuster, New York: 2000.

Palmer, Abram Smythe. Studies in Biblical Subjects Series, issue 2: Jacob at Bethel, London: 1899.

Vargo, Joseph & Joseph Iorillo. *The Gothic Tarot Compendium.* Monolith Graphic, Cleveland, OH: 2007.

Waite, Arthur Edward. *The Pictorial Key to the Tarot.* Barnes & Noble Books, New York: 1995
   -- *The Doctrine and Literature of the Kabalah.* Theosophical Publishing Society, London: 1902.

Printed in Great Britain
by Amazon